Guide to the Recommended
COUNTRY INNS
of N

```
║█║██║█║║███║██║║█
     D1488991
```

"More guests come to our inn with Elizabeth's book tucked under their arm than any other guidebook. They feel what we know—Elizabeth has been to her inns and she tells it as it is."
—*Paul and Louise Ebeltoft, innkeepers,*
Copper Beach Inn, Ivoryton, Connecticut

"A look at the most charming way to spend your vacation."
—Philadelphia Daily News

"Spotlights pleasant houses where—as visitors to New England know— handcrafted quilts, antique furniture, home-cooked meals, and spectacular mountain scenery are the norm. . . "
—The Tampa Tribune, Florida

"We like to recommend Elizabeth's book because it is one of the best. She makes sure she checks on each inn before a new edition is printed."
—*Sandy and Jack Allembert, innkeepers,*
Four Columns Inns, Newfane, Vermont

"Not a guide you flip through lightly. Get comfortable in a cozy wing chair. . . . Just when you think you've found the perfect inn, you'll turn the page and discover another one."
—Sunday Call-Chronicle, Allentown, Pennsylvania

". . . can help you plan a sojourn in New England."
—Travel & Leisure

"This is a volume that is the best of its type in a crowded field."
—The Chattanooga Times, Tennessee

". . . the definitive reference for finding a well-laid board and a warm bed to follow."
—Eastern Airlines Review, F.Y.I.

"Squier beckons travelers to these charming inns with explicit directions."
—Travel Agent

The "Guide to the Recommended Country Inns" Series

"The guidebooks in this new series of recommended country inns are sure winners. Personal visits have ensured accurate and scene-setting descriptions. These beckon the discriminating traveler to a variety of interesting lodgings."
—*Norman Strasma, publisher of* Inn Review *newsletter*

The "Guide to the Recommended Country Inns" series is designed for the discriminating traveler who seeks the best in unique accommodations away from home.

From hundreds of inns personally visited and evaluated by the author, only the finest are described here. The inclusion of an inn is purely a personal decision on the part of the author; no one can pay or be paid to be in a Globe Pequot inn guide.

Organized for easy reference, these guides point you to just the kind of accommodations you are looking for: Comprehensive indexes by category provide listings of inns for romantic getaways, inns for the sports-minded, inns that serve gourmet meals . . . and more. State maps help you pinpoint the location of each inn, and detailed driving directions tell you how to get there.

Use these guidebooks with confidence. Allow each author to share his or her selections with you and then discover for yourself the country inn experience.

Editions available:

Guide to the Recommended Country Inns of
New England • Mid-Atlantic States and Chesapeake Region
South • Midwest • Arizona, New Mexico, and Texas
Rocky Mountain Region • West Coast

Guide to the Recommended
COUNTRY INNS
of New England
Tenth Edition

by Elizabeth Squier
illustrated by Olive Metcalf

A Voyager Book

The Globe Pequot Press

Chester, Connecticut 06412

ISBN; 0-87106-819-2
Library of Congress card number: 73-83255

Manufactured in the United States of America
Tenth Edition/Second Printing

Contents

For Arthur,
who knows why I have
dedicated this book to him.
With love always,
Elizabeth.

How This Guide Is Arranged

The inns are listed by states, and alphabetically by towns within each state. The states are arranged in the following order: Connecticut, Rhode Island, Massachusetts, Vermont, New Hampshire, and Maine. Before each state listing is a map and special index to help you in planning a trip, and on page 443 is a complete index to every inn in the book. There are also several special-category indexes that will help you locate the inns that are just right for you.

The following abbreviations are used:

EP: European Plan. Room without meals.

EPB: European Plan. Room with full breakfast

AP: American Plan. Room with all meals.

MAP: Modified American Plan. Room with breakfast and dinner.

BYOB: Bring Your Own Bottle.

In the write-ups you will, from time to time, find some pointing fingers: ☞ ☞ . While I have not rated the inns, when I found something particularly outstanding or different, I inserted a ☞ as a special note.

At the end of the write-ups you will find this symbol:

E: Stands for Elizabeth.

This was to give me the opportunity to add an individual note on a special, personal delight.

How to Enjoy This Guide

When I first started writing *Guide to the Recommended Country Inns of New England* back in 1973, country inns were relatively scarce. Since that time, however, the number of country inns has been rapidly growing as more and more people have tired of the monotony of motels and thruway hotels and have begun searching for the infinitely more warming pleasure of a good country inn.

Therefore, as I have begun the research for each edition of this guide, it has become more and more difficult for me to wade through the volumes of mail from new country inns. I have had to be increasingly selective in choosing the best inns in each state. Do not be distressed if an inn you like is not in this guide. Please understand that my definition of a country inn is that it must have lodging as well as good food, and it must have a certain ambience that appeals to me. I prefer that the inns I select serve at least two meals a day and be open most of the year, but I have made exceptions when an inn seems just too special to leave out of this guide.

By my descriptions and comments I have tried to indicate the type of atmosphere you can expect to find in an inn, whether it would be a fun place to bring your children to, or whether it would be more appropriate to leave the children at home. Do not forget that the very reason you are passing up a motel or a hotel is for the bit of adventure and surprise you will find sitting in a weathered farmhouse, eating country cooking, chatting with a discovered friend, and finding new delight in a very old tradition.

Although I make every attempt to keep this guide up to date, please realize that prices and menus are subject to change, as are innkeepers. If you are planning to stay overnight, or even to have a special dinner out, I recommend that you call ahead for reservations so that you will not be disappointed. Many of the inns are quite small, and it would be a shame to travel a long distance and not get in.

With prices fluctuating so widely in today's economy, I quote an inn's current low and high rates only. This will give you a good indication, though not exact, of the price ranges you can expect. I have not included the tax rate, service charge, or tipping suggestions for any or the inns. Be sure to inquire about these additional charges when you make your reservations. Be prepared to pay a deposit when you make your reservation at most of the inns.

About pets: Most of the inns do not accept pets, but give an inn a call before you go. They may be able to make arrangements for you.

And a special note hopefully to dispel a rumor that has been going about. *There is no charge of any kind for an inn to be in this guide.*

So, enjoy! This *Guide to the Recommended Country Inns of New England* was compiled for you, fellow lovers of New England country inns.

Elizabeth

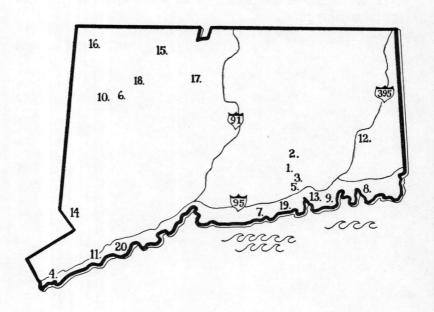

Connecticut

Numbers on map refer to towns numbered below.

Olive Metcalf

The Inn at Chester
Chester, Connecticut
06412

Innkeepers: David and Elise Joslow
Telephone: 203-526-4961
Rooms: 47, all with private bath.
Rates: $80 per room, EP.
Facilities: Open all year. Breakfast, lunch, dinner, Sunday brunch, full
   license. Elevator, sauna, exercise room, tennis court, jogging track,
   billiard room, bicycles, three conference rooms. Lake nearby. All
   major credit cards accepted.

The years 1776–1778 were the beginning of the Inn at
Chester, but, of course, John B. Parmelee who owned the house
then had no idea that 200 years later it would become a fine
country inn.

All the guest accommodations are lovely. They were decorated by Elise, who is an author herself and a fine one. She also
writes the inn's brochures. Some of the rooms have sitting areas,
and ☛ four have fireplaces. There is an elevator to take you up
and down from your room. This is a ☛ good inn for the handicapped. Twenty-six rooms are equipped for handicapped guests.

During the warm months the outside terrace is a perfect spot
to enjoy fine dining or a cocktail. There are three private dining

rooms and three that are open to the public. The largest dining room is in what was once a barn, a fantastic, high-ceilinged room with dark wood and a huge fireplace. A small greenhouse is attached to it. This makes a magnificent setting for the marvelous food.

An interesting breakfast selection is Bircher Muesli, a hearty alpine favorite made of oats, hazelnuts, and fresh fruits. My favorite lunch choice is the really good black bean soup with the proper accompaniments of chopped egg, minced onions, and sherry. At dinnertime the rooms are candlelit. For a starter, try the Mushroom Strudel. It is pure ambrosia. The inn also serves Rack of Lamb for one, which is done to perfection. The Port with Plums also is outstanding. Leave some space for dessert; all of them are made here and each one is divine.

The inn has piano music seven nights a week, and on special holidays an a cappella choir sings from the balcony in the main dining room.

There are large and small conference rooms, a billiard room with a fireplace, and an exercise room. Have a massage or take a sauna. It's all right here for you.

How to get there: Take Exit 6 off Route 9 and turn west on Route 148. Go 3.2 miles to the inn. In a private plane, fly in to the Chester Airport.

❋

E: *Elise and I are both cat happy. She has a Burmese named Arthur, a name I happen to love, and a flat-coated retriever called Raffles.*

The dog nuzzled my leg. The fire sent out a glow.
The drink was good. Only at an inn.

The Inn at Goodspeed's Landing, Gelston House

East Haddam, Connecticut
06423

Innkeepers: David and Elise Joslow
Telephone: 203-873-1411
Rooms: 3, plus 3 suites, all with private bath and telephone.
Rates: $80 to $125, including continental breakfast.
Facilities: Open all year. Full breakfast available, lunch, dinner, Sunday brunch, bar and lounge. Banquet facilities. Handicapped access to dining room. Boating, fishing, shopping, and theatre nearby. All major credit cards accepted.

When you approach the iron swing bridge to cross the Connecticut River, the first thing you see is the Goodspeed Opera House. Right next to it is The Inn at Goodspeed's Landing, more commonly known as the Gelston House. Let me tell you, it is an impressive sight.

Built in 1854, the inn has seen many changes, not only to

itself but also to the area surrounding it. In 1876 William Goodspeed built the Goodspeed Opera House. It was many things over the years before it became what it is today—a renowned theatre where "Annie," "Man of La Mancha," and others began. Three musicals a year are produced here, from spring through fall.

The inn, thanks to David and Elise, who also own the Inn at Chester on the other side of the river, has been ☞ restored back to its original beautiful classic structure. Inside, the inn has been updated with a complete ☞ sprinkler system and interior fire escapes from all the guest rooms and suites. This is an excellent feature to find in an old beauty like this. The guest rooms and two-room suites have been nicely remodeled, and there are lush thirsty towels, sleigh beds, good reproductions, and a variety of antiques. All this and a view of the beautiful Connecticut River, too.

You descend from your room down a magnificent grand staircase that deposits you in the ballroom. Nice for a bride or for that dramatic entrance you always wanted to make. You can dine in here or in the porch with floor-to-ceiling windows overlooking the river. You also can dine in the Bank Room or Winter Garden. I love the Summer Garden, open from spring until fall, which has its own informal specials including pitchers of beer. Shaded by trees and umbrellas and overlooking the river, it is a relaxing and fun place to be.

There is a lot to do in this area. Go shopping or antiquing or wandering down pretty country roads. The food here is grand. Do give the inn a try. It really is a gem.

How to get there: From I-95 take Exit 69 onto Route 9 north. Or from I-91 take Route 9 south. Follow Route 9 to Exit 7 and then follow the signs to the Goodspeed Opera House.

∽

E: *Remember those hearty Sunday dinners we used to have with roast beef, or chicken, or some other meat? Well, you can get good meals just like them here at the inn.*

Griswold Inn
Essex, Connecticut
06426

Innkeepers: Bill and Victoria Winterer
Telephone: 203-767-0991
Rooms: 18, all with private bath and telephone; 4 suites.
Rates: $68, double occupancy; $90 to $110, suites; continental break-
fast included.
Facilities: Open all year. Closed Christmas Eve and Christmas Day.
Lunch, dinner, Sunday brunch, children's menu, bar. All major
credit cards accepted.

Essex is a very special town right on the Connecticut River.
Although it was settled long before the Revolution, Essex is still
a living, breathing, working place, not a re-created museum of a
town. The first warship of the Continental Navy, the *Oliver
Cromwell,* was built and commissioned here in 1776.

"The Gris," as the inn is fondly called by everyone, is the
highlight of anyone's trip to Essex. When you come in from the
cold to the welcome of crackling fireplaces, you are doing
what others have done before you for 200 years. You can lunch
or dine in the cool dimness of the Library or the Gun Room. A
special spot is the Steamboat Room where the mural on the far
wall floats gently, making you feel that you are really on the river.

Their collection of Currier & Ives is museum-size and quality. There is music almost every night, old time banjos, sea chanteys, Dixieland jazz, or just good piano; but never rock 'n' roll.

In the bar is a great, old-fashioned popcorn machine. Bill Winterer gives popcorn to all the children who come in. Do ask for some. It's one of many personal touches that make this nice kind of inn such a special place.

The Hunt Breakfast is the renowned Sunday brunch at the inn. This bountiful fare is worth a trip from anywhere. The selection is extensive, with enough good food to satisfy anyone's palate.

The guest rooms are old, but nice. The *Oliver Cromwell* suite is in the main building, with a woodburning fireplace, comfortable couches, a four-poster bed, and a lovely bar for your very own. There is a very nice view of Middle Cove from here.

Down the river in Old Saybrook Bill owns the Dock, a fine seafood restaurant.

How to get there: Take the Connecticut Turnpike to Exit 69, and follow Route 9 north to Exit 3. Turn left at the bottom of ramp to a traffic light, turn right, and follow this street right through town to the river. The inn is on your right, about 100 yards before you get to the river.

✳

E: My favorite thing about The Gris? Love that popcorn machine in the bar.

The Homestead Inn
Greenwich, Connecticut
06830

Innkeepers: Lessie Davison and Nancy Smith
Telephone: 203-869-7500
Rooms: 19, plus 6 suites, all with private bath, color television, clock
radio, and telephone.
Rates: $80 single; $95 to $150, double; $135 to $150, suites; continental
breakfast included.
Facilities: Inn open all year. Dining room closed Christmas Day, New
Year's Day, and Labor Day. Full breakfast, lunch Monday through
Friday, dinner seven days a week, bar. All major credit cards ac-
cepted.

There are very good reasons why this lovely Victorian inn
has been chosen as the 🦅 best country inn in the country.
Jacques Thiebeult is the French chef who oversees the superb
food served here. Richard (Dick) Perchak, the head maître d',
makes you feel like royalty. I think we all need this kind of treat-
ment once in a while.

The dining room is elegant in a rustic fashion; beams, brick
walls, fireplaces, skylights, and well spaced tables with comfortable chairs. A simple bunch of flowers is on each table.

The inn's rooms are beautifully refurbished and each has a

name. William Inge wrote "Picnic" while staying at the inn in the 1950s, and the name of the room he stayed in is the Picnic Room. I stayed in this one too. The Poppy Room is a single with the smallest bathtub I believe was ever made. The Tassle Room has his and her desks, the Sleigh Room has old sleigh beds, and the Robin Room has delicate stencils on the walls. They were found under six layers of wallpaper dating back to 1860. The Bride's Room has a queen-sized canopy bed.

The Independent House is the ☛ newest addition to the inn. There are eight glorious rooms out here. The bathrooms are large and have tub, shower, and bidet. All the rooms have porches and the furnishings are wonderful. The Cottage has a lovely suite and two other bedrooms, all very nice and quiet.

La Grange is the dining room and the food is fabulous. Besides the extensive menus there are many specials. One that I had was ☛ poached fresh Dover sole, the best I have ever eaten. Another dinner offering is "Black Angus" Sirloin, Béarnaise. A real winner is Mélange de Fruits de Mer au Safrin—lobster, shrimp, scallops, and mussels in a creamy saffron sauce. The presentation of the food is so ☛ picture perfect, you could almost eat the plate.

One of the luncheon dishes is escallops of veal, served with chestnuts, cream, and cognac. Some of the hors d'oeuvres are fresh poached Arctic salmon or a pot of snails with cream, Pernod, and herbs. The desserts, needless to say, are spectacular.

Do I like it here! I just wish I lived a bit closer.

How to get there: Going north or south on I-95, take Exit 3. Go north about 200 yards to a light and turn left. Then turn left on Horseneck Road, go to the deadend, and turn left. Go under the turnpike and up a hill. The inn is on your right.

☙

E: The ironstone place settings in Wedgwood's Chinese Bird pattern and the beautiful stemware are for me.

Copper Beech Inn
Ivoryton, Town of Essex, Connecticut
06442

Innkeepers: Paul and Louise Ebeltoft
Telephone: 203-767-0330
Rooms: 4 in inn, 9 in carriage house, all with private bath.
Rates: $70 to $125, double occupancy, continental breakfast included.
Facilities: Open all year. Restaurant closed on Mondays, Christmas Eve, Christmas Day, and New Year's Day. Dinner, full license. Greenhouse cocktail lounge open on Friday and Saturday. All major credit cards accepted.

The magnificent copper beech tree that shades the front lawn of this wonderful inn was the inspiration for the name.

The rooms in the inn, with their unbelievable old-fashioned bathrooms and numerous, soft fluffy towels, are so nice. Comfortable beds and antiques all add to the charm. The rooms in the carriage house are ☞ spectacular. Louise has an eye for color and perfection. I could write a whole article on her selection of shower curtains for the Jacuzzi tubs that are in here. All the rooms are different. The beds are queen-sized. Some are four-poster and some are canopied. There are wing chairs, couches, and loveseats in the rooms, and each room has a porch to sit on.

Back to Louise's color choices: ☞ The wallpapers are breathtakingly beautiful.

The four dining rooms have comfortable Chippendale or Queen Anne chairs. The dining porch, which is my favorite, is done in white wicker. The ☞ spacious tables are set far apart for gracious dining. Fresh flowers are everywhere and the waiters serving the excellent food are friendly and courteous.

There are at least thirteen appetizers to choose from, each one better than the next. The soups that follow are superb. The lobster bisque has chunks of lobster in it, as it should. Entrees read like poetry and taste even better. My friend Linda ordered baked scallops and shrimp served with a sauce of white wine, shallots, mushrooms, cream, Swiss and Romano cheeses, and fresh tarragon. It was perfection. I had ☞ roast duck with a sauce of peaches, duck stock, and champagne—very different and very good. The swordfish is always excellent, but then so is everything you eat here.

Now for dessert. ☞ Rich chocolate mousse with white spongecake coated in dark chocolate, served with a fresh raspberry sauce. Oh my. There are several more such gems, plus lovely exotic coffee selections or espresso. The wine list is impressive, with something for everyone.

How to get there: The inn has recently added limousine service from open marinas, buses, trains, and local airports. If you're driving, the inn is located one mile west of Connecticut Route 9, from Exit 3 or 4. Follow the signs to Ivoryton. The inn is on Ivoryton's Main Street, on the left side.

❋

E: *A turkey sandwich to go after a sumptuous dinner is my idea of a perfect Thanksgiving.*

> *One good night in a country inn*
> *can keep the mind in quiet order*
> *for many moons.*

The Litchfield Inn
Litchfield, Connecticut
06759

Innkeeper: Rose Marie McCafferty
Telephone: 203-567-4503
Rooms: 30, all with private bath, air conditioning, television, telephone, and smoke alarm.
Rates: $60 to $70, double occupancy, EP.
Facilities: Open all year. Dining room closed Christmas Day. Breakfast, lunch, dinner, Sunday brunch, bar, lounge. Gift shop. Handicapped facilities. All major credit cards accepted.

The first thing that greets you as you enter the inn is the nine-foot chandelier over the delicately carved main staircase. How nice to be a bride and make your royal descent here. Breathtaking, I'm sure.

There are singles, doubles, and suites, all beautifully furnished in Early American style. They all have air conditioning, smoke alarm, television, and telephone. Some even have their own bar. There also are rooms for the handicapped.

The Tapping Reeve Room is the inn's main lounge and bar, offering choice beverages and a luncheon menu that features soups and overstuffed sandwiches. There is live entertainment here Thursday through Sunday all year long. The Terrace Room with greenery and sunlight is another place for lunch. What a menu! I found a favorite dish of mine here: ☛ chilled beef tenderloin, served with horseradish-sour cream dressing and red potato salad. The crepes and egg dishes are spectacular.

And now to dinner. The main dining room is lovely with its wide-planked floors and well-spaced tables. It's such a wonderful setting in which to savor the food. The menus change four times a year. One appetizer while I was here was fresh asparagus in puff pastry with a hollandaise sauce. It was so good. I then chose the lemon sole in a light herb sauce. Delicious! Of course there are many other selections. Be sure to cap off your meal with a cup of ☛ Royal Kona Hawaiian coffee. It is very interesting. Only domestic wines are served here at the inn.

Sunday brunch (reservations are a must) is beautifully done. From Steamship Round and four or five other hot dishes to assorted salads and a dessert table. Oh my!

How to get there: From I-84 in Danbury, take Route 7 north to Route 202 to Litchfield. The inn is on the left.

〜

E: *The four lovely fireplaces in the inn keep you warm on a cold winter's day.*

Madison Beach Hotel
Madison, Connecticut
06443

Innkeepers: Betty and Henry Cooney, Sr., Kathleen and Roben Bagdasar-
  ian
Telephone: 203-245-1404
Rooms: 28, all with private bath; 4 suites; all with air conditioning and
  cable television.
Rates: In season, $75 to $95, single; $85 to $120, double; $125 to $195,
  suite; continental breakfast included. Off season, $60 to $80; single; $70 to $105, double; $125 to $175, suite; continental breakfast
  included.
Facilities: Closed October 31 to April 15. Lunch, dinner, bar, lounge,
  conference room. Private beach on Long Island Sound. All major
  credit cards accepted.

    If you are fortunate enough to own a boat, do come to Mad-
ison, drop your anchor, and row right in to the Madison Beach
Hotel. If you don't own a boat, you don't need to hesitate to come
here. The hotel is very easy to reach and should not be missed.
    This Victorian beauty dates back to the 1800s. It has had
many uses and a lot of names, but it has never been better than
it is today. The whole inn has been refurbished with an abundance of tender love and care.

14

Each of its rooms and magnificent suites has its own entrance and balcony overlooking the Long Island Sound and beach. The rooms are large and airy and furnished with antique oak bureaus and wicker and rattan furniture. Soft puffs cover the wicker so you just sink into comfort. The four suites are absolutely breathtaking; each has its own kitchen, and the views from all of them are just wonderful.

There is a distinct nautical flavor to the wharf dining room and the lovely crow's-nest dining room on the upper level. The luncheon menu is extensive. The lobster salad roll is huge and even I could not quite finish it. Several cold salad plates are offered. These are so nice on a hot day. For dinner they have queen- or king-sized cuts of roast prime ribs of beef, served with horseradish sauce. This is such a nice way to serve beef. The stuffed veal chop is different and very good. From the sea there are sixteen entrees, each one sounding more enticing than the next.

The beach is private, seventy-five feet of it. The water is clear with no undertow, so the children are safe. There is good fishing off the inn's pier. Or sit on the porch in one of the many wicker rockers and just enjoy where you are.

How to get there: From I-95 take Exit 61 onto Route 79. Go to Route 1 (Boston Post Road), turn left to West Wharf Road at the Madison Country Club. Go to the end of it, and here is the inn.

E: *There is good entertainment by a trio every Friday and Saturday night.*

Olive Metcalf

Stevens Inn at Cafe Lafayette
Madison, Connecticut
06443

Innkeeper: AJ Belmont
Telephone: 203-245-2380
Rooms: 5, with 2 shared baths.
Rates: $45 to $60, double occupancy, continental breakfast included.
Facilities: Open all year. Lunch, dinner, Sunday brunch, bar. Sailing, swimming, and fishing nearby. MasterCard, Visa, and American Express accepted.

In 1837 the inn was built as the Madison Methodist Church, made of local timber and all handfitted by local craftsmen. In the early 1920s it was converted into an inn. In 1964 Al and Nancy Belmont bought the inn and added the restaurant. Twenty years later the current owners bought it and made the son of the Belmonts, AJ, the innkeeper. Nice for him, as he was raised here. He is a nice young man who knows how to run a successful inn.

There are four dining rooms. One that I like in particular is the ☞ Greenhouse. My favorite lunch here is always delicious. AJ had eggs Benedict one day I was here and they looked very good. A good many selections are on the menu. Champagne brunch on Sunday includes a split of champagne. Very nice indeed.

The dinner menu is extensive. Hors d'oeuvres include pâté, fondue, and smoked salmon, to name a few. Soups are excellent. Lobster bisque is a winner. Beef stroganoff, Wiener schnitzel, and veal sauté are just three examples of the delicious entrees. Rack of lamb is always good and on weekends they have ☛ leg of lamb. I have had their fillet of sole, which is very fresh. And then there are the French regional specials, such as bouillabaisse and duckling with bing cherry sauce. No matter what you order, the food here is delectable. In summer come and dine outside on the lawn. On Friday nights you'll find music and dancing.

The rooms are nice with attractive wallpapers. The shared baths are a good size. You can relax in a common room where there is a television, and continental breakfast is set up in another room.

This is an in-town inn, so you'll find it's busy at lunchtime. The pub is fun; it is a good meeting place for friends.

How to get there: From I-95 take Exit 61. Turn onto Route 79, going toward Route 1 and Madison center. Go left on Route 1, and at the next corner, at Wall Street, turn left. The inn's driveway is just beyond the post office.

✸

E: *The infamous Reverend Hayden of this church was tried for the murder of a young lady parishioner in 1879, but he was acquitted. Rumor has it that his ghost still hangs around the attic.*

Olive Metcalf

The Inn at Mystic
Mystic, Connecticut
06335

Innkeeper: Jody Dyer
Telephone: 203-536-9604
Rooms: 5, all with private bath, in two houses.
Rates: $95 to $135, double occupancy, EP.
Facilities: Open all year. Breakfast, lunch, Sunday brunch, dinner every
    night except on Christmas Eve and Sundays from December 1 to
    April 1. Bar, lounge. Room service available. Swimming pool, ten-
    nis, canoes, sailboats. All major credit cards accepted.

Every time I think about this beautiful spot I want to go back
there. The views from the inn extend from Mystic Harbor all the
way to Fishers Island; they are absolutely breathtaking.

The inn and gatehouse are situated on eight acres of land
amid pear, nut, and peach trees and ☛ English flower gardens.
From the Victorian veranda—furnished, of course, with beautiful
old wicker—the view of the natural rock formations and ponds (I
watched birds have their baths) and beyond to the harbor is
worth a trip from anywhere.

Built in 1904, the inn is elegant. The large living room has
walls covered with magnificent pin pine imported from England
and contains lovely antiques and comfortable places to sit. The

rooms in both the inn and the gatehouse are beautifully done. Some have fireplaces. My room had a canopy bed, and was it ever comfortable! They all have interesting baths with ☞ whirlpool soaking tubs or Thermacuzzi spas. One has a view across the room to the harbor. Now that's a nice way to relax.

The Flood Tide restaurant has ☞ executive chef Peter Schroll at the helm with his lovely wife, Sandy, who orchestrates the Tableside Classics prepared or carved at your table. Never have I seen a whole roast chicken for two on any menu except here. What a nice idea. I had baked stuffed two-tail Maine lobster—two claws and two tails and very good. My friend Charlie Nafie had soft-shell crabs and he declared them excellent. Pork tenderloin with lingonberries almost got me. All the food is memorable. The ☞ luncheon buffet is lavish or ask for a ☞ picnic basket to take out sightseeing. They have thought of everything to make your stay pleasant. Sunday brunch, as you can imagine, is a bountiful affair.

The lounge is pleasant for lighter fare and is right at the swimming pool. A piano player provides music on a parlor grand piano every night and Sunday brunch. A wedding up here would be ambrosia.

How to get there: Take Exit 90 from I-95. Go 2 miles south through Mystic on Route 27 to Route 1. The inn is here. Drive up through the motor inn to the inn at the top of the driveway.

༄

E: *I really could go on and on and on. The inn is just lovely, and so is the whole staff.*

olive Metcalf

Lighthouse Inn
New London, Connecticut
06320

Innkeeper: Don Tillett
Telephone: 203-443-8411
Rooms: 27 in main building, 24 in carriage house, all with private bath, telephone, and television.
Rates: $95 to $175, double occupancy, continental breakfast included.
Facilities: Open all year. Breakfast, lunch, dinner, Sunday brunch. Elevator. Private beach. All major credit cards accepted.

The mansion, known as "Meadow Court," was completed in 1902. In 1928 it became the Lighthouse Inn. And what an inn it is!

The accommodations are sumptuous. There are 🖝 no two rooms alike. Many of the antiques were found in flea markets and auctions in Connecticut and surrounding states. Numerous quality reproductions are also featured in the rooms. You will find armoires with television sets concealed in them, canopy and four-poster beds, wicker pieces, Victorian wing chairs, quilt racks, and more. The fireplaces are nonfunctional, but they are filled with 🖝 glorious baskets of silk flowers. Many of the rooms have the most beautiful wreaths I have ever seen. Twenty-six of the rooms in the main building have whirlpool tubs. The staircase that goes to the upper floors is truly a masterpiece. This is an inn not to be missed.

☞ Saturday night dancing is here. Why, oh why, isn't there more of it everywhere? Music in the lovely Meadow Court Lounge is also fun, and all of the people are so nice. The inn provides a fine setting for seminars and any type of corporate gathering. Wherever you are, it's all just glorious.

The dining rooms are spacious. Waiters and waitresses know their business, and food presentation is done so well. I had ☞ clams casino, which were served in a beautiful way. My friend Arneta had the inn's famous clam bisque. I tasted it, and oh my, I can see why it's famous. We both enjoyed the excellent tenderloin of beef special.

On a nice day, guests can wander through a meadow down to a private beach. And at all times of the year, inn guests enjoy the inn's proximity to Mystic Seaport Museum and Marinelife Aquarium, the U.S. Coast Guard Academy, U.S. Naval Submarine Base, and much more.

I get good reports all the time about this inn. Don't miss this one.

How to get there: Take I-95 north to Exit 82. Turn right, and at the second stoplight turn right onto Colman Street. At the end of the street turn left onto Bank Street. Take the second right onto Montauk Avenue. At the end of the street turn right onto Pequot Avenue. At the first stop sign turn right onto Lower Boulevard. The inn is in a half block, on the right.

✷

E: *After forty some years, they still have the chef who prepares their famous* *Delmonico potatoes.*

Olive Metcalf

Boulders Inn
New Preston, Connecticut
06777

Innkeepers: Carolyn and Jameson Woollen
Telephone: 203-868-7918
Rooms: 5, all with private bath, in the inn; 8 cottages with fireplaces.
Rates: $80, single; $130, double; MAP; EP rates available in the off
    season.
Facilities: Open all year. Breakfast, lunch, and dinner from Memorial
    Day to Labor Day. After Labor Day, breakfast, dinner Wednesday
    through Saturday, Sunday brunch. Bar. Swimming, boating, ten-
    nis, bicycling, hiking, and cross-country skiing nearby. All major
    credit cards accepted.

The stone boulders from which the inn was made jut right
into the inn, and so the name, Boulders Inn.

If you have the energy, take a hike up Pinnacle Mountain
behind the inn. From the top of the mountain you'll be rewarded
with a 🐾 panorama that includes New York state to the west
and Massachusetts to the north. The inn has a dog, Zoara, who
may be on hand to guide you along one of the mountain's hiking
trails.

If you're not a hiker, you can enjoy the marvelous countryside right from the inn. There is an outside terrace where, in

summer, you may enjoy cocktails, dinner, and ☛ spectacular sunsets. The Woollens have added on to the dining room, making it octagonal in shape, which affords a wonderful view of the lake. The spacious living room has large windows, and its comfortable chairs and couches make it a nice place for tea or cocktails. All the guest accommodations have a view either of the lake or of the woods and are tastefully furnished. ☛ There are eight cozy cottages, all with fireplaces.

The food is excellent with all baking done right here. The desserts are grand. Be sure to try the Chicken Cashew Crepe at Sunday brunch. Delicious. Dinner has several entrees. One favorite is Boeuf Bourguignon, morsels of beef sautéed in cognac and baked in a rich sauce of burgundy wine, fresh mushrooms, and herbs.

How to get there: From New York take I-84 to Route 7 in Danbury and follow it north to New Milford. Take a right onto Route 202 to New Preston. Take a left onto Route 45 and you will find the inn as you round onto the lake.

ঔ৯

E: *Tweek is a black inn cat. Curl up in a chair with a book and Tweek will join you.*

In the autumn, especially as one ages,
a firelit tavern in an excellent inn cannot be bettered
by the smallest mansions in Christendom.

The Hopkins Inn
on Lake Waramaug
New Preston, Connecticut
06777

Innkeepers: Franz and Beth Schober
Telephone: 203-868-7295
Rooms: 9, 7 with private bath; one apartment.
Rates: $39 to $47, double occupancy, EP.
Facilities: Inn open April to November. Restaurant closed January
   through March. Breakfast for house guests only, lunch, dinner, bar,
   lounge. Private beach on lake. Golf, tennis, and horseback riding
   nearby. No credit cards accepted.

Overlooking lovely Lake Waramaug sits this inn surrounded
by majestic trees on particularly beautiful grounds. The inn has
glorious, unmatched views of the lake.

In season there is ☞ dining under the magnificent maple
and horse chestnut trees, and dine you will. The inn has
a ☞ trout pond where you can pick the fish you fancy, and next
you have Trout Meunière; fresher fish would be hard to find.

Franz is the chef, and a few of his specials include Lamb
Curry, Veal Piccata or Milanaise, and Boeuf Bourguignon. Those
are for lunch. For dinner how about bay scallops in a special

24

garlic sauce, and backhendl with lingonberries. And there is always a special or two.

The dining rooms are cheerful. The fireplace has ceramic square tiles across the mantel, and the decorations are wine racks full of wines from all over the world. Naturally their wine list is quite impressive and, pleasantly, fairly priced.

There is a private beach down at the lake for use by inn guests. Bicycling, hiking, horseback riding, golf, and tennis are available nearby.

The rooms are very clean, neat, and country-inn comfortable. Almost all of the rooms have a view of the lake.

How to get there: Take I-84 to Route 202 East to Route 45 in New Preston. Turn left on Route 45 and follow it 2 miles past the lake. Take your first left after the lake. Then take the second right onto Hopkins Road.

❋

E: *Strawberries Romanoff, Meringue Glacé, Coupe aux Marrons, and homemade cheesecake. Need I say more.*

"The best landscape in the world
is improved by a good inn in the foreground."
—Dr. Samuel Johnson

The Inn on Lake Waramaug
New Preston, Connecticut
06777

Innkeepers: John and Karen Koiter
Telephone: 203-868-0563, 212-724-8775
Rooms: 25, all with private bath, air conditioning, and television.
Rates: $75 to $95, per person, double occupancy, MAP. Package plans available.
Facilities: Open all year. Breakfast, lunch, dinner, bar. Indoor pool, sauna, game room, cross-country skiing, ice skating, boating, lake swimming. Tennis, golf, horseback riding, and downhill skiing nearby. All major credit cards accepted.

The second largest natural lake in Connecticut fills part of the view you have from this old Colonial inn that dates back to 1795. There are enormous 100-year-old sugar maples and a magnificent Hawthorn tree.

There is so much to do here both inside and outside the inn. Winter is a fairyland. The innkeepers keep an ☛ area on the lake cleared for skating. Cross-country skiing starts just outside the door. Downhill skiing is but twenty minutes away. And how about a 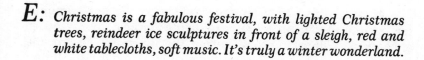 horse-drawn sleigh ride, compliments of the inn? Summer brings boating and swimming or just enjoying the shaded lawns and sandy beach. The inn has a showboat that takes you around the lake. A nice way to see it all. Bicycles are also available. Nearby are golf, tennis, and horseback riding.

Inside the inn is year-round fun. A 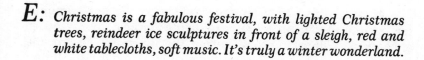 heated swimming pool with a whirlpool lagoon plus a sauna snuggle up to the Barefoot Bar. The game room has pool, Ping-Pong, electronic and other games, and even a juke box.

The Sand Bar on the patio at the beach is open in summer. During winter's blustery weather a glowing fireplace in the inn and drinks from Dudley's Tavern will keep you warm.

The dining rooms are large and well appointed, serving good food all year round. On one occasion I had Steak Diane, tender beef laced with brandy, mustard, and mushrooms, and oh, so good.

For antique lovers there is a gracious old fireplace made from the bricks that once were ballast on English sailing ships.

This is a wonderful place for the whole family or just one tired "inn creeper" like me. I arrived at a long day's end and spent about an hour in the pool. What a way to relax.

How to get there: From New York take I-84 to Route 7 in Danbury and follow it north to New Milford. Take a right onto Route 202 to New Preston. Take Route 45 west and follow signs to the inn. From Boston take the Massachusetts Turnpike to I-86. Follow it to I-84. Exit from I-84 onto Route 4 in Farmington. Continue on Route 4 to Route 118, and in Litchfield, pick up Route 202 and follow it to Route 45 West.

❈

E: *Christmas is a fabulous festival, with lighted Christmas trees, reindeer ice sculptures in front of a sleigh, red and white tablecloths, soft music. It's truly a winter wonderland.*

Silvermine Tavern
Norwalk, Connecticut
06850

Innkeeper: Francis C. Whitman, Jr.
Telephone: 203-847-4558
Rooms: 10, all with private bath.
Rates: $52 to $58, single; $68 to $74, double; continental breakfast
　included.
Facilities: Open all year. Restaurant closed Tuesdays from September to
　May. Lunch, dinner, Sunday brunch, bar. Television in parlor. All
　major credit cards accepted.

Although the colonial crossroads village known as Silvermine
has been swallowed up by the surrounding Fairfield County towns
of Norwalk, Wilton, and New Canaan, the Silvermine Tavern still
lies at the heart of a community of great Old World beauty. It has
a remarkable way of sweeping you worlds back in time.

This is one of the most popular dining places in the
area, ☞ known for delicious New England traditional food.
Thursday night is set aside for a fantastic buffet supper featuring
steaks, fried chicken, and many salads, all of which you top off
with a great array of desserts. Sunday buffet brunch features
twenty different dishes. Some of the inn specialties are Oysters
Country Gentlemen, Scallops Nantucket, mussels steamed in

wine, and roast duckling with an apple cider sauce. The food may be savored in one of the six dining rooms or on the riverside deck, which is open from June through September. On the old millpond below, the ducks and swans wait, hoping for some leftovers.

Silvermine Tavern is furnished with old oriental rugs antiques, old portraits, and great comfortable chairs and sofas surrounding the six huge fireplaces. The main dining room is decorated with over 1,000 antiques, primarily old farm tools and household artifacts. Also in here is an 1887 Regina music box. The drop of a coin will turn a huge disk and the music will begin. This is a really fun antique.

The guest rooms are comfortably furnished, many of them with old fashioned tester beds. One of my favorite rooms has its own deck overlooking the lovely millpond.

If you wish, you can stroll by the waterfall and feed the ducks and swans on the millpond. Across the road from the Tavern you will find the Country Store, run by Frank's wife. It has a back room that is a museum of antique tools and gadgets. It also has a fine collection of Currier & Ives prints. Do take a leisurely drive around the back roads near the inn, too. They are a delight. Also in this area you have the well-known Silvermine Guild of Artists.

How to get there: From the Merritt Parkway take Exit 39 onto Route 7 south. Go south to the second traffic light and turn right onto Perry Avenue. Follow it to a stop sign and turn left. The inn is on the right.

E: *In the front parlor, in front of a cheery fire, you can enjoy sherry and petit-fours at the end of your day. This is the life.*

Olive Metcalf

Norwich Inn
Norwich, Connecticut
06360

Innkeeper: Francis X. Acunzo
Telephone: 203-886-2401
Rooms: 65, including suites, all with private bath.
Rates: $75 to $100, per room; $100 to $150, suites; EP.
Facilities: Open all year. Breakfast, lunch, dinner, Sunday brunch, bar, lounge. Croquet, badminton, tennis court, swimming pool, spa. Executive retreat and conference center. Cross-country skiing and 18-hole golf course adjacent to inn. All major credit cards accepted.

The Norwich Inn began as a hotel in 1929 and has a colorful past. For the present it has been totally refurbished and it is truly elegant. The inn is a lovely red brick building on a hill, surrounded by huge elms, maples, and oaks. The grounds are beautifully manicured.

Everything you could possibly want is here. The magnificent restaurants are beautifully decorated. The Prince of Wales Bar has a log-burning fireplace, and the Windsor Room is set up for games. The Hunt Room, a meeting room, is done in English decor. There are other conference rooms on the lower floor. The Grand Ballroom is so nice for weddings, banquets, and meetings. The Sunroom is a tranquil place to have a cocktail, and the deck is so lovely. It overlooks the Norwich Golf Course. Lunch, dinner, and Sunday brunch are served here in warm weather months. For a special party, there is a pit for a clambake. Lobster, clams, mussels, corn, and potatoes cook all day and are so good.

Best of all is the fabulous spa, which features the best exercise equipment. There are life-cycle bikes, herbal wraps, whirlpool and sauna, hydrotherapy equipment, and massages. Aerobics, aquacise, and dancing are fun. The spa food is delicious; you would never know that it's low in calories. The owners are experienced in spas, as they own The Greenhouse Spa in Dallas, the California Terrace, and Spa Monte Carlo in Monaco.

I love chintz, and the huge lobby has chintz upholstered armchairs and sofas. An enormous bird cage in which two white Mexican fantail doves live is the focal point of the room. Their names are Patti and Mike.

The seventy-five rooms and suites are just so lovely. Many have raised four-poster beds, all new, of course, and very comfortable. You'll need to use the stepstool that is thoughtfully placed here to climb up into bed. What luxury.

This is a different type of inn, business and pleasure together.

How to get there: From the Boston area, take I-95 south. Take Exit 83 onto Route 32 north. The inn is in 1.2 miles on the left side. From New York, take I-95 north to Exit 76 onto I-395. Take Exit 79A onto Route 32 north. The inn is 1.5 miles north, on the left side.

✹

E: *Fran, the innkeeper, is really on top of everything. This is why the inn runs so well. And having music from the fifties piped into the inn is such fun.*

Olive Metcalf

Bee and Thistle Inn
Old Lyme, Connecticut
06371

Innkeepers: Bob and Penny Nelson
Telephone: 203-434-1667
Rooms: 11, 9 with private bath.
Rates: $56 to $92, double occupancy, EP.
Facilities: Closed Christmas Day and after New Year's Day for two
    weeks. Breakfast. Lunch and dinner every day except Tuesday.
    Sunday brunch, bar, lounge, library. All major credit cards accepted.

This lovely old inn, built in 1756, sits on five and one-half acres bordering the Lieutenant River in historic Old Lyme, Connecticut. During summer the abundant flower gardens keep the inn filled to overflowing with color.

The guest rooms are all tastefully decorated. Your bed, maybe a four-poster or canopy, is covered with lovely old quilts or afghans. The bath towels are big and thirsty. How I love them.

There are six fireplaces in the inn. The one in the parlor is most inviting, a nice place for a cocktail or just good conversation. On Saturdays there is ☛ a harp player in here, and she is excellent.

☛ Breakfast in bed is an especially nice feature of the inn. ☛ Freshly squeezed orange juice is a refreshing way to start any day. Muffins made fresh each day, buttery crepes folded with strawberry or raspberry preserves, and much more. Lunch is interesting and inventive. One item is cold sliced duck served with a basil and tomato mayonnaise and melon. Sunday brunch is really gourmet. ☞ Stir-fried duck and pheasant are glorious. I could eat the menu. And, of course, dinners here are magnificient. Candlelit dining rooms, ten appetizers, and entrees such as fresh tuna baked with shrimp and artichoke hearts and served with a sauce made of white wine, lemon, tarragon, and shallots. The list goes on and on. The menu changes seasonally, each time bringing new delights.

This is a fine inn in a most interesting part of New England. You are in the heart of art, antiques, gourmet restaurants, and endless activities. Plan to spend a few days when you come.

How to get there: Traveling north on I-95, take Exit 70 immediately on the west side of the Baldwin Bridge. At the bottom of the ramp, turn left. Take the first right at the traffic light, and turn left at the next light. The inn is the third house on your left. Traveling south on I-95, take Exit 70 and turn right at the bottom of the ramp. The inn is the third house on your left.

૭

E: *You can walk down to the river with a book, or just sit and watch the water. It's beautiful down here.*

Old Lyme Inn
Old Lyme, Connecticut
06371

Innkeeper: Diana Field Atwood
Telephone: 203-434-2600
Rooms: 13, all with private bath, telephone, and clock radio.
Rates: $75 to $100, continental breakfast included.
Facilities: Closed January 1 to 14. Dining room closed Mondays. Lunch, dinner, bar. All major credit cards accepted.

Sassafras is the inn cat who has a neat lounge named after her. Here you'll find television, games, books, and a lovely fireplace for your enjoyment, along with comfortable chairs and couch. The Victorian bar room has a back bar that is over one hundred years old, which was found by the innkeeper in Philadelphia. There is a ☛ beveled mirror over it that most museums would covet. A ☛ raw bar is offered in here for light suppers. A very cozy and comfortable room.

The rooms here at the inn are grand. The new wing has eight rooms. The beds are all four-posters. All rooms have telephones and clock radios, Victorian couches and/or delightful wing chairs. You will find mints on your pillow at night.

There are four separate dining areas and the food is superb. The menu, of course, changes with the seasons, but I'd like to

34

give you just a few ideas. At lunch one appetizer that appealed to me was Oysters Toscanini, oysters poached in white wine with prosciutto, mushrooms, and shallots, glazed with Gruyère and cream. There also are nice salads and sandwiches. Try Two Bird Sandwich—chicken and duck salad with herbs and walnuts served on pumpernickel. Delicious.

Dinner is spectacular. Their Old Lyme Inn Pasta is so divine I won't even describe it. You must come and try it. Veal of the day, loin of lamb in puff pastry, it just goes on. The desserts have been written up in food magazines and have won awards. That's how good they are. Continental breakfast is served to guests every day except weekends when a breakfast buffet is offered.

The inn can handle small conferences, weddings, parties, reunions, and such. It would be a lovely place to have a wedding, and is easy to find just off Interstate 95. There is much to do and see in this pretty town and area.

How to get there: Traveling north on I-95, take Exit 70 immediately on the west side of the bridge. At the bottom of the ramp turn left. Take the first right at the traffic light, and turn left at the next light. The inn is on the right. Traveling south on I-95, take Exit 70. At the bottom of the ramp turn right. The inn is on the right.

✳

E: *Do look around the inn. It is full of fascinating things.*

The Elms
Ridgefield, Connecticut
06877

Innkeepers: Robert and Violet Scala
Telephone: 203-438-2541
Rooms: 20, all with private bath, television, and telephone.
Rates:$78, single; $90 to $120, double occupancy; EPB.
Facilities: Open all year. Closed Wednesdays and Christmas Day. Lunch, dinner, Sunday brunch, bar. Piano entertainment on Fridays, Saturdays, and at Sunday brunch. All major credit cards accepted.

In 1760 a master cabinetmaker built this charming colonial house that is now known as The Elms. It is on a historical site, for it was here that the Battle of Ridgefield was fought during the Revolution. Since 1799, when the house became an inn, the same loving care and artistry that marked its beginning has been applied to every phase of its operation.

Peter, the maître d', is very informative. It is always nice to have such a person in a country inn. He has been with this family-owned inn for the past six years. The dining rooms are all on the first floor of the original inn. The brochure says, ☞ "To partake of a meal is no mundane experience in eating, but rather an adventure in dining." Very well stated, for the food and wines are stupendous. The lunch menu features good soups, salads, pastas, omelettes, curries, and on and on. Then for dinner there are about sixteen appetizers alone, plus soups, salads, and pastas. For entrees there are always specials. I had ☛ Veal Francesca, and it was delightfully served by courteous waiters. There is something for everyone. The desserts are sinfully good, but the topper for me (because I am allergic to caffeine) was ☛ decaffeinated espresso. A great ending to a perfect evening.

☛ Noel Regney plays music from the 1940s and '50s. It's delightful background music, for he does not play too loud. Noel also wrote a song. Do ask him for it. More inns would be wise to find a good piano and player. It really adds to the charm and warmth of the inn.

The newly refurbished guest rooms have all the modern conveniences, but still are rich in the mellow mood of yesteryear. Four-posters, canopies, and brass beds are the order here.

How to get there: The inn is located at 500 Main Street in Ridgefield. From Route 7 take Route 35 right into town.

E: ☛ *Nice to have family-owned and -run inns and a staff that stays for years.*

Stonehenge
Ridgefield, Connecticut
06877

Innkeepers: David Davis and Douglas Seville
Telephone: 203-438-6511
Rooms: 11, plus 2 suites, all with private bath, color television and telephone. Guest cottage, guest house.
Rates: $85 to $115; suites $170; double occupancy, EP.
Facilities: Open all year. Closed Tuesday and New Year's Day. Breakfast, lunch, dinner, Sunday brunch, bar, lounge. Swimming pool. All major credit cards accepted.

The setting for Stonehenge is serenely beautiful. The old white farmhouse overlooks the pond, which is bedecked with swans and aflutter with Canada geese and ducks stopping in on their migratory journeys. The Stonehenge Room, which once was a porch, faces the pond and has a great view. This is where ☞ breakfast is served, a lovely way to start your day.

In the inn's sumptuous addition are two suites and two glorious rooms that are almost suites. The suites have facilities for light cooking. They all are color coordinated and oh, so comfortable. All of the rooms in the inn, the guest cottage, and guest house have been refurbished in an elegant fashion. Most of the rooms have queen- and king-sized beds. Two have working fireplaces.

The chef, Jean-Maurice Calmels, is French born and trained, and nonpareil. Address yourself seriously to the food. The appetizers are unusual. I had the Mushroom Crepe Mornay. Another in my party had the ☞ inn's own smoked sausage in a pastry crust with a mustard wine sauce. The soups are poetic. The ☞ trout is live. "How long ago?" I asked. "About five minutes," was the reply. "The time it takes to come from the 'trout house.'"

This is fine gourmet dining. The luncheon selections are superb. The inventive touch with vegetables, the care taken with the sauces, all reflect the dedication with which M. Calmels approaches his task.

The dining room is beautiful by day or night, but for a quiet dinner à deux, reserve a table in the bar. There ☞ Len Gendal plays wonderful piano. He is excellent.

If you are tired of the "same old thing," book yourself into Stonehenge for a long weekend and find out what "haute cuisine" is all about. It is expensive, but worth every centime.

How to get there: From the Merritt Parkway, take Exit 40. Go north on Route 7. The inn's sign is in 13 miles, on the left. From I-84, go south on Route 7. The inn's sign is in 4½ miles on the right.

❀

E: *My favorite room is the big one in the front of the main house. Any season, any weather, it is a home away from home with wine and cheese waiting and breakfast served on the spot.*

olive Metcalf

West Lane Inn
and
The Inn at Ridgefield
Ridgefield, Connecticut
06877

Innkeepers: Maureen Mayer and Henry Prieger
Telephone: West Lane 203-438-7323
    Ridgefield 203-438-8282
Rooms: 20, with private bath, air conditioning, and television; some with
    fireplace.
Rates: $90 single; $100, double; EPB.
Facilities: West Lane Inn open all year. The Inn at Ridgefield closed
    Mondays. Lunch, dinner, Sunday brunch, bar, lounge, piano
    nightly. American Express, MasterCard, and Visa accepted.

We have a first here, two separate inns next door to each
other. West Lane Inn has the rooms and serves breakfast and a
light menu from the pantry. The Inn at Ridgefield serves delicious lunch and dinner.

Rich oak paneling and lush carpeting along with a crackling
fire greet you as you enter West Lane. The bedrooms are luxurious, with individual climate control, color television, radio, and

telephone. Each room has either one king- or two queen-sized beds. Some have working fireplaces. These are really nice on a cold night.

The breakfast room is bright and cheerful, serving freshly squeezed orange juice. A West Lane breakfast special is yogurt with bananas, honey, and nuts. Cold cereals in the summer, and hot cereals in the winter; Danish, muffins, or toast; or a poached egg are offered. Everything is done very nicely. The pantry selections are available from noon until late in the evening. There are tuna fish salad plates, several sandwiches like grilled cheese— even peanut butter and jelly—and more. There also are desserts.

The ends of the old wooden wine and whiskey crates that line the porch of The Inn at Ridgefield let you know there are good things inside. Henry is the innkeeper here. Dinner features hors d'oeuvres like Pâté of Pistachio and Truffles with Sauce Cumberland, Onion Soup Calvados Gratinée, or cold vichysoisse. Then entrees such as frogs legs (they are really good), fresh Dover sole, Châteaubriand, and roast rack of spring lamb follow. There are wonderful salads and desserts. Crepes Suzettes for two is an old favorite. And believe me, there are more, plus good coffees.

Both inns are just around the corner from the famous Cannon Ball House, which was struck by a British fieldpiece during the Revolution. There are quite a few stores to browse in, as well as antique stores. The Aldrich and Hammond museums are in town, and you are close to several fine summer theaters. Ridgefield is such a pretty town to visit.

How to get there: Coming north from New York on Route 684, or Route 7 from the Merritt Parkway, get off on Route 35 and follow it to Ridgefield. The inns are on Route 35 at the south end of town.

✻

E: *These are two lovely inns. Do come and try them both.*

Old Riverton Inn
Riverton, Connecticut
06065

Innkeepers: Pauline and Mark Telford
Telephone: 203-379-8678
Rooms: 12, all with private bath.
Rates: $50 to $78, double occupancy, EPB.
Facilities: Open all year. Restaurant closed Mondays, Christmas Day, and first three weeks in January. Lunch, dinner, bar. Dining room has wheelchair accessibility. All major credit cards accepted.

The Old Riverton Inn was originally opened in 1796 by Jesse Ives. It was on the post road between Hartford and Albany, and was known as Ives Tavern. It has passed through many hands since then, and the hands that now have it are very capable.

The Grindstone Terrace was enclosed to make it useful all year. The floor of this room is made of grindstones, which, according to 100-year-old records, were quarried in Nova Scotia, sent by ship to Long Island Sound, and then up the Connecticut River to Hartford. From there they were hauled by oxen to Collinsville, where they were used in the making of axes and machetes. A lot of history is here. Once Riverton was known as "Hitchcocksville," because the famous Hitchcock factory is here. It is open each day except Sunday until 5 P.M.

42

The colonial dining room has, of course, Hitchcock chairs and a ☞ lovely bow window chock-full of plants. I sat here for luncheon one day and had delicious broiled scrod. The menu offers a lot of choices. Chicken salad plate looked really enticing. Dinner appetizers, such as the homemade soups, also are good. I had the onion soup and it was delicious. There are several seafood entrees, each one looking better than the next. Other specialties of the inn include Boneless Breast of Chicken Marengo, Veal Français, and Veal Maison. Chef Leo Roy really has a way with food.

A stained glass window is in the bar. In charge of this charming room is a ☞ bartender from the Philippines who, like most of the help, has been here for years.

There is a ☞ working fireplace in one bedroom. It's a large room with a sitting area and queen-sized bed. A few rooms have canopy beds. Mints on the pillows at night is a very special touch I love. A comfortable lounge and library is on this floor, providing you with games, tons of books, and lots of quiet.

Antiques, galleries, a general store, the Hitchcock Museum, the Seth Thomas factory outlet, the Tartan Shop, Kitchen Shop, not to mention the Cat Nip Mouse Tearoom, are all here.

How to get there: The inn is 3½ miles from Winsted. Take Route 8 or Route 44 to Winsted. Turn east on Route 20, and it is approximately 1½ miles to the inn.

∾

E: *One room has a "new" old tub that's a pip. Go and see.*

Under Mountain Inn
Salisbury, Connecticut
06068

Innkeepers: Marget and Peter Higginson
Telephone: 203-435-0242
Rooms: 7, all with private bath.
Rates: $75 to 98.50, per person, double occupancy, MAP.
Facilities: Open all year. Full English breakfast and dinner for houseguests. For the public, dinner Thursday through Monday during summer and fall, and Friday and Saturday during winter. Swimming, canoeing, skiing, fishing, and golf nearby. All major credit cards accepted.

Under Mountain Inn was built in the early 1700s. Wood found in the attic was known as "king's wood" because of its special width. It now is the paneling on the front of the bar.

The house is colonial in style and has been 🖙 lovingly restored. Each of the seven guest rooms has 🖙 posturpedic mattresses. There are queens, doubles, and twins, so take your choice. Marget has a wonderful collection of stuffed animals, and you will find one or two on your bed. What a homey feeling this added touch provides. You also will find sherry and mints in your room for your enjoyment.

There are three acres of grounds, so in the summer you can

wander out under the trees and enjoy their beauty. Shading the inn and terrace is a tree that is rumored to be the oldest thorned locust in Connecticut.

The dining rooms are charming. There are three plus one private one. Peter is the chief. You may start with Scottish salmon or one of Peter's good soups. Go on to entrees such as roast goose with chestnut stuffing, crabmeat au gratin in a pastry shell, beef steak and kidney pie . . . I could go on and on. Desserts are homemade and scrumptious. The menu, of course, changes seasonally.

There is much to do in this area of Connecticut. The inn has ☞ brochures to help you plan your day. You will find canoeing, fishing, swimming, horseback riding, tennis, skiing, and more. There also are many good private schools in this area.

How to get there: Take Route 41 north for 4 miles from Salisbury. The inn is on the left. From New York state, take I-684 to Route 22, then Route 44 to Route 41.

❃

E: *Coco and Sugar are the two inn dogs. They surely are a handsome pair.*

Well cooked, well served, and well eaten,
a meal at a good country inn.

Simsbury House
Simsbury, Connecticut
06070

Innkeeper: Dick Clark
Telephone: 203-658-7658
Rooms: 30, plus 4 suites, all with private bath, telephone, and television, in two buildings.
Rates: $80 to $125, double occupancy, EPB.
Facilities: Open all year. Lunch, dinner, Sunday brunch. Lounge, conference rooms, handicapped access. Shopping and antiquing nearby. All major credit cards accepted.

Built in 1820, Simsbury House recently stood vacant for twenty-four years while vandals, time, and weather took their toll. But today, after a lot of hard work, frustration, and expense, it has been beautifully transformed into a fine inn and restaurant.

Relati es of the former owners provided ☞ old photographs of the house that were a good reference as it was restored. Two local craftswomen made leaded glass windows to match the originals. The oak parquet flooring in the inn *is* the original. The furniture consists of antiques and fine handmade reproductions from England. For example, the four-poster mahogany beds were carved by English cabinetmakers, and they are beauties. Most of them are king-sized and oh, so comfortable.

Twelve hundred rolls of wallpaper and five thousand yards of fabric were used in restoring the inn and carriage house. The color schemes—blue, green, rose, and burgundy—recur among the rooms. The suites in the carriage house are sumptuous. One has a whirlpool tub. This is the life! All the rooms are different and each one has an outside terrace.

The inn has a ☞ sprinkler system throughout, as well as smoke detectors. There are two rooms for the handicapped.

The dining room, divided into three sections, has an emerald green cotton print, a matching colored linen, and an English wool plaid on the walls. It is a wonderful place to savor the food prepared by the chef, a graduate of the Culinary Institute. Breakfast, lunch, Sunday brunch, and dinner are quite an undertaking, but he does it all so well. The menus are grand, with something for everyone. The chef insists on the freshest ingredients and emphasizes light sauces for his seasonal menus of game, seafood, lamb, and veal. One time for brunch I had ☞ crabmeat in phyllo, and it was so good. Fisherman's stew at dinner is also excellent. Desserts, well, one I had here was ☞ chocolate and raspberries. I would drive hours just for it.

How to get there: From I-84 take Exit 39 onto Route 10 and go to Simsbury. The inn is on the left. Its address is 731 Hopmeadow Street.

❧

E: *The whole inn, staff, and area are just lovely. Don't miss this one.*

Yankee Pedlar Inn
Torrington, Connecticut
06790

Innkeepers: Arthur and Gerald Rubens
Telephone: 203-489-9226
Rooms. 75, all with private bath, air conditioning, television, sprinkler
   system, and smoke alarm.
Rates: $54, single; $64, double; EP. Package plans available for off-
   season weekends.
Facilities: Open all year. Breakfast, lunch, dinner, bar, lounge. All major
   credit cards accepted.

The Yankee Pedlar is a bit different from the other inns in
that it is an in-town inn. There were, at one time, many such
inns, but now only a few survive. Nice that this inn was a sur-
vivor.

There is a wood sign in the dining room written by an English minister, "Fate cannot harm me—I have dined well to-day."
And so will you, as the food here is very good. One specialty of the
house is ☛ Sauerbraten with Potato Pancakes, and, boy, do I
love it. The veal is so tender you can cut it with your fork. All
breads and desserts are prepared right here. The inn has a
beautiful ☛ silver serving cart now used to hold vintage wines.
A nice way to present them.

All of the rooms are beautifully furnished with Hitchcock colonial furniture. Dorothy Rubens decorated six of the newer rooms, and they are lovely with hand-stencilled walls and fine furniture. Dorothy really has done an outstanding job. And one of the rooms has a fireplace. A beauty.

The lobby-living room has a large fireplace over which is mounted a pair of 1935 skis. They belonged to J. Franklin Ellis, the first ski instructor in the Mohawk ski area. The skis are not much, but he made them work.

There is much to do while visiting this inn. The Cornwall and Bull's covered bridges are nearby. You also have the Lime Rock races, but best of all is just driving around this beautiful section of country.

How to get there: From I-84 pick up Route 8 North at Waterbury. Take Route 8 to Exit 44 at Torrington. From Hartford, take Route 44 to Route 202 to Torrington. The inn is right in the center of town.

E: The staff really tries to satisfy your every wish.

*Man has tendencies of many temperatures,
the warmest of which is hospitality.*

Olive Metcalf

The Captain Stannard House
Westbrook, Connecticut
06498

Innkeepers: Arlene and Ed Amatrudo
Telephone: 203-399-7565
Rooms: 6, all with private bath; suite.
Rates: $55, single; $60 to $70, double; EPB.
Facilities: Open all year. Breakfast only meal served. BYOB. No pets, and no children under 6. Bicycles, lawn games. Swimming, boating, golfing, tennis, and restaurants nearby. All major credit cards accepted.

The inn dates back to 1850 and has been known by many names. It's a beautiful old charmer of a house. ☛ Floor-to-ceiling windows and a magnificent staircase with an interesting newel post are but a few of its fine features.

The rooms are very attractive. All have handmade afghans, color-coordinated sheets, and extra pillows and blankets. A lovely canopy bed is in one room. ☛ Plenty of towels are available; this alone is a nice touch. A radio and a clock are in each room, and fresh flowers, fresh fruit, cheese and crackers, and mints are provided. Hand-drawn stencils decorate each bedroom. In the two-room suite, one room is a lovely bedroom, and the other room across a hall is the living room with a comfortable hideabed, so a family could stay here. The private bath for this suite has an old-fashioned clothes wringer for a towel rack, very quaint. There's a guest office on the second floor for your use—a very nice feature for the business traveler.

Breakfast of fresh juices, fresh fruits in season, homemade goodies, and hot and cold cereals is served in the antique shop or your room. The breakfast trays are really unbelievable, with candlesticks and all. Finger towels are the placemats and napkins. There's a refrigerator for guests to use and a set-up bar. Wicker baskets full of ice are in a freezer. You will also find a color television, piano, automatic disc organ, reading material, and playing cards at your disposal.

If you want, you can buy the antiques that are for sale in the inn.

How to get there: Take I-95 to Exit 65. Turn toward Westbrook Center. Go west on Route 1 for ⁴⁄₁₀ mile. The inn is on the left, on the corner of South Main and Kingfisher Lane.

❀

E: *This is a nice area to walk in, and it's just a short walk to the beach.*

> *If all inns were alike*
> *they simply would not be inns.*

olive Metcalf

Water's Edge Inn
Westbrook, Connecticut
06498

Innkeeper: Charles Nehme
Telephone: 203-399-5901; out of state; 800-222-5901
Rooms: 20, plus 11 suites, all with private bath, cable television, and
  direct dial telephone
Rates: $70 to $190, per room.
Facilities: Open all year. Breakfast, lunch, dinner, Sunday brunch, bar
  and lounge. Room service available. Entertainment on holidays and
  special occasions. Conference and banquet rooms. Swimming and
  boating. All major credit cards accepted.

  There is a song that says, "This one's for me." Well, here it
is, and what a gem! Sitting up high, overlooking ☛ Long Island
Sound, the inn is a turn-of-the-century resort. With its own spar-
kling private beach, it offers swimming, plus boating on the inn's
fleet of catamarans, sailfish, and paddle boats.
  The dining room is decorated in soft shades of peach, rose,
and gray. The food is ☛ magnificent. One appetizer that offers a
little of everything is the Coastal Seafood Sampler. It's wonderful.
The seafood and lobster bisque with crab is excellent. There is a
choice of several salads. I had the ☛ scrod entree one night and

duckling another. Both were very good. I love the way the food is arranged so prettily on the plates.

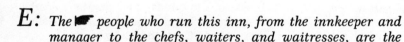 Sunday brunch is a delight. Chefs make Belgian waffles to order, as well as omelettes with almost anything inside. Roast beef, roast turkey, fish, fruit, and vegetables are also offered. The pastries will really finish you. I know they did my friend Arneta and me. Wow, were they good!

There's an outdoor patio for cocktails and dining in summer. It is just fabulous with its view of the Sound. The lounge is warm in feeling, and has a nice fireplace besides. The bar has comfortable chairs and has the style of a pub.

The rooms and suites are sumptuous. Most of them have a king- or a queen-sized bed. All have comfortable chairs and views of something pretty. Some have a balcony and there are wet bars in the suites.

The health club, which opens in 1987, will have platform tennis, day and night tennis courts, indoor and outdoor swimming, and sauna. There are banquet and conference rooms for ten to 200 persons. The inn's grounds are very nice for a walk. And there is much to do in this lovely area—marinas, state parks, the lovely town of Essex nearby, and much more.

How to get there: From I-95, take Exit 65 at Westbrook. Go south to Route 1, then go east approximately ¼ mile and look for the inn's sign.

❀

E: The *people who run this inn, from the innkeeper and manager to the chefs, waiters, and waitresses, are the nicest people I've met in a long time.*

Olive Metcalf

Cotswold Inn
Westport, Connecticut
06880

Innkeepers: Mike and Martha Kirk
Telephone: 203-226-3766
Rooms: 3, 1 suite, all with private bath, color cable television, and telephone.
Rates: $165 to $195, per room, EPB.
Facilities: Open all year. Breakfast and Sunday brunch. Many nearby restaurants. BYOB. Swimming, sauna, racquetball, and theaters nearby. American Express, MasterCard, and Visa accepted.

    The Cotswold Inn is a rare gem quietly tucked among the historic homes of downtown Westport in beautiful Fairfield County. The ☛ innkeepers are here to help you in any way they can, with suggestions where to dine and shop; passes to the attractive nearby YMCA for swimming, saunas, and racquetball; and information about how to obtain tickets to the Westport Country Playhouse. And if you need a secretary, the innkeepers will get one for you.
    Furnishings in the inn are ☛ sumptuous. The area rug in the living room is pink, beige, and blue. The fireplace is white brick with niches built in for a book or vase. All of the furniture and appointments are accurate reproductions of the originals.

The whole inn is color coordinated, squeaky clean, and just so lovely. An elegant country home is a good way to describe it. Don't miss the gardens, as they are just beautiful.

The guest rooms have names. Bedford is done in smoke blue and cream with a queen-sized canopy bed. Jesup is moss green and white and Sherwood is china blue. Both have queen-sized four-poster beds. The Wheeler Suite is apricot and white with a canopy bed and a sleigh bed in the adjoining room. ☞ Fresh flowers and bedside mints, ☞ oversized fluffy towels, and imported scented soaps are lovely touches in all the rooms to make you feel pampered. Very nice gift baskets are available here at the inn.

Breakfast is a full one and just delicious. Complimentary wine and cheese are served upon request in the early evening. A well-known classical guitarist, Jeannie MacPhee, plays for Sunday brunch.

How to get there: From Route 1 in Westport turn right on Myrtle Avenue and look for the signs for the inn. It is at 76 Myrtle.

⤵

E: *Fresh-squeezed orange juice is a nice way to start your day.*

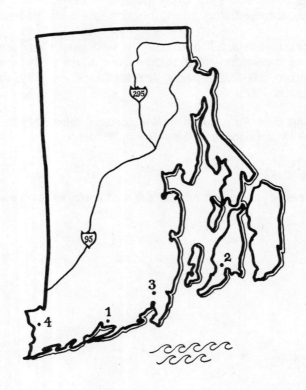

295

95

1

2

3

4

BLOCK
ISLAND

Rhode Island

Numbers on map refer to towns numbered below.

olive Metcalf

The General Stanton Inn
Charlestown, Rhode Island
02813

Innkeepers: Janice and Angelo Falcone
Telephone: 401-364-8888
Rooms: 15, 14 with private bath.
Rates: $50 to $75, double occupancy, EP.
Facilities: Open all year. Breakfast, lunch, dinner, bar, lounge. Flea
    market on premises April to October. Five miles to ocean beach.
    American Express, MasterCard, and Visa accepted.

One of the oldest continuously run inns in America is in the
little state of Rhode Island, dating back to 1667. That's old, folks.
From the mid-1800s until well after the repeal of Prohibition, the
inn was a mecca for gamblers from all over the country. Many
nationally known names are in the guest books, including future
presidents, generals, and theater people. This information came
from their brochure.

☛ Janice, the historian, hostess, and chef, needs no encour-
agement to talk about the Stantons. The General is buried in the
family cemetery on the grounds of the inn. There have been
only ☛ five owners of this property since the Indians owned the
land.

The five dining rooms are a bit different from each other.

58

There is a collection of old hats in one and a lovely sleigh in another. Each one is homey and comfortable. The girls serving the meals wear long gowns from years gone by and certainly have the perfect look for this old inn.

The food is so very good. I had a jumbo shrimp cocktail. The snails are nice and garlicky, and the scallops are freshly harvested from nearby waters. One menu phrase I love is "Mrs. Stanton's Old-Fashioned Baked Hickory Glazed Ham."

The inn's lounge area has entertainment on Friday and Saturday, and there's a television in here.

This is a charming, old, old inn; come and enjoy the past.

How to get there: From I-95 take Exit 92 onto Route 2. Follow Route 2 south a short distance to Route 78 (Westerly By-pass), which leads directly to Route 1. The inn is located 12 miles north on Route 1.

E: *The history of the area and the Indians is spectacular. So are the innkeepers.*

The cheers of millions are for politicians,
while the quiet appreciation of a well-cooked
chop is but for a few.

olive Metcalf

The Inn at Castle Hill
Newport, Rhode Island
02840

Innkeeper: Paul McEnroe; Jens Thillemann, general manager
Telephone: 401-849-3800
Rooms: 10, all with private bath.
Rates: Depending on the season, rates range from a low of $50 to a high
of $242, double occupancy, continental breakfast included.
Facilities: Inn open all year. Restaurant closed December through
March. Lunch and dinner served daily from May through October.
April through November, dinner served Thursday, Friday, and Sat-
urday. Sunday brunch served from April through November. Bar.
Entertainment. Live jazz on Sunday afternoons. Swimming from
inn's private beach. All major credit cards accepted.

Newport is a fabulous place to visit any time of the year. And
to be able to go to Newport and stay at The Inn at Castle Hill is
a rare treat. I have always loved the warm atmosphere of this inn.
It was built as a private home in 1874 and has been little changed
over the years. Thirty-two acres of shoreline right on the entrance of Narragansett Bay offer a natural setting for almost anything a person could desire. The views from any place, in or about
the inn, are breathtakingly beautiful. ☛ The Atlantic Ocean and
the bay are at your feet.

As for things to do, there is everything. Newport is the home of America's Cup Races and the Tennis Hall of Fame, and it is famous for its great "cottages" lining the waterfront.

The inn has four dining rooms. The small one with only six tables, each set with different serving plates, is very special. Another is a light and airy oval room, which, like the others, looks over the water. The chef is very good, and the food he creates is delicious. The menu changes seasonally. Veal, beef, lamb, fowl, and seafood are prepared many ways and are beautifully served. Every day there are three homemade soups, together with an endless variety of appetizers. The inn has always had a ☞ sumptuous ten-course New Year's Eve dinner, which is now held on November 30 with all their old fanfare of December 31.

The Tavern is a different room, with a beauty of a bar and a view unmatched, if you love the sea. There are Chinese teak and marble tables in the living areas, and the bannister on the staircase is its own delight.

Almost all the rooms are quite large and beautifully furnished. The paneling is magnificent, as are the oriental rugs that have been left here.

Innkeeper McEnroe has refurbished the entire inn with wallpapers that are color coordinated with spreads and drapes, plus thick towels. Here the view outside is not enough for our innkeeper. He cares about the interior look, too.

How to get there: From the north take Route 138 into Newport, and follow Thames Street about 4½ miles to Ocean Drive. Look for the inn's sign on your right. From the west come across the Newport Bridge and take the scenic Newport exit that goes into Thames Street.

∽

E: *The 10-mile ocean drive is among the most strikingly beautiful areas in New England. And do remember that Sunday brunch is very active with jazz.*

Olive Metcalf

Larchwood Inn
Wakefield, Rhode Island
02879

Innkeepers: Francis and Diann Browning
Telephone: 401-783-5454
Rooms: 19, 10 with private bath, in two buildings.
Rates: $30 to $65, EP.
Facilities: Open all year. Breakfast, lunch, dinner, bar, tavern. Swimming, fishing and skiing nearby. All major credit cards accepted.

Over the fireplace in the homey bar is carved "Fast by an Ingle Bleezing Finely," a quotation from the Scots' Robert Burns. ☛ His birthday, January 25th, is celebrated here, and every year a couple of pipers come over from Connecticut to help the party along. The Scottish flavor is all over this homelike country inn.

The Tam O'Shanter Cocktail Lounge serves up a delectable lunch that includes huge sandwiches, good salads, hamburgers, and quiche. There are four other lovely rooms for dining or private entertaining. Dinner ideas are rack of lamb for one or two, lots of fresh fish, and a ☛ beefeater's special, a thick slice of prime rib Angus. Come summer the meals are served on the covered patio in the garden.

Some of the rooms are in the Holly House across the street. It is the same age as the inn; both were built in the 1830s. It so well done. Diann has a real touch. The wallpapers are glorious and one room is an especially lovely salmon color. All of the inn's guest rooms have been individually decorated and are beautifully furnished.

The inn is situated in the heart of Rhode Island's beautiful South County. Saltwater beaches for bathing, fishing, and sunning are close by. In the winter it is only a short drive to Pine Top and Yawgoo Valley for skiing.

Rhode Island isn't all that big, you know, so it's never very far from anywhere to the Larchwood Inn.

How to get there: Take I-95 to Route 1. Exit from Route 1 at Pond Street, follow it to the end, and the inn will be immediately in front of you.

*

E: Pipers and Haggis is a Scottish man's dream come true.

> *When you have but one night to spend,*
> *which inn to choose is as difficult*
> *as the choice you had years ago*
> *at the penny candy counter,*
> *and equally rewarding.*

Olive Metcalf

Shelter Harbor Inn
Westerly, Rhode Island
02891

Innkeepers: Jim and Debbye Dey
Telephone: 401-322-8883
Rooms: 24, all with private bath; some with fireplace; some with television.
Rates: $68 to $88, single, $58 to $78, double occupancy; EPB.
Facilities: Open all year. Lunch, dinner, Sunday brunch, bar. Two paddle tennis courts with night lighting. Private beach. Summer theaters nearby. All major credit cards accepted.

If you would like a three-mile stretch of uncluttered ocean beach located just a mile from a lovely old country inn, find your way to Rhode Island and the Shelter Harbor Inn. Bring the children. When they're not playing in the ocean surf, there's a salt pond near the inn for them to explore.

Eight of the guest rooms are in the restored farmhouse, and ten more are located in the barn. The rest of the rooms are in the coach house, which is a lovely recent addition to the inn. There is a large central living room here that opens onto a spacious deck—how ideal for families. Or if your business group is small, have a meeting right here. There is also a library with comfortable leather chairs where you can relax with a book. The coach house is a wonderful addition.

The menu reflects the location of the inn, and at least half the items offered are from the sea. ☞ The Finnan Haddie is specially smoked in Narragansett. You can choose your place to eat, from the formal dining room, the small private dining room with a fireplace, or the glassed-in terrace room. The sun porch has been turned into a pub bar. There is a delightful old wood stove to warm you, and Debbye's plants are everywhere. If weather permits, take a drink out to the secluded terrace.

If you can tear yourself from the beach, there is much to see around here. You are about halfway between Mystic and Newport. The ferry to Block Island leaves from Judith Point. It is an hour-long ride, and when you arrive on Block Island you will find it a super spot for bicycling. You can charter boats for fishing, or stand at the edge of the surf and cast your line into the sea. In the evenings there is Theater by the Sea in nearby Matunuck, or the Heritage Playhouse in Hopkinton.

How to get there: Take I-95 to Route I. Follow Route 1 out of Westerly for about 5 miles. The inn is on the right side of the road when you're heading northeast.

∽℘

E: *On a clear day you can see Block Island from the third floor of the inn. There's a hot tub up here, plus a barbecue grill.*

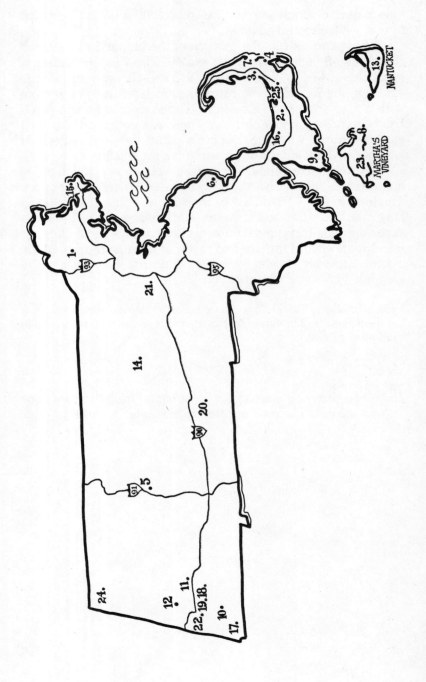

NANTUCKET

MARTHA'S
VINEYARD

Massachusetts

Numbers on map refer to towns numbered below.

Olive Metcalf

Andover Inn
Andover, Massachusetts
01810

Innkeeper: Henry Broekhoff
Telephone: 617-475-5903
Rooms: 33, 23 with private bath, some with running water; all with air
conditioning, television, and telephone. One suite.
Rates: $39 to $49, single; $61 to $71, double; $110, suite; E.P.
Facilities: Closed last two weeks of August. Dining room closed on
Christmas Day. Breakfast, lunch, dinner, Sunday brunch, bar. Ac-
cessible to wheelchairs. Elevator, barbershop. All major credit cards
accepted.

The Andover Inn is part of the campus of Phillips Academy.
It is privately owned and offers twenty-four-hour desk service,
an ☞ elevator, dry cleaning services, photocopying, and box
lunches. Room service is available, as are baby sitters, medical
services (a doctor is on twenty-four-hour call), safety deposit
boxes, taxis, and wake-up service. There is ☞ limousine service
to and from the airports, and these stretched Cadillacs can be
rented for other activities such as weddings, proms, or an evening
on the town. Now that's the way to travel in style!

You expect ivy-covered buildings here, and you get them in
abundance. Upon entering the inn you are in the reception area

with a fireplace and comfortable couches. The bar is in the right corner of this room, and it is one of the nicest I've visited. The stools with ☞ armrests are overstuffed, and honest, you hate to leave them.

The rooms all have modern conveniences, such as color television, air conditioning, direct dial phones, radios, and full baths. All of them have nice views.

The dining rooms are lovely and the china used is Villeroy and Boch Luxembourg. Siena is the pattern. It is porcelain and looks just like pink marble. The breakfast menu is extensive. ☞ Freshly squeezed orange or grapefruit juice is a nice way to start the day. Dinner selections include hot and cold appetizers, salads, and entrees from the sea or land. Try the specialty of the inn, Shrimp Flambée. There are lots more.

Sundays bring ☞ Rijsttafel, an original Indonesian dish served late in the day. It consists of dry steamed rice and an indefinite number of side dishes and sauces. The menu tells you how to eat it. I was overwhelmed and delighted by it. Do go and give it a try. It's worth a trip from anywhere, and reservations are a must.

How to get there: The inn is 25 miles north of Boston on Route 28, near the intersection of Routes 93 and 495.

❀

E: ☞ *Monday through Saturday evenings guests enjoy light classical music on the grand piano.*

Olive Metcalf

Cobb's Cove
Barnstable Village, Massachusetts
02630

Innkeeper: Evelyn Chester
Telephone: 617-362-9356
Rooms: 6 suites, all with private bath.
Rates: $129 to $149, double occupancy, EPB.
Facilities: Closed mid-January to mid-February. Full breakfast, dinner
    by reservation only to house guests. BYOB. No credit cards hon-
    ored, but checks will be accepted.

The moment you walk in the door and are greeted by Evelyn
and Henri-Jean, you know you have happened on a distinctive
and delightful inn. You are taken to your suite, and what a marvelous view you have. ☛ The third-floor suite has the biggest
skylight I have ever seen. It goes from almost the gable down to
the eave. There is a couch in front of this skylight where you can
sit and see all of Cape Cod Bay, Sandy Neck, and all the way to
Provincetown Light. The other suites also have grand views, deliciously comfortable beds, and all the extras you expect at an
extraordinary inn. The baths all have ☛ whirlpools, so relaxing
after a day of travel. The soaps and bubble bath are pear-scented,
a nice touch. Plenty of big towels and good, soft pillows.
The inn is on a very secluded and scenic piece of property.

The bay is right at hand. The inn was built of twelve-by-twelve-foot rough-cut timbers and many of the walls are done in rough burlap. The keeping room has a large Count Rumford shallow fireplace, comfortable chairs, and wonderful smells that come from Henri's kitchen. There is a terrace full of bird feeders made by Harry Holl of the Scargo Pottery. Harry also made many of the kitchen things Henri uses, including a huge salad bowl that is a rare beauty. In summer, breakfast is served on the terrace.

The dining room-library has a long hutch table that seats fourteen quite comfortably. Dinner is served in three or five courses. One night I was there it started with delicious mussels, then a special cauliflower dish done Henri's way. This was followed by a ☛ fish (cod, I believe, and you can only believe because Henri reveals no kitchen information at all) so white and so tasty you wonder why you had ever eaten meat. Next came a salad, and finally a crème caramel for dessert, topped off by a great cup of espresso coffee, an Henri specialty.

This is fine dining, and believe me, the innkeeper who joins you for every course is the reason this inn is such a success.

How to get there: Take Exit 6 off Route 6. Turn left on Route 132 North to Route 6A. Go about 3 miles and pass through the light in the middle of Barnstable Village. After you pass the church on your left, look for a sign saying "Cobbs Cove." Turn left and within 100 yards on your left you will see a driveway marked "Evelyn Chester." Take this drive to the inn.

❧

E: *Vickey is the inn cat. He was given this name when he was very small and before anybody knew he was a male.*

Olive Metcalf

Inn of the Golden Ox
Brewster, Massachusetts
02631

Innkeepers: David and Eileen Gibson
Telephone: 617-896-3111
Rooms: 7, all share bathroom facilities.
Rates: $40 to $50, double occupancy, continental breakfast included.
Facilities: Open all year. Dinner served Thursdays through Sundays
from December 1 to the end of February. No food served in March.
Dinner daily the rest of the year. Bar, lounge. American Express
accepted.

David and Eileen are both graduates of the ☞ Culinary Institute of America and that, for starters, is a good indication of the
food that is served here. There are three lovely dining rooms, the
Cranberry Room, the Bay Room, and the Brewster Room. It really does not matter where you eat, for the food is excellent.

Here's just a hint of the food to expect. For appetizers there
are ☞ Mousseline of Seafood with Sauce Americaine and chowder of the day, and the others are equally tantalizing. And for
dinner, sauerbraten the way it should be served, roast duckling
with orange and cranberries, and a variety of veal and fresh fish
dishes prepared with a lot of imagination. All the desserts, of
course, are homemade and delectable.

You are sure to enjoy the generous cocktails served in the lovely relaxed atmosphere of the Decoy Lounge. All the common rooms are quiet and tastefully decorated, as are the seven sleeping rooms.

The inn was originally a church, completed in 1828. In 1852 the growing congregation prompted the church's move to larger quarters, which have since become the Brewster General Store. The original church was converted to an inn, and the Golden Ox was born. The church steeple was removed and sold for one dollar and seventy-five cents. Things were surely different back then.

How to get there: Take the Sagamore Bridge across Cape Cod Canal and follow signs for Mid-Cape Highway (Route 6) to Brewster Exit 10. Take Route 124 north to Route 6A.

E: *Okemo is a beauty of an English setter and Slinkey is a black cat.*

The good morning greeting
and the good night good wish
can only be found in a country inn.

The Captain's House Inn
of Chatham
Chatham, Massachusetts
02633

Innkeepers: Cathy and Dave Eakin
Telephone: 617-945-0127
Rooms: 10, all with private bath; one suite.
Rates: $90 to $130, per room, EPB.
Facilities: Closed December 1 to February 1. Breakfast only meal served.
BYOB. Restaurants, swimming, and sailing nearby. No children under 12. All major credit cards accepted.

Cathy and Dave are the two very ambitious young innkeepers of this beautiful sea captain's house that dates back to 1839. They never stop making improvements, and this, of course, makes it very comfortable for you. They try to think of everything to make your stay perfect.

Breakfast is the only meal here, and it is one you will long remember. It is served in their lovely light and airy dining room. Two or three live-in 🖙 English girls from the hotel management college in England are the staff, and they are so very pleasant. Good restaurants for lunch and dinner are in the area, and you

74

will be given full directions on how to get there, plus a 🖝 card introducing you to the restaurant signed by Dave or Cathy—very thoughtful.

Dave is a 🖝 licensed captain with the Coast Guard and, weather permitting, will take the guests out in their twenty-three-foot Seacraft Sports Fisherman. This is a wonderful way to see the Monomoy wildlife preserve.

The ambience of the whole inn is terrific. The rooms are named after ships that were sailed by Captain Hiram Harding who built the house. They are 🖝 clean and well appointed with beautiful furniture. The Eakins are always adding "new" beds. They really are old, expensive, and beautiful four-poster canopy beds. The good mattresses and reading chairs ensure that your stay is comfortable. One room has a fireplace. Three of the rooms are in the Captain's Cottage, and one of these has a fireplace.

This whole area offers many activities, fishing, swimming, boating, or just plain loafing. Whether you enjoy being relaxed or energetic, it's a nice place for it here.

How to get there: Take Route 6 (Mid-Cape Highway) to Route 137, Exit 11, and south to Route 28. Turn left to Chatham Center. Follow the rotary out of town on Route 28 toward Orleans. The inn is on the left in about one-half mile.

∽

E: *The inn dogs are Lily Marlene and Daisy Mae.*

How good of you to have asked me in.

Olive Metcalf

The Queen Anne Inn
Chatham, Massachusetts
02633

Innkeeper: Guenther Weinkopf
Telephone: 617-945-0394
Rooms: 30, all with private bath.
Rates: $96 to $146, per room, continental breakfast included.
Facilities: Inn open all year. Dining room closed December 1 until mid-April. Dinner. Tennis courts, meeting rooms. Swimming and boating nearby. Fishing tours can be arranged. MasterCard, Visa, and American Express accepted, but personal checks preferred.

Guenther has a fine inn. The rooms are so very comfortable. On the garden side the rooms have ☞ private balconies, which are a nice addition to the inn. Rooms looking south have a good view of Oyster Pond Bay.

There is a very pleasant lounge to relax in, and then there is the Earl of Chatham, the dining room, serving the most unbelievable food you can imagine. The help is beautifully trained. The chef has a ☞ briefing with them each night, so they can explain each course.

I have never seen appetizers presented this way. There were four different mousses. I tried Sea Bass and Salmon Mousse with lobster sauce. I really wanted them all. And such different soups.

I had cold leek and cream of carrot soup, thick and sumptuous. There is a very complete herb garden at the inn, and all the herbs are used in the kitchen.

Several different sorbets are served before the entree. Cantaloupe, grapefruit, and kiwi sorbets are but a few. I had lobster and medallions of veal, and oh, were they good. All this time you are looking at a magnificent dessert cart with an unbelievable array of sweets. I finally had to choose and had chocolate mousse topped with strawberries in Grand Marnier and real whipped cream. A snifter of Rémy Martin and I could hardly leave the table.

I needed a walk and there are nice places to go. The water is close at hand and every Friday night band concerts are held in nearby Kate Gould Park. What a nice way to meet the other guests.

The inn has a twenty-six-foot cabin cruiser, on which there are trips to Nantucket and Monomoy Islands. Guenther is a Coast Guard–licensed skipper, and the boat is equipped with radio and radar. The inn also has three all-weather Har-Thu tennis courts in a beautiful parklike setting, a resident tennis pro, pro shop, and private lessons. Add to this a six-foot TV screen in the downstairs lounge, and your vacation is complete.

How to get there: From Route 6 take Exit 11, go south on Route 137 to its end, take a left on Route 28 to Chatham Center. At your first traffic light, in about three miles, go right on Queen Anne Road. The inn is on your right.

✱

E: *Imagine receiving this lovely place for a wedding gift. True. It happened in 1840.*

The Town House Inn
Chatham, Massachusetts
02633

Innkeepers: Russell and Svea Peterson
Telephone: 617-945-2180
Rooms: 24, all with private bath, television, refrigerator, and telephone;
2 have water beds; 2 cottages have fireplace and air conditioning.
Rates: $85 to $125, double occupancy, EPB.
Facilities: Closed December until Washington's Birthday. Full breakfast, lunch June through September, beer and wine license. Friday night band concerts, golf, tennis, and beaches nearby. All major credit cards accepted.

The front porch that overlooks Main Street beckons me. The 4th of July parade, one of the summer's biggest events, goes right by the front door. Best seat in town is the porch of this inn.

The original structure dates back to the 1820s. Remains of the foundation still can be seen in the cellar, and some of the original woodwork is here. The carved moldings and wood trim depict harpoon and oar motifs. The floors are made of hemlock, and the original walls, recently exposed, have hand-painted scrolling.

The ☛ rooms are immaculate; matter of fact, the whole inn is. If you have always wanted to try a water bed, here is your chance. I think they are neat. The rest of the beds are very comfortable, also. All of the linens and towels are laundered right here by Svea. She likes to hang them out, when weather permits, for that ☞ lovely smell of fresh air.

Breakfast is not a ho-hum thing here. Russ bakes the muffins and Svea does wonders with Scandinavian goodies. Favorites are Svea's ☞ Finnish pancakes with a fresh fruit melange on top and her French toast with apricots.

The restaurant is called Two Turtles. Using her mother's recipes, Svea prepares Swedish pickled herring and Swedish meatballs as well as desserts. The chef provides a nice array of appetizers and main courses. Some specialties have been deluxe-cut Western lamb chops, scampi cooked with Svea's homegrown dill, and, of course, fresh fish. This is some lunch!

How to get there: Take Route 6 (Mid-Cape highway) to Exit 11, Route 137 south to Route 28 and east to the center of downtown Chatham. Watch for the Eldredge Library on your left. The inn is next door at 11 Library Lane.

❧

E: *Children are welcome and there are baby sitters available.*

Deerfield Inn
Deerfield, Massachusetts
01342

Innkeeper: Paul J. Burns
Telephone: 413-774-5587
Rooms: 23, all with private bath and air conditioning.
Rates: $75 to $80, single or double occupancy, EP.
Facilities: Open all year. Closed Christmas Day. Breakfast, lunch, dinner. Cocktail lounge, two bars. Elevator. Color television in lounge. Museum, Deerfield Academy, historic house tours nearby. All major credit cards accepted.

Some years back a serious fire did extensive damage to this lovely old inn, but alumni of Deerfield and many others banded together and rebuilt the inn. They did such an exquisite job the federal government has designated the inn a ☛ National Historic Site.

☛ The rocking chairs on the front porch somehow let you know how lovely things will be inside. The parlors are beautifully furnished with mostly twentieth-century copies or adaptations. The Beehive Parlor, done in shades of blue, is a restful place for a cocktail or two. The main dining room is spacious, serving the kind of food befitting the setting. The chef prepares a daily special, taking advantage of seasonal and local market offerings. He also does magic things with veal, chicken, and fish.

The luncheon menu has some interesting and quite different offerings, such as Lamb Brochette, marinated lamb with vegetables on a skewer, and very good. There is also Chicken Mandarin Salad that will light up your day. By the way, all the baking is done right here.

The bedrooms are joys, ☞ Beauty-Rest mattresses, matching bedspreads and drapes, comfortable chairs, ☞ and good lights for restful reading or needlework. The baths have been color coordinated with the rooms they serve. Little to nothing has been left to chance in this restoration.

There is a coffee shop on the lower level, which gives off onto an outdoor garden. Perfect spot for informal meals, and a place the children will love.

How to get there: From I-91 take Exit 24 northbound. Go 6 miles north on Route 5. At the sign for Old Deerfield Village take a left. The inn will be on your left just past the Academy.

❋

E: *For an old "inn creeper" like me this inn is the icing on the cake.*

An unlit hearth in a good tavern is warmer by equators than a blazing fire where there is no love.

Winsor House Inn
Duxbury, Massachusetts
02332

Innkeepers: David and Patricia O'Connell
Telephone: 617-934-0991
Rooms: 2, plus 1 suite, all with private bath and telephone.
Rates: $70 to $90, double occupancy, EPB.
Facilities: Open all year. Breakfast, lunch, dinner, Sunday brunch from
first Sunday in October to Mother's Day. Bar and lounge. Boating,
fishing, and swimming nearby. All major credit cards accepted.

Winsor House was built in 1803 by the Winsor family as a
private residence. In 1932 part of the family turned the house
into an inn. Now the O'Connells have restored it to its original
loveliness. This really would be a wonderful place for a wedding.
From the sitting room full of books and comfortable couches and
chairs to the lovely bedrooms, this is a very nice place to be.

The dining room has a 🐾 double fireplace. There's a smaller
one in a smaller dining room. They provide a warm and cozy
atmosphere for the superb food. There were four of us at the
table, David and Pat, Paula Schaeffer, and me. We all ordered a
different appetizer, soup, entree, and dessert, and then we shared
our food. What a great way to taste a lot of dishes from the menu,
and what a treat it all was. Really, the food is beyond belief. It is

so ☛ well prepared. The veal is perfectly tender. ☛ The lobster fettucine was the best I have ever had. As you may guess, the chef always has specials, too.

The pub has a lighter menu. The carriage house is used for brunch and breakfast. The menus for these meals are delightful and include ☛ fresh fruit and fresh juices. I think they make a big difference to a breakfast. Summer lunch is served outside on the patio. The swing chairs are unique and made at the state prison.

The bar in the pub is just great. Grandma and Grandpa Winsor lean out a window behind the bar watching all. You must come and see them. There are pewter mugs hanging on a wall with names and numbers of the members of the Unwinders Club. I love the name. I met a few of the members and they only had nice things to say about the inn and its keepers. There is a glorious fireplace in here. I'm planning to return for a winter unwinder.

How to get there: Take Exit 11 off Route 3 south. Bear right at the end of the ramp onto Route 14. Follow Route 14 until it ends. Bear right onto Washington Street.

∽

E: *Going from the pub to the dining room you'll see a full-length portrait of Daniel Winsor. Amazing how much he looks like David O'Connell.*

The Nauset House Inn
East Orleans, Massachusetts
02643

Innkeepers: Diane and Al Johnson
Telephone: 617-255-2195
Rooms: 14, 8 with private bath.
Rates: $35 to $80, double occupancy, EP.
Facilities: Open April 1 to October 31. Full or continental breakfast only
    meal served. BYOB. Restaurants, antique shops, bicycling, hiking,
    and ocean beach nearby. MasterCard and Visa accepted.

    Nauset Beach at East Orleans is the first of the great Atlantic
beaches that rim Cape Cod; rolling dunes, dashing surf, and
wide swaths of sand run southward for more than ten miles.
There are quiet, out-of-the-way coves that offer the beachgoer an
ideal place to sun and picnic, or just to relax and enjoy. If your
tastes are for fresh water, there are dozens of inland ponds at
hand.
    Breakfast is the only meal served here, but it is a real 🖙 old-
fashioned country one, and so good. One beautiful morning I had
the best French toast that I had tasted in a long time.
    A unique feature of the inn is its 🖙 1908 conservatory filled
with plants and flowers and a dolphin fountain. The very com-

fortable wicker furniture makes this a great spot to while away a summer evening.

The guest rooms are nice and cozy. One has a balcony and some have a sitting area. It's great to come back to a lovely inn like this after a day on the beach or in a boat. The patio offers a view of the sea that is so tranquil.

The Johnsons have two dogs, Roo and Winnie, who are fun dogs. They will pick up small stones and bring them in to the guests.

There's so much to do in this area. There is a multitude of good restaurants, antique stores, and shopping spots for your every need. It's a great area for biking, hiking, boating, and fishing, and, of course, for enjoying the beautiful beach. And if you want a less active day, drive out to Provincetown. It is not too many miles away and well worth the trip.

How to get there: From the Mid-Cape Highway (Route 6), go to Main Street in East Orleans. Turn right onto Beach Road, and the inn is on your right.

E: *You must see the instant relatives in each room!*

*Snug in a country inn, I have finally found
the perfect topping to a windy Cape Cod day.*

The Charlotte Inn
Edgartown, Massachusetts
02539

Innkeepers: Gery and Paula Conover
Telephone: 617-627-4751
Rooms: 25 plus 2 suites, 22 with private bath; some with fireplace.
Rates: In season, $110 to $250; off season, $40 to $195; suite $250 in
August and $195 rest of year; double occupancy, EPB.
Facilities: Open all year. In season, lunch and dinner. Off season, din-
ner on weekends. Sunday brunch year round. Reservations a must.
Gift shop and gallery. Sailing, swimming, fishing, golfing, and ten-
nis nearby. All major credit cards accepted.

The start of your vacation is a forty-five-minute ferry ride to
Martha's Vineyard. It's wise to make early reservations for your
automobile on the ferry. There also are cabs if you prefer not to
take your car.

When you open the door to the inn you are in the
☛ Edgartown Art Gallery, with interesting artifacts and paintings, both watercolor and oil. This is a well-appointed gallery
featuring such artists as Ray Ellis who has a fine talent in both
media. The inn also has an unusual gift shop.

Four of us had dinner in the inn's lovely French restaurant
named L'Etoile. The food was exquisite. ☛ Capon breast stuffed

with duxelles, spinach, and sun-dried tomatoes with coriander mayonnaise was the best I have had. I tasted everyone's food— nice occupation I have. Rack of lamb, served rare, with red wine rosemary sauce, and accompanied by potato and yam gratin was excellent. They also have a special or two, but then everything is so special, the word does not fit. At brunch the cold cucumber soup was served with chives and followed by entrees like blueberry soufflé pancakes with crème fraîche. For breakfast I had a strawberry crepe that I can still remember vividly. Freshly squeezed juices and fruit muffins. . . . Heaven!

The rooms are authentic. There are Early American four-poster beds, fireplaces, and the carriage house is sumptuous. The second-floor suite with fireplace I could live in. Paula has a touch with rooms—comfortable furniture, down pillows, down comforters, and all the amenities. As an example, the shower curtains are eyelet and so pretty. As a finishing touch, there are plenty of large towels.

Across the street is the Garden House, and it is Edgartown at its best. The living room is unique and beautifully furnished, and has a fireplace that is always set for you. The rooms over here are just so handsome. Paula, by the way, has green hands, and all about are gardens that just outdo each other.

How to get there: Reservations are a must if you take your car on the ferry from Woods Hole, Massachusetts. Forty-five minutes later you are in Vineyard Haven. After a 15-minute ride, you are in Edgartown, and on Summer Street is the inn.

❁

E: *Gery and Paula are special innkeepers, but they do need the help of Andrew and Morgan, the dogs, and Oscar and Cricket, the cats.*

Coonamessett Inn
Falmouth, Massachusetts
02541

Innkeeper: Joe Badot
Telephone: 617-548-2300
Rooms: 25 suites, all with private bath.
Rates: $60 to $115, per room, EP; EPB in summer only.
Facilities: Open all year. Breakfast, lunch, dinner, bar. Parking. All major credit cards accepted.

In 1796, in a rolling field that sloped gently down to a lovely pond, Thomas Jones constructed a house and barn that was to become Coonamessett Inn (Indian, for "the place of the large fish"). The framework of the house is finished with wooden peg joints, and much of the interior paneling is original. Many of the bricks in the old fireplaces are thought to be made of ballast brought from Europe in the holds of sailing ships. Hanging in the inn are many paintings by the primitive American artist, Ralph Cahoon. They represent much of the history of the Coonamessett.

The food is excellent, offered from a large, varied menu, and served by friendly waitresses. Breakfasts are memorable.

Luncheons attract a lot of people, as the inn's food reputation travels far and wide. The famous Coonamessett Onion Rings are glorious. Dinner appetizers are many, including clams casino—my favorite after lobster—and baked imported brie with basil pesto. A real winner, and judged to be the ☞ best in the East, is the lobster bisque, and I'll second it. It's really almost better than I make! And dinner entrees are great, with fresh lobster meat, Cape Cod lobster pie, or cold boiled lobster. There are other seafood dishes, and meat eaters are not forgotten either. There are beef, lamb, and veal entrees, plus the chef's special ☞ homemade fresh pasta of the day.

The guest suites have recently been refurbished. They have a sitting room, bedroom, modern bath, color television, and touch-tone telephones. They are furnished with period antiques and colonial pine and cherry reproductions. These are cottage suites, as there are no guest rooms in the inn itself.

I love the Cape off season, and it is good to know that no matter what day I decide to come, I will receive a cordial welcome here. The inn grounds are beautiful and are kept in mint condition year round. All around you will see the loveliest array of grass, trees, flowers, shrubs . . . and peace. Don't forget the peace.

How to get there: Take Route 28 at the bridge over the canal, and go into Falmouth. Turn left on Jones Road, and at the intersection of Gifford Street you will see the inn.

⌇

E: *I wish I lived closer, because I like the whole thing, starting with the flower arrangements, fresh every other day, that are done by a man who really knows how to arrange. He is helped by Tess, the inn dog, who is a beauty. He is of the Bouvier breed.*

Mostly Hall
Falmouth, Massachusetts
02540

Innkeepers: Jim and Carolyn Lloyd
Telephone: 617-548-3786
Rooms: 7, 5 with private bath.
Rates: $50 to $90, per room, EPB.
Facilities: Closed three weeks in February. Breakfast only meal served.
Menus available for nearby restaurants. BYOB. Children over 16 are
welcome. Bicycles. Beaches, ferries to islands, four-mile ocean bike
path, summer theaters nearby. No credit cards accepted.

Mostly Hall is an authentic New Orleans home built in 1849
by Captain Albert Nye as a wedding present for his southern
bride. There are floor-to-ceiling windows and thirteen-foot ceilings. Slowly revolving Bombay fans make this handsome inn
even more special.

You will find a spinet piano and a Victorian couch in the
living room. There are oriental rugs and a pair of couches covered
in a striped blue velvet. I felt right at home. I have a big comfortable chair at home in the same fabric.

The guest rooms are very different. The walls are ☛ covered
with sheets, and they look terrific. The beds are very comfortable,
perfect for a good night's sleep.

Maybe dinner will be served in the off-season. Now it is breakfast only, but what a breakfast. During the summer it is served on the lovely porches that surround the inn. Jim is the grill man and Caroline does the rest. Ham rolls with spinach, topped with cheddar cheese sauce. French toast stuffed with walnuts and cream cheese. Eggs Benedict soufflé. Cheese blintz muffins with hot blueberry sauce. What a list, and these are just a few of the breakfast dishes they prepare.

You can walk from the inn to the village center. Do sample their library and shops. Visit the church with a bell cast by Paul Revere. Restaurants are close at hand, and so are the beaches and ferries to the islands.

How to get there: Take Route 28 to Falmouth. Go left on Route 28 south. It is 500 yards to the inn. The address is 27 Main Street. The inn is on the right, set well back from the road.

✻

E: *There is a lovely gazebo at the rear of the property, watched over by Yuki, the Samoyed.*

"Enough," he cried
and left with all speed
for the neighborhood inn.

olive Metcalf

Windflower Inn
Great Barrington, Massachusetts
01230

Innkeepers: Barbara and Gerald Liebert, Claudia and John Ryan
Telephone: 413-528-2720
Rooms: 13, all with private bath, many with fireplace.
Rates: $55 to $77, per person, double occupancy, MAP.
Facilities: Open all year. Breakfast, dinner, full license. Reservations a
    must. Swimming pool. Golf, tennis, downhill and cross-country ski-
    ing, music, and theater nearby. No credit cards honored, but per-
    sonal checks accepted.

Great Barrington was settled in the eighteenth century, and
today is a lovely resort town. The inn was built in 1820, and is
Federal in style.

I like the large living room. It has a white brick fireplace,
couches, and a huge coffee table covered with magazines. Very
conducive to 🖙 loafing. There also is a reading or game room
with a piano.

The guest rooms are spacious. All the beds are new and
some have canopies. Fireplaces are in some of the rooms. The
room on the first floor has its own entrance from the terrace and
a large stone fireplace. It's a lovely room.

The dining room features Currier & Ives snow scenes on the

walls and a coffeepot bubbling on the mantel all day. In the late afternoon you can have your choice of tea or cocktails with a grand assortment of hors d'oeuvres.

Barbara and Claudia, mother and daughter, are the chefs. Every evening they give you a choice of three entrees, and each one is cooked fresh. Roast Duck with Plum Sauce, Salmon with Sorrel Sauce, and Veal Marsala with Peppercorns are just a few hints of what you might expect. The ☛ vegetable garden is a seventy-by-ninety-foot spread of delights. John was ready to go out and pick raspberries when I saw him. He is the only one who picks them because he's so careful that they don't get bruised. ☛ Barbara makes any dessert you can think of with raspberries and chocolate (one of my favorite combinations).

The country club across the street is available for golf and tennis. The inn's own swimming pool is very relaxing, and in summer you have Tanglewood, Jacob's Pillow, and the Berkshire Theater nearby.

How to get there: The inn is on Route 23, 3 miles west of Great Barrington.

∽&

E: *The wraparound porch is so nice. Dinner is served out here in summer.*

> *Our sympathy for the hardships*
> *of our forbears should be somewhat mitigated*
> *by the fact that they had the best*
> *of country inns.*

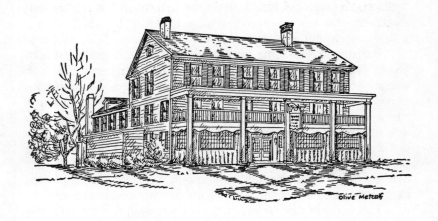

The Morgan House
Lee, Massachusetts
01238

Innkeepers: Beth and Bill Orford
Telephone: 413-243-0181
Rooms: 13, one with private bath.
Rates: $30 to $85, double occupancy, EPB.
Facilities: Open all year. Lunch, dinner, bar, lounge. American Express, MasterCard, and Visa accepted.

The Morgan House is another of my few in-town inns. Very nice to have in any town. The inn has a long and interesting history dating back to 1826 when it was built as a private home. In 1853 it was converted into a stagecoach inn, and an inn it has remained.

The lobby is papered in ☞ old registration sheets, many of them showing the names of the noted visitors over the past 100 years, such as Ulysses S. Grant, Robert E. Lee, Buffalo "Bill" Cody, Horace Greeley, and George Bernard Shaw. Many of the pages are beautifully decorated in flowing script advertising the bill at the local opera house.

The guest rooms are furnished with early American pieces. The walls are stenciled, and everything is clean and crisp. There is a porch on the second floor looking over Main Street for the guests' use. Wicker chairs make an afternoon here extremely delightful.

Now for the best part, the food. The veal is butchered and pounded here in the inn's kitchen. You just know it will be good. The menu shows thirteen different appetizers to go with the entrees, every one of which is prepared here. One different entree you should try is the Yankee Pork Chops, two generously cut chops served with a dressing of apples and raisins. All breads and desserts are created in the kitchen. An example is Pear Helen, ice cream capped with half a pear, laced with chocolate sauce, and topped with a dab of sweet whipped cream.

You can host a small meeting or special occasion in the Coach Room on the second floor. The room can accommodate fifty people.

There is so much to do in this lovely part of the world I just may write a book on the subject.

How to get there: From the Massachusetts Turnpike, take Exit 2. Follow Route 20 west one mile to the center of Lee. The inn will be on your left.

❋

E: *The inn is famous for its New England Duckling. The young duckling is brushed with imported mustard, topped with Provolone cheese, roasted to a delicate crispness, and finished with a special Triple Sec sauce. Yum yum.*

olive Metcalf

The Candle Light Inn
Lenox, Massachusetts
01240

Innkeepers: Robert Artig and Marsha Heller
Telephone: 413-637-1555
Rooms: 8, all with private bath.
Rates: $50 to $120, double occupancy, EP.
Facilities: Open all year. Lunch, dinner, Sunday brunch, piano bar. Pub
with entertainment on weekends. All major credit cards accepted.

The Candle Light Inn was built in the early 1900s by a wealthy Englishman as a wedding present for his daughter who, by the way, never set foot in it. The location of the inn is very convenient as it is right in the center of town and just three minutes from Tanglewood. It's also fun to go watch the dancing at Jacob's Pillow or browse in the local crafts shops and galleries.

Christmas is a time of royal splendor here at the inn. They ☛ decorate for each season, but Christmas is just something special and worth a trip from anywhere.

An old wagon and an old double sled are on the lawn, Tiffany lamps are on the porch, and a lovely flower cart is in the entrance hall. Straight ahead is the bar, and what a bar, done pub-style with some of the ☛ greatest stemware I have ever seen.

The dessert cart sits at the entrance of one of the dining rooms with a beautiful array of all homemade desserts, each one better than the next. There is a gracious fireplace in this dining room. Napery is bluest white. The chairs are comfortable, and the food divine. All the food is fresh and cooked to order; nothing frozen in this chef's kitchen except the ice cubes. And it is good! The luncheon menu features some great choices. Angel hair pasta with tomatoes, garlic, and olive oil, plus interesting sandwiches and burgers. Breast of Chicken Pot Pie is yummy. For a dinner appetizer I discovered Pâté de Strasbourg Foie Gras with Truffles. Wow! Dinner entrees like Shrimp, Lobster, and Scallops Mornay, and Boneless Breast of Chicken Amandine are a delight. The poultry, veal, beef, and lamb selections are varied and good.

Flowers are all over the inn, with Boston ferns at the windows, and fuchsias in abundance, usually hanging together with impatiens. And the backyard in summer is a wealth of blooms.

How to get there: The inn is at 53 Walker Street. Turn into Lenox on Route 7-A, off Route 7.

$$*$$

E: *The marble counters in some of the bathrooms are really nice.*

> *Man has tendencies of many temperatures,*
> *the warmest of which is hospitality.*

The Gateways Inn
Lenox, Massachusetts
01240

Innkeepers: Lilliane and Gerhard Schmid
Telephone: 413-637-2532
Rooms: 8, all with private bath; one suite with fireplace.
Rates: $80 to $110, double; $200, suite; continental breakfast included.
Facilities: Open all year. Restaurant closed Sundays and Mondays in winter. In summer, dinner by reservation preferred. Free guest privileges at Haus Andreas. MasterCard and Visa accepted.

The Gateways began as a mansion built for Harley Procter of Procter and Gamble, the Ivory soap magnate. It is in the shape of his favorite product, a cake of soap. It is square and flat on top.

Chef-owner Gerhard was the winner of both ☞ a silver and a gold medal in the 1968 International Culinary Competition, and three Olympic gold medals in 1976. Gerhard also had the honor of preparing Boston's royal luncheon for Queen Elizabeth during her bicentennial visit in 1976. To add to the laurels, the Gateways rates ☞ four stars in the Mobil Guide.

Want a few hints of what to expect? Lobster cocktail, mussels vinaigrette, and smoked salmon are some of the appetizers. Chilled vichysoisse and bisques are some soups. These are followed by wonderful salads and entrees like veal sweetbreads,

Veal Contina, steaks, Salmon Continental, rack of lamb, fish, game, poultry, and specials of the house. The desserts are fabulous. I really cannot say enough about his creations. You'll have to try them for yourself.

Two bedrooms, with their high ceilings, are perfect for the massive furniture with which they are furnished. The other bedrooms, equally lovely, have colonial-style furniture. Color-coordinated towels add just the right final touch. The suite is called the Fiedler Suite because Arthur Fiedler stayed in it so many times. It is lavish in its appointments, and worth all it costs to spend a night in.

The sister inn, Haus Andreas, is named for the Schmids' son, and is but five miles away. It is a lovely, old colonial mansion with a charming pastoral view. Here you will have complimentary guest privileges entitling you to swim, play tennis, and ride bicycles.

How to get there: Take Route 7 to Route 7A. The inn is on Route 7A, one block away from the intersection of Routes 183 and 7A.

E: *The oval windows beside the front door and the magnificent stairway alone are worth a visit here.*

The Village Inn
Lenox, Massachusetts
01240

Innkeepers: Clifford Rudisill and Ray Wilson
Telephone: 413-637-0020
Rooms: 28, 25 with private bath.
Rates: $50 to $120, double occupancy, EP.
Facilities: Open all year. Breakfast, afternoon tea, dinner Wednesday
   through Sunday, Sunday brunch. Late after-concert suppers on
   Friday and Saturday. Village Tavern. Skiing, tennis, golfing, swim-
   ming, horseback riding, fishing, hiking, Tanglewood, and Jacob's
   Pillow nearby. MasterCard and Visa accepted.

There is a saying here at the inn, "If you can't be a house
guest in the Berkshires, be ours." This surely would be a fine
choice. The rooms are so clean and cheerful. The inn's walls are
covered with stenciled wallpapers, the maple floors have oriental
rugs, and antiques are found throughout the inn.

The Village Tavern was built in the old cellars of this 1771
house, and is furnished with seats made from church pews. On
those blustery winter days there is a cheery fire to go with your
drink. The living room, called the Common Room, is a delightful
place to sit and listen to the grand piano being played. There is a
nice television and reading room for your comfort.

A real first is an authentic English tea served from 3:30 to 5:00 every day with homemade scones, pastries, and small tea sandwiches. To make it perfect, you are provided with Devonshire-style clotted cream.

Breakfast is a thing of joy. Any inn that serves eggs Benedict with a glass of champagne gets my hearty applause. Another clap of the hands goes for their Irish coffee. There are many other good things to eat here. The dinner menu begins with such specialties as snails sautéed in brandy and white wine on toasted crusts with a shallot and garlic cream, and smoked Maine trout with horseradish cream. The summer menu offers your choice of cold fresh fruit soup (blueberry, raspberry, or strawberry), followed by fresh Columbia River poached salmon with a gingered hollandaise sauce, or Fresh Vegetable Plate, steamed and lightly sautéed vegetables. This dish is not seen often enough on a menu.

The inn is near many activities, churches, shops, the library, and the bus stop.

How to get there: Take Route 7A off Route 7 and turn on Church Street in Lenox. The inn is on the right.

❋

E: *Once a month on Sunday afternoons the inn features chamber music concerts. All this and English tea. Oh my.*

Olive Metcalf

Wheatleigh
Lenox, Massachusetts
01240

Innkeepers: Susan and Linfield Simon
Telephone: 413-637-0610
Rooms: 17, all with private bath.
Rates: $95 to $325, double occupancy, continental breakfast included.
Facilities: Open all year. Dinner served Tuesday through Sunday, lounge. Children over 8 are welcome; pets are not. Swimming, tennis, cross-country skiing. All major credit cards accepted.

In the heart of the beautiful Berkshires, overlooking a lake, amid lawns and gardens on twenty-two self-contained acres stands the estate of Wheatleigh, former home of the Countess de Heredia. The centerpiece of this property is an elegant private palace fashioned after an Italian palazzo. The cream-colored manse re-creates the architecture of sixteenth-century Florence. You must read the brochure of Wheatleigh, for it says it all so well.

Patios, pergolas, porticos, and terraces surround this lovely old mansion. The carvings over the fireplaces, ☛ cupids entwined in garlands, are exquisite. In charming contrast, the inn also has the ☛ largest collection of contemporary ceramics in the New England area. There are many lovely porcelain pieces on the walls. In the dining room are tile paintings weighing over 500 pounds. They are Doultons from 1830; this was before it became Royal Doulton. They are just beautiful.

There is a service bar in a lovely lounge, and boy, you sure can relax in the furniture in here. It has a wonderful fireplace and the views from here are glorious. And imagine a ☞ great hall with a grand staircase right out of a castle in Europe. There are also exquisite stained glass windows in pale pastels, plus gorgeous, comfortable furniture. From the great hall you can hear the tinkle of the fountain out in the garden.

The rooms are ☞ smashing with lots of white dotted swiss and eyelet material for the canopy beds. Do you long for your own balcony overlooking a lovely lake? No problem. Reserve one here.

At the entrance to the dining room the homemade desserts are beautifully displayed along with French champagne in six sizes from a jeroboam to a small bottle for one. This is very nice indeed. I chose grilled quail on young lettuce leaves and raspberries for a dinner appetizer; it was superb. Tartare of fresh tuna was so beautifully presented, just like a Japanese picture, and delicious. I also had chilled fresh pea soup with curry and sorrel, followed by monkfish coated with pistachios, sautéed, with red wine sauce. Homemade sorbets are very good, but then, so is everything here.

How to get there: From Stockbridge at the Red Lion Inn where Route 7 turns right, go straight on Prospect Hill Road, bearing left. Go past the Stockbridge Bowl and up a hill to Wheatleigh. From the Massachusetts Turnpike, take Exit 2, and follow signs to Lenox. In the center of Lenox, take Route 183, pass the main gate of Tanglewood, and then take the first left on West Hawthorne. Go one mile to Wheatleigh.

∽

E: *Susan's description of the inn is "elegance without arrogance," and Lin's is "the ultimate urban amenity." Mine is "a perfect country inn."*

Olive Metcalf

Jared Coffin House
Nantucket, Massachusetts
02554

Innkeepers: Philip and Margaret Read; manager, Don Terry
Telephone: 617-228-2400
Rooms: 58; 9 in main house; 16 simpler rooms in Eben Allen Wing; 3
    rooms in Swain house, connected to the Eben Allen Wing; 12 rooms
    in Daniel Webster house across the patio; 18 rooms in two houses
    across the street.
Rates: $50, single; $95 to $135, double; EP.
Facilities: Open all year. Breakfast, lunch, dinner, taproom. Eben Allen
    Room for private parties. Near swimming and tennis. All major
    credit cards accepted.

It is well worth the thirty-mile trip by ferry, or the plane trip
from Boston or New York, to end up at the Jared Coffin House.
Built as a private home in 1845, the three-story brick house with
slate roof became an inn only twelve years later. The inn passed
through many hands before it came to the extremely 🐾 capable
ones of Philip and Margaret Read.

The public rooms at the inn reflect charm and warmth. The
furnishings are Chippendale and Sheraton, and showing the results of the world-wide voyaging by the Nantucket whalemen are
Chinese and Japanese objets d'art and furniture.

104

To add to the charm are many fabrics and some furniture that have been made right here on the island. In addition to the main house, there are several other close-by houses that go with the inn. All are done beautifully for your every comfort.

☛ The taproom, located on the lowest level, is a warm, happy, fun place. Here you meet the local people and spin yarns with all. Old pine walls and hand-hewn beams reflect a warm atmosphere. Luncheon is served down here with good burgers and great, hearty soups. During the winter this is a nice spot for informal dinners.

The main dining room, papered with authentic wallpapers, is quiet and elegant. Wedgewood china and pistol-handled silverware make dining a special pleasure, and reflect the good life demanded by the nineteenth-century owners of the great Nantucket whaling ships.

The inn is located in the heart of Nantucket's Historic District, about one-eighth mile from a public beach, and one mile from the island's largest public beach and tennis courts. It's a pleasant three-mile bicycle ride to superb surf swimming on the South Shore.

How to get there: To get to Nantucket, take a ferry from Hyannis (April through January) or Woods Hole (January through March and summer months). First call 617-540-2022 for reservations. Or take a plane from Boston, Hyannis, or New York. The House is located 2 blocks north of Main Street, and 2 blocks west of Steamboat Wharf.

✳

E: *The size and the quantity of the luxurious bath towels pleased me greatly. The housekeeping staff does a wonderful job, and the exquisite antiques reflect their loving care.*

Olive Metcalf

The Woodbox
Nantucket, Massachusetts
02554

Innkeeper: Dexter Tutein
Telephone: 617-228-0587
Rooms: 3 doubles and 6 suites, all with private bath, in two buildings.
Rates: $90 to $140, double occupancy, EP.
Facilities: Open Memorial Day to Columbus Day. Full breakfast, dinner, beer and wine license. Swimming, boating, biking nearby. No credit cards honored, but personal checks accepted.

For thirty-six years there has been a Tutein running this inn. Built in 1709, it is the oldest inn on Nantucket Island. What a treat to be here.

The suites are unique. In an old building like this, you cannot change the structure to modernize it, so the bathrooms have been very inventively fit in. Very pretty and comfortable. The suite I was in had a ☛ fireplace in the living room, two bedrooms, one with a huge canopy bed, and a lovely little private patio. It was hard to leave.

There are three dining rooms in the inn. I'm sure I had dinner in what must be the oldest public dining room in New England. The room has two ☛ "king's boards" on the wall of the immense, almost walk-in fireplace. Today the fireplace holds an old cradle with dried flowers. The china is old and there are nice touches on the tables like your own peppermill and cute little glass chicken holders for salt. Tall candlesticks add to the charm of this inn.

They are famous for their popovers and I believe it, having devoured quite a few. The food is truly gourmet. One of the appetizers was Gravlax—fresh salmon in a fresh dill marinade. Naturally the entrees include the catch of the day; I had fresh sea bass that was delicious. My dinner companion had lamb noisettes, which were so tender and good. The house salad dressing is excellent. Dessert, well, the best white chocolate mousse I have ever had.

The inn's breakfast is a great way to start the day. A tent card lists "Our Morning Breakfast Bubbles—Mimosas and Champagnes." Oh my. The pancakes and waffles come with blueberries, strawberries, peaches, or apples. Those wonderful popovers come with any egg dish.

How to get there: Take the ferry to Nantucket or fly from New Bedford. It's only 25 minutes. The inn is at 29 Fair Street. You can walk to it from the ferry.

E: *The powder room must be seen. There are no words to describe it.*

Country Inn at Princeton
Princeton, Massachusetts
01541

Innkeepers: Don and Maxine Plumridge
Telephone: 617-464-2030
Rooms: 6 suites, all with private bath.
Rates: $110 and $130, double occupancy, continental breakfast included.
Facilities: Inn open all year. Dining rooms closed Mondays and Tuesdays. Dinner served Wednesday through Sunday. Sunday brunch. No children under 12. American Express, MasterCard, and Visa accepted.

"The year 1890 had a certain charm and way about it," says the inn's brochure, and it is so right. The inn is a ⬛ Victorian delight. It was built with meticulous attention to every detail by Charles G. Washburn, an industrialist and outspoken senator, and a close friend of Theodore Roosevelt.

The parlor-living room is exquisite with swirling Casa Blanca ceiling fans with chandeliers, Victorian chairs and couches that are beautifully upholstered, and oriental rugs. The fireplace is massive and so cozy on a chilly night. All through the inn you will find ⬛ greenery and fine arts displayed with taste.

During the warmer months, guests can enjoy cocktails on the expansive wraparound veranda or garden terrace. There are three elegant dining rooms. The Library Den, striking in its Chinese Ming red wallcoverings, is available for private dining or small parties up to twelve guests. There is the Garden Room; there's also the more formal Washburn Room. There is so much to look at and enjoy. From the dining room windows you have a distinct view of Boston's twinkling lights.

Award after award keeps being presented to the inn and their five-star chef, Frank McClelland. And rightly so, for the food is spectacular. It is Country French cuisine, both creatively and lovingly prepared. On a recent visit I had for a first course the Vermont Lamb Prosciutto with White Truffle Oil. Excellent! Soup or salad is the second course, and I had the Washburn Salad, which is a little different each night. The main course is always splendid. If you inform the inn, Chef Frank will treat you to a menu tasting. Half portions of various first and second courses—what a way to taste his glorious food—topped by the Grand Dessert, a sampling of about four of the beauties. Oh my. The soufflé is also not to be missed.

I keep returning to sample the new magic created by the chef.

How to get there: From just north of Worcester take I–190 to Exit 5. Follow Route 140 north to Route 162 and turn left to Princeton. At the blinker by the post office, turn right. The inn is on the right just up the hill.

❋

E: *The accommodations are six extremely* *spacious parlor suites. They are sumptuous. Each one is different, and I could live forever in any one of them.*

Yankee Clipper Inn
Rockport, Massachusetts
01966

Innkeepers: Bob and Barbara Wemyss Ellis
Telephone: 617-546-3407
Rooms: 28, plus 6 suites, all with private bath, air conditioning, and
  telephone, in two buildings.
Rates: In season, $121 to $169, double occupancy, MAP; $60 to $75,
  double occupancy, EPB.
Facilities: Closed November 30 until December 27. Full breakfast, din-
  ner, BYOB. Only wine allowed in dining room. Heated saltwater
  pool, tours in powerboat. Fishing, boating, and shopping nearby.
  MasterCard and Visa accepted.

When you are lucky enough to be here and see a ☞ sunset,
you will be overwhelmed. It's a golden sea and sky, with the town
of Rockport in the distance. No camera could truly capture this
scene. Wait a while longer, and the moonlight on the sea is an
awesome sight.

Three buildings make up the Yankee Clipper. The inn is an
oceanfront mansion. Here the rooms have antique furniture, oriental rugs, and some canopy beds. Some rooms have porches.
You're sure to enjoy the TV lounge with cable TV and a really big
screen. All meals are served in this building.

The Quarterdeck has 🖝 large picture windows providing a panoramic view of the ocean. Upholstered chairs are placed in front of the windows. Sit back and relax; it's almost like being on a ship that does not move. All of the rooms in this building are beautifully furnished. Some of the rooms in the Bullfinch House have waterviews. If you stay here you are on the EPB plan; the other buildings are MAP.

The 🖝 glass-enclosed dining room has marvelous views that are matched by the marvelous food. I started my dinner with an appetizer of chicken fingers served with a honey mustard sauce. Chilled Melon Soup was different and 🖝 Yankee Clipper Scrod is a young cod fillet topped with scallops, cheddar cheese, and Galliano sauce. Delicious. I was determined to make room for dessert. I had a hard time choosing, but chocolate won. I had the 🖝 Grand Marnier Soufflé, layers of chocolate cream molded on a base of chocolate cake, and covered with a glaze of dark chocolate.

To work off some of the calories, you might want to swim in the heated saltwater pool at the inn. The inn also offers sightseeing tours in its powerboat. In the area there are whale-watching trips, fishing, and in the town of Rockport, fantastic shopping. It really is fun to walk around here.

And when you return to the inn, be sure to say hello to Rusty, the beautiful, well-trained inn dog.

How to get there: Take Route 128 north and east to Cape Ann. Route 128 intersects Route 127 at two points. The second one is shorter. After taking the second one, go about 4 miles to the "corners" where you should see a sign for the inn.

࿊

E: *Over the mantel is a portrait of Mehitable Lamon, Barbara's great-great-grandmother. That's really going back.*

Olive Metcalf

The Dan'l Webster Inn
Sandwich, Massachusetts
02563

Innkeeper: Steve Catania
Telephone: 617-888-3622
Rooms: 42, all with private bath.
Rates: $54 to $115, per person, MAP. $50 to $165, double occupancy,
   EP.
Facilities: Closed Christmas Day only. Breakfast, lunch, dinner, Sunday
   brunch, bar, lounge. Swimming pool, gift shop. Doll museum, glass
   museum. Heritage Plantation, and beaches nearby. All major credit
   cards accepted.

A 250-year-old linden tree, complete with bird feeders, stands
outside the Conservatory, one of the inn's three lovely dining
rooms. This is a glassed-in room, overlooking a beautifully landscaped courtyard and swimming pool. The Webster Room has
china cabinets to display ☞ old Sandwich glass on loan from the
museum. There's a portrait of Daniel Webster's second wife in
here. The Heritage Room has a huge open fireplace and a grand
piano on the stage for your entertainment. A ☞ dance band is
here on weekends, and they surely sounded good to me.
   These dining rooms provide the perfect atmosphere for the
excellent food. Breakfasts are hearty, with eggs, six different

omelettes, sausage, croissants, fruit, and much more. The lunch menu lists salads, sandwiches, and quite a few hot choices. Dinner is an adventure. The hors d'oeuvres list is extensive. I had clams casino and also tasted the escargots, which were served en croute with mushrooms, garlic, and herb butter. There are four veal offerings, chicken, ten different seafood specials, and, of course, beef. I had Châteaubriand, very nice because it was served for one. It was very good. Desserts are sinful, and there are special coffees.

The Devil 'n Dan Tavern is a cozy spot, with stained glass windows and very nice wooden bar stools. There are tables and chairs here for those who are not barflies.

All the guest rooms are a little different. Most have Hitchcock furniture. Some have canopy beds. All of the beds are comfortable. The new Webster Suite on the third floor of the inn has two bedrooms and two bathrooms. One bath has a Jacuzzi, and the other has a steam tub.

In the lovely Fessenden House next door are four suites. I was in the Captain Ezra Nye Suite. A whirlpool tub is in each of these suites as is a marble fireplace. They are beautifully furnished with classic antiques. I had to go up two steps to get into bed. Oh my, I do like it here.

How to get there: Go over the Bourne Bridge to a rotary; go ¾ of the way around it, taking the Route 6A exit that parallels the canal. Stay on this road until you come to the third set of lights. This is Jarves Street. Go right, then right again onto Main Street. The inn is on the right, close to the corner.

✳

E: *A split of wine is waiting in each guest room. How nice.*

The Weathervane Inn
South Egremont, Massachusetts
01258

Innkeepers: Anne and Vincent Murphy
Telephone: 413-528-9580
Rooms: 10, all with private bath.
Rates: $70, per person, EP, $130, MAP.
Facilities: Closed three weeks in spring and three weeks in late fall. Breakfast, dinner, Sunday brunch, bar, lounge. Swimming pool, antiques shop, outside games. MasterCard, Visa, and Diners Club accepted.

The Weathervane began its existence as a farmhouse in 1785. The original fireplace, which served as a heating and cooking unit, boasts a beehive bake oven. These are rarely seen today, but were a real necessity in those early times. The inn has been included in the ☛ National Register of Historic Places.

The sign over the bar says, "Kiss the Cook." Anne is the chef, daughter Trish is the pastry chef, and they are both pretty enough to kiss. Some of Anne's specials are Rock Cornish Hen with Kiwi Sauce, Duckling with Black Cherries, and ☛ Pork Tenderloin Normandy (an apple and Calvados concoction). There also are veal and fish entrees and ☛ vegetarian dishes if you let them know in advance. Trish's department turns out fresh fruit

114

pies, cheesecake, and chocolate chip walnut pie. Sound good? Well, it's even better eating. The dining room is cozy and attractive with nice napery and candles.

The inn is so fresh and clean in every corner that you know you have good innkeepers at hand. One of the rooms is named the Norman Rockwell Room because Anne has three of his works on the wall. The first has two youngsters looking at the moon. The second has the youngsters, now a bit older, at the soda fountain, and in the last they are even older at the registrar's desk getting a license to marry. Anne has some other Rockwell paintings at various places in the inn.

There is ☛ one room that needs special mention. It is over the kitchen and has a tiny bathtub with a shower.

All the public rooms are comfortable, and there is so much to do in this area all year that you could stay and stay. Be sure to visit the antiques dealer in the barn.

Bear is the inn dog and is perfect for the part. He is an English cocker spaniel.

How to get there: Follow Route 7 to Route 23 west. You are now 3 miles from South Egremont. The inn will be on your left.

⊷

E: *There are canopy beds in the new wing. The rooms are color coordinated, and finding cordials in them is a nice surprise.*

> *Man's cruelty to man knows almost no horizons.*
> *His continued existence, however, is justified*
> *when he says to a stranger, "Come in."*

 alive Metcalf

Federal House
South Lee, Massachusetts
01260

Innkeepers: Robin and Ken Almgren
Telephone: 413-243-1824
Rooms: 7, all with private bath and air conditioning.
Rates: $55 to $135, double occupancy, EPB.
Facilities: Closed one week in spring. Full breakfast in summer only;
   continental breakfast served during the rest of the year. Dinner,
   Sunday brunch, bar, lounge. Skiing, golf, and tennis nearby. All
   major credit cards accepted.

   Ken is the innkeeper/chef of Federal House. He worked for
one of my favorite people, Albert Stockli, of the Stonehenge Inn
in Ridgefield, Connecticut, who has now gone to his reward.
   The Federal House was built in 1824 by Thomas O. Hurlbut,
whose family came to America in 1635. It remained in this family
until 1948, when it became a summer home for family members
who resided in New York City. Today it has been restored to the
original country elegance it once had. Its architectural style is
Greek Revival.
   The rooms are spacious, ☞ air conditioned, and have large
windows. The wallpapers are lovely, and so are the Victorian

couches. Some of the antiques came from the original Hurlbut home, and some were handed down in the innkeepers' families.

Dinner, as well as Sunday brunch, is served in a choice of three lovely rooms—the original dining room, front parlor, or billiard room. No matter which one you choose, the tables are set with fine silver, tall candles, and ☞ fresh flowers that are just beautiful. The food, as you would expect in this elegant atmosphere, is glorious. No prepared foods are used. All the sauces and condiments are made right here. There are appetizers like cherrystones broiled with herb butter, cherrystones served on the half shell, and their own ☞ smoked trout with horseradish sauce. Dinner entrees include veal prepared two luscious ways, Escallope of Salmon with Caviar, and Chicken à la Kiev. To accompany your meal, choose a wine from the fine wine cellar. The inn also has a full license for other drinks.

Both Ken and Robin have had extensive training mostly in four-star restaurants, so it is no wonder this is a grand inn.

How to get there: South Lee is 4 miles from Lee and 1 mile from Stockbridge. The inn is on Main Street (Route 102).

❀

E: *The Federal House is soon to be listed in the National Register of Historic Places.*

Olive Metcalf

The Inn at Stockbridge
Stockbridge, Massachusetts
01262

Innkeepers: Lee and Don Weitz
Telephone: 413-298-3337
Rooms: 7, 5 with private bath.
Rates: $50 to $160, double occupancy, EPB.
Facilities: Closed a few months in winter or spring. Full breakfast, dinner by reservation on weekends. BYOB. Swimming pool. All major credit cards accepted.

There is a small red and gold sign by the side of the road directing you into the lane that leads to this lovely inn with stately white columns. Wonderful spot.

The living room-library has soft sofas and chairs, and is done in an intriguing blue print. Plenty of books and a fireplace are at hand. A room as cozy as this makes me want to curl up with a book or needlework.

Lee's dining room is beautiful, from the gleaming mahogany table to the sideboards groaning under the weight of her silver services. It is just grand. There is a real country kitchen, spacious and clean. What a wonderful place to cook.

And cooking is something Lee knows a lot about. Her breakfast is a real treat. Eggs Benedict, Breakfast Soufflé (a ham, cheese, and egg soufflé), and French Toast with Grand Marnier Whipped Butter are a few of the treats Lee makes to start your day. These are accompanied by home-baked goodies and fresh fruit and served on bone china. Mimosas are served on Sunday. The patio is a good place to savor breakfast in the summer.

The rooms are colorful and pleasant. They have king-sized or twin beds, double pillows, and ☛ heavy, thirsty, color-coordinated towels. You'll be pampered by such nice touches as turned-down beds and a mint on your pillow. Sheer comfort and joy.

There are twelve acres to roam about in and a large swimming pool to relax in. The trees that surround the whole scene are beautiful.

Lee sometimes can be coaxed to play her piano. This is quite a treat. Moto, the inn dog, likes it too.

How to get there: From the Massachusetts Turnpike, take Exit 2 onto Route 102 to Stockbridge. At the intersection of Routes 102 and 7, take Route 7 north 1.2 miles to the inn's driveway. (Look for the small red and gold sign on your right after you pass under the turnpike.)

༄

E: *Cheese and wine in the afternoon. Lovely.*

olive Metcalf

The Red Lion Inn
Stockbridge, Massachusetts
01262

Innkeeper: Betsy M. Holtzinger; Church Davis, Director of Lodging
Telephone: 413-298-5545
Rooms: 110, 80 with private bath; 6 suites in summer, 2 in winter.
Rates: $37 to $110, winter; $46 to $150, summer; double occupancy;
EP.
Facilities: Open all year. Breakfast, lunch, dinner, bar. Heated swimming pool. Elevator. Accessible to wheelchairs. Pink Kitty Gift Shop. All major credit cards accepted.

The Red Lion Inn is a four-season inn. In summer you have the Berkshire Music Festival at Tanglewood and the Jacob's Pillow Dance Festival, both world renowned. The inn's own ☞ heated swimming pool is a nice attraction. Fall's foliage is perhaps the most spectacular in New England; in winter there are snow-covered hills; in spring come the lovely green and flowers. All go together to make this a great spot anytime of year.

The inn is full of lovely old antiques. The halls are lined with antique couches, each one prettier than the next. From a four-poster, canopy bed to beds with great brass headboards, all the rooms are marvelously furnished and comfortable as sin. Whether in the inn itself or in one of the inn's adjacent houses, Stafford

House and Ma Bucks, you will love the accommodations. The wallpaper in Ma Bucks is a delight. All rooms have extra pillows, which I love.

Excellent food is served in the lovely dining room, or if you prefer, in the Widow Bingham's Tavern. There is an almost hidden booth designed for lovers in here.

The Lion's Den is downstairs with entertainment nightly, and it has its own small menu. In warm weather the flower-laden courtyard with its Back of the Bank Bar is a delightful place for food and grog.

Be sure you find an opportunity to visit The Red Lion Inn.

How to get there: Take Exit 2 from the Massachusetts Turnpike and follow Route 102 west to the inn.

E: *Norman Rockwell lived in Stockbridge. The Corner House is a step down the street, so do not miss this great museum of this wonderful artist's works.*

olive Metcalf

Colonel Ebenezer Crafts Inn
Fiske Hill, Sturbridge, Massachusetts
01566

Innkeeper: Pat Bibeau
Telephone: 617-347-3313
Rooms: 6, all with private bath; 2 suites.
Rates: January 2 through June, $85 to $90; July through October, $95 to $100; November to January 1, $90 to $95; suites higher; double occupancy, continental breakfast included.
Facilities: Open all year. Afternoon tea. Publick House nearby for other meals. Small swimming pool. Near Old Sturbridge Village. All major credit cards accepted.

In Colonial times the finest homes were usually found on the highest points of land. Such a location afforded the owners commanding views of their farmland and cattle. It also set them above their contemporaries. So David Fiske, Esquire, a builder, built this house in 1786 high above Sturbridge. The house was magnificently restored by the management of the Publick House and named after the inn's founder, Colonel Ebenezer Crafts.

Accommodations are wonderful. There are two ☞ queen-sized canopy beds that are real beauties. Some beds are four-posters. ☞ Terrycloth robes are placed in your room for your comfort. The wallpapers are subtle and elegant. The cottage suite was furnished by the Sturbridge Yankee Workshop. It joins the main inn by a short breezeway. It has a living room, bedroom, bath, and color television.

Provided for your relaxation is a nice living room with a baby grand piano, a color television with a videocassette recorder and movies, and a good library of books and *National Geographic* magazines that are always a pleasure to read or look through.

Your breakfast of freshly baked muffins, fresh fruit, juice, and coffee comes with a copy of the morning paper. In the afternoon, tea, sherry, and sweets are served. Or you can go two miles down the road to the famous Publick House in Sturbridge for a full breakfast. Here too you can have lunch and dinner and enjoy the lovely bar and cocktail lounge. You will find a gift shop and an incredible bake shop. Do not miss taking some treats home.

How to get there: Take Exit 3 from I–86, and bear right along the service road into Sturbridge. Continue to Route 131 where you turn right. Turn left at Hall Road and then right on Whittemore Road, which becomes Fiske Hill Road.

E: *Ask Pat to show you the Underground Railroad of Civil War Days. The slave hole is still here.*

There is no definition of a proper inn.
Like night and day it either is or is not.

Olive Metcalf

Publick House
Sturbridge, Massachusetts
01566

Innkeeper: Buddy Adler
Telephone: 617-347-3313
Rooms: 16 plus 9 suites, all with private bath, air conditioning, and
   telephone.
Rates: January 2 through June, $70 to $110; July through October, $82
   to $125; November through January 1, $77 to $119; suites higher;
   double occupancy, EP.
Facilities: Open all year. Breakfast, lunch, dinner, bar. Complimentary
   high tea for all guests. Ramp to restaurant. Television in lounge.
   Gift shop. Near Colonel Ebenezer Crafts Inn and Old Sturbridge
   Village. All major credit cards accepted.

It's a real pleasure to me to keep coming back to the Publick
House and finding it always the same, always excellent. As a
matter of fact, very little has changed here in the last 200 years.
The green still stretches along in front of it, and the trees still cast
their welcome shade. The Publick House is still taking care of the
wayfarer, feeding him well, providing a comfortable bed, and
supplying robust drink.

The Publick House calendar is fun to read. Throughout the
year there are special celebrations for holidays. They *do* keep

Christmas here! All twelve days of it. The Boar's Head Procession is truly unique, complete with a roast young suckling pig, a roast goose, and plum pudding. Wow!

Winter weekends are times for special treats, with chestnuts roasting by an open fire, and sleigh rides through nearby Old Sturbridge Village, a happy step backward in time.

The guest rooms are decorated with period furniture, while the penthouse suite has the modern conveniences of a television and king-sized bed. The wide floorboards and beamed ceilings have been here since Colonel Ebenezer Crafts founded the inn in 1771.

The barn, connected to the main house with a ramp, has been transformed into a restaurant. Double doors, topped by a glorious sunburst window, lead into a restaurant that serves hearty Yankee cooking such as delicious Lobster Pie. There is a little musician's gallery, still divided into stalls, that overlooks the main dining room. Beneath this is an attractive taproom, where a pianist holds forth, tinkling out nice noises.

A blueberry patch and a garden that covers more than an acre of land provide the inn with fresh fruit and vegetables during the summer.

I found my way by following my nose around behind the inn to the Bake Shoppe, where every day fresh banana bread, sticky buns, deep-dish apple pies, corn bread, and muffins come out of the ovens to tempt me from my diet! Take some along for hunger pangs along the road.

How to get there: Take the Massachusetts Turnpike to Exit 9. The Publick House is located on the Common in Sturbridge, on Route 131. From Hartford, take I–84 to I–86, Exit 3, which brings you right into Sturbridge.

E: *The inn's good jams, mustards, relishes, chowders, and more can now be enjoyed at home. They are beautifully packaged and mailed to you wherever you wish.*

Longfellow's Wayside Inn
Sudbury, Massachusetts
01776

Innkeeper. Francis J. Koppeis
Telephone: 617-443-8846
Rooms: 10, all with private bath, air conditioning, and telephone.
Rates: $47.50, single; $52.50, double, EP.
Facilities: Open all year. Closed Christmas Day. Breakfast for house
    guests only, lunch, dinner, bar. No room service or television. Pets
    limited, horses boarded. Gift shop, museum. All major credit cards
    accepted.

☛ Since 1959 Francis Koppeis has been the innkeeper here,
and what a wonderful job he does. Once you meet him you will
understand why this famous old inn functions so well and so
happily.

Eight generations of travelers have found food and lodging
for "man and beast" at the Wayside Inn. Route 20 is the old
stagecoach road to Boston, now well off the beaten track. The inn
looks much as it did 280 years ago, and still supplies the traveler
with hearty food and drink and a comfortable bed.

As with many old buildings, "improvements" were made to
the inn in the nineteenth century, but a complete restoration in
the 1950s afforded the opportunity to put many things back the

way they were in the beginning. Now part of the inn serves as a museum with priceless antiques displayed in their original settings.

There are a large dining room, and several smaller ones, a bar, a gift shop, and a lovely walled garden. At the end of the garden path is a bust of Henry Wadsworth Longfellow, who was inspired by the inn to link together a group of poems known to all schoolchildren as "Tales of a Wayside Inn."

Henry Ford bought 5,000 acres surrounding the inn in 1925, and since then this historic area has been preserved. A little way up the road stand a lovely chapel, the little red schoolhouse that gained fame in "Mary Had a Little Lamb," and a stone gristmill that still grinds grain for the rolls and muffins baked at the inn. I bought some of their cornmeal because the muffins I ate at the inn were exquisite. This is a most interesting building to visit as all of the equipment in the mill is water-powered.

As a final touch, the inn boasts of the oldest mixed drink in America. It is called "Coow Woow." You must taste it to discover how well our forefathers lived.

How to get there: From Boston, take the Massachusetts Turnpike to Route 128 north. Take Exit 49 west onto Route 20. Wayside Inn Road is 11 miles west, just off Route 20. From New York, take the Massachusetts Turnpike to Route 495, and go north to Route 20 east. It is approximately 8 miles to Wayside Inn Road.

✳

E: *Only in my country inns do you normally find the inn-keeper. And here, when you find Francis, you find a real winner.*

Olive Metcalf

The Williamsville Inn
West Stockbridge, Massachusetts
01266

Innkeepers: Kathleen and Geoffrey Riefe
Telephone: 413-274-6118
Rooms: 8 rooms and one suite in winter; 6 additional rooms in summer; all with private bath.
Rates: $89 to $150, double occupancy, EP.
Facilities: Closed last three weeks in April and first three weeks in November. Breakfast, afternoon tea, dinner. Tavern. Swimming pool, clay tennis court. No pets or small children. MasterCard and Visa accepted, but personal checks preferred.

Built in 1797 as a farmhouse, this inn is the second oldest house in the hamlet of Williamsville. It is a charmer.

You will find ☛ fireplaces all over the inn; so important in this part of the world where there is so much winter. The fireplaces in the dining rooms are raised hearth and especially warming. There also are fireplaces in two bedrooms, the sitting rooms, and the tavern.

The garden room is a lovely sitting room with a ☛ puzzle going most of the time, books, television, and a music center with stereo and tapes. The comfortable chairs and couches make this such a cozy room for afternoon tea. Tom Ball's Tavern, which is a delight, has nice stencils on the walls.

The guest rooms and suite are so attractively styled and furnished with a sense for old-fashioned grace and comfort.

There are three candlelit dining rooms for your pleasure. Service is unhurried and the food is outstanding. There are seven appetizers. Salmon mousse with green mayonnaise was yummy, and the onion soup is baked to perfection with Swiss and Gruyère cheese and croutons. Here are just a few ideas of the entrees. Boneless chicken stuffed with artichokes, mushrooms, and Gruyère cheese, or scallops baked in a delicately flavored cream sauce with stoneground wheat crumbs. And this is a real winner. ☛ Boneless shell steak coated with crushed peppercorns and served with a brandy cream sauce.

Desserts, of course, are freshly made. Lemon angel pie is so good, and nice liqueur parfaits are always in order. Eating my way through New England is so much fun.

So much to do in this area, from skiing, theater, and antiques, to just loafing at this lovely inn.

How to get there: Take the Massachusetts Turnpike to Exit 1, which puts you on Route 41. Turn left toward Great Barrington. The inn is 4 miles south of the turnpike on your right. From the New York Thruway, follow directions for Berkshires Spur, Exit 33. Go south on Route 22 to Route 102, east on Route 102 to Route 41, south on Route 41 toward Great Barrington.

⊷

E: *Fresh flowers all around the inn. How nice.*

Lambert's Cove Country Inn
West Tisbury, Massachusetts
02575

Innkeeper: Marie Burnett
Telephone: 617-693-2298 (Mailing address: Box 422, RFD, Vineyard Haven, MA 02568)
Rooms: 15, all with private bath.
Rates: In season, $95 to $110; off season, $55 to $85; double occupancy, continental breakfast included.
Facilities: Open all year. Dinner daily in season, Thursday through Sunday off season. Sunday brunch. BYOB. Tennis court. Swimming, cross-country skiing, and pond ice skating nearby. Weekly booking preferred in summer, but will take three-day bookings. All major credit cards accepted.

At the end of a tree-shaded country road you will find this gem of an inn. The original house was built in 1790 and over the years it was enlarged and a carriage house and barn added. Today the carriage house and barn have been beautifully renovated for guest use, and half of the rooms are here.

One of the rooms in the carriage house has a ☞ greenhouse sitting room at one end. Nice to have your cocktails in here and look up at the stars. All of the rooms in the inn are done with imagination. The mattresses are new, and there are plenty of ☛ pillows and lush color-coordinated towels.

When you enter the inn you are in an elegant center hall done in soft beige. Up a magnificent staircase and you are in a restful sitting area with wicker furniture and bookcases full of books. There also is a delightful library, a huge room with walls lined with volumes of books, and furnished with tables for games and really comfortable furniture. On a cold day a fire in the fireplace here feels great.

A big deck opens from the library and dining room and looks out on an apple orchard. There are five decks in all at this inn.

☛ Brunch is fun at a place like this. Blueberry Pancakes, Sourdough French Toast with Strawberries, Poached Sole with Scallop Mousse, steak and eggs . . . lovely. Or do come for dinner and try Kebab of Fresh Tuna and Peppers, Grilled Baby Back Ribs, or Curried Shrimp sautéed with Apples and Cream. No matter what you order it will be good.

This is real country. Walk twenty minutes to the Lambert's Cove beach, or just walk anywhere. It's just a beautiful part of the world.

How to get there: Take the ferry to Martha's Vineyard from Cape Cod. After driving off the ferry, take a left, then a right at the next stop-sign intersection. Stay on this road for 1½ miles to Lambert's Cove Road, on your right. Three miles from this point look for the inn's sign, on the left.

∽

E Boots, the inn cat, is a real character.

olive Metcalf

Le Jardin
Williamstown, Massachusetts
01267

Innkeeper: Walter Hayn
Telephone: 413-458-8032
Rooms: 6, all with private bath.
Rates: $65 to $85, EP.
Facilities: Closed January. Dinner, Sunday brunch, bar. All major credit
    cards accepted.

The grounds are so pretty at this inn. The backyard has
picnic tables and in front are Hemlock Brook and a nice pond.
There are a lot of sugar maples on the property, which Walter
taps and then makes ☛ his own maple syrup.

The rooms are lovely. There are four working fireplaces with
glass doors for safety. One of the rooms, the one where I always
want to stay, has a ☛ whirlpool tub. What heaven it is to relax
in.

Sports fans will love the ☛ forty-six-inch TV screen in the
bar and lounge. It's a most attractive room, with comfortable bar
stools and tables.

Terry Perry is the manager of the dining rooms and she does
a superb job. They are real beauties. Fresh, crisp napery, a fresh
flower on each table, and plants hanging in the windows provide

132

the perfect cozy, but still elegant, atmosphere for the magnificent food. The cuisine is French. Some of the hors d'oeuvres are snails in garlic butter, oysters baked with spinach and Pernod, and ☛ Beluga Malosol caviar. I had the onion soup baked in a tureen. Very hot and good. The frog legs were done to perfection. There also are jumbo shrimp baked with a hint of garlic and crisp Long Island duckling with apples. A real zinger is ☛ sirloin flamed in cognac and laced with coarse black pepper. Rack of lamb is beautifully served with tender vegetables and fresh mint sauce.

And the desserts . . . well, just imagine a French restaurant. I'm not about to spill the beans and tell you what to expect. Come on up and see for yourself.

How to get there: The inn is right on Route 7, just 2 miles south of Williamstown, on the right.

❋

E: *Strider is a beautiful red setter. He's getting old, but what a nice dog he is.*

*Who can refuse the beckoning
of a cozy country inn?*

133

Old Yarmouth Inn
Yarmouth Port, Massachusetts
02675

Innkeeper: Shane E. Peros
Telephone: 617-362-3191
Rooms: 5, all with private bath, 2 suites.
Rates: $55 to $85, double occupancy, continental breakfast included.
    Off-season package plans available.
Facilities: Open all year. Lunch, dinner, bar. Theater and beaches
    nearby. All major credit cards accepted.

Whenever I get the feeling that I want to step back in time, I go to the Old Yarmouth Inn. It is the oldest inn on Cape Cod. Built in 1696 as a wayside staging inn, it has had many owners, but it maintains its charm. The building sags a bit, and when you come in it is like savoring a bit of yesterday, with old leather suitcases, quaint, papered hat boxes, dusty coats, hobnail boots, and ancient horse brasses, all combining to carry you back to the olden days.

There is salt air here, flowers, sunshine, some days a little fog. You can dine indoors or out at the Old Yarmouth Inn, and seafood is, of course, a specialty of the house.

I love eating here because their salad bar is so good. All their salad ingredients, vegetables, and herbs come fresh from the

134

garden; flaky pastries, rich cakes, and hot breads burst from the ovens. Let me tell you about one recent holiday menu. Fresh fruit cup or piping hot French onion soup were among the appetizers. Oven-roasted fresh New England turkey with country dressing and hot cranberry sauce, or roast prime ribs of beef from ☞ rare to medium, or roast leg of lamb were three of the entrees you could have. All dinners included choice of butternut squash, green beans amandine, or baked or whipped potato, salad bar, and a loaf of home-baked bread. All this plus a divine dessert and coffee. What a nice place to come for any holiday. Just be sure you reserve well ahead.

You are only four miles from the famous Cape Playhouse at Dennis, one of the original "straw hat" theaters. There are several fine beaches nearby, and fishing, boating, and day trips to Nantucket and Martha's Vineyard can be arranged.

How to get there: Leave Route 6 (Mid-Cape Highway) at the Yarmouth Port Exit to Route 6A. Turn right, and one mile will bring you to the Old Yarmouth Inn.

❧

E: *The antique bug is gonna bite me, sure's I live, if I keep coming back to Yarmouth Port.*

> *The aroma of freshly baking bread told me surely*
> *I was awakening in a good country inn.*

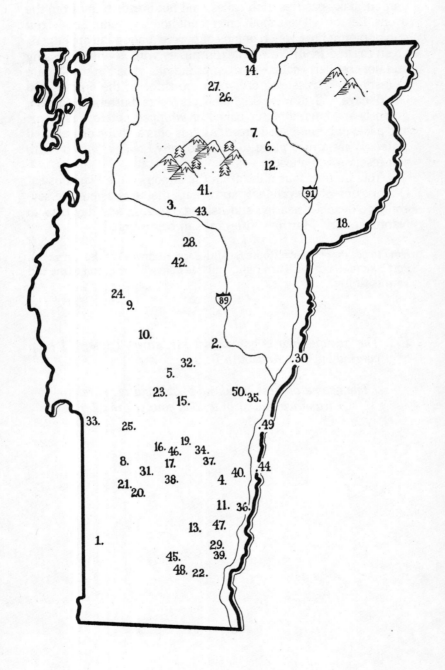

Vermont

Olive Metcalf

The Arlington Inn
Arlington, Vermont
05250

Innkeepers: Paul and Madeline Krozel
Telephone: 802-375-6532
Rooms: 13, all with private bath.
Rates: $48 to $125, double occupancy, EPB.
Facilities: Open all year. Lunch, dinner, Sunday brunch, bar and lounge.
  Fishing in the famous Battenkill. MasterCard and Visa accepted.

If you want to go back in time, this is the inn to do it in. You can recapture the gracious living of the Victorian period in this historic Greek Revival mansion. It was built in 1848 by Martin Chester Deming. The lovely rooms in the inn are named after Deming family members. There are Sylvester's study, Pamela's suite, Martin Chester's room, Sophie's room, Mary's room, and (I love this name) Chloe's room. The rooms are beautifully furnished and very comfortable.

The parlor or sitting room has a wonderful red oriental rug on the floor and, in the winter, a fire roaring in the fireplace. The whole inn is magnificent.

The dining rooms are well appointed. There is a new solarium for dining that's perfectly lovely. Plants, fountains, and beautifully landscaped outside. The best part, of course, is

138

the food. There are eight appetizers. I love garlic and the escargots are divine. So is the Fettucine à la Parma. The soups and salads are very special. They have a house dressing I would love to steal, it is so good. The main courses vary from day to day. Salmon, baked with tomato and spinach butter cream sauce, or stuffed with shrimp and topped with a creamy dill sauce. Get the idea? It's great. Sunday brunch is inventive, with a really super menu. Spinach and mushroom salad with a lemon and Pommery mustard dressing is just one selection. You really must go.

How to get there: The inn is located on Route 7 in the middle of Arlington.

❋

E: *The tavern has live entertainment on Friday and Saturday nights. If you get tired, there's a huge oversized rocking chair out on the porch.*

In the autumn, especially as one ages,
a firelit tavern in an excellent inn cannot be bettered
by the smallest mansions in Christendom.

Olive Metcalf

West Mountain Inn
Arlington, Vermont
05250

Innkeepers: Mary Ann and Wes Carlson
Telephone: 802-375-6516
Rooms: 13, 11 with private bath; 1 suite; 1 apartment with housekeeping facilities.
Rates: $110 to $140, double occupancy, MAP.
Facilities: Open all year. Breakfast, dinner, bar. James Walker Stoneware Studio in the stable-barn. Hiking, cross-country skiing, fishing, swimming. All major credit cards accepted.

Wes and Mary Ann are really the ideal innkeepers. From the minute you arrive until you leave you feel at home.

The inn is always being updated. There is a new lovely suite of rooms with a fireplace. There also is a new room and bath with ☞ complete facilities for the handicapped. The nicest touch is the thought. There are too few people who care enough to spend a bit more for other people's comfort.

Wes loves ☞ exotic goldfish. They are in the ponds around the inn and in a huge aquarium inside that is so nice to watch. Wes also raises African violets. He puts one in each room and invites you to take it home with you. The ☞ bowl of fruit, chocolate bar, and trail map are also for your pleasure.

The rooms, all named for famous people, are quite different. I have stayed in the Norman Rockwell Room, which is up in the treetops. Icelandic comforters and wool blankets are provided to keep you toasty warm.

The inn prepares great dinners. Wes has some excellent wines in an extensive wine cellar. They are the perfect complement to the meal.

This inn is truly in the country, with 150 acres of trees, trails, pastures, and ponds, all on the mountainside overlooking the village of Arlington. Cross the trout-filled Battenkill River, wind your way over the bridge, which is flower-laden in summer, go by the millhouse, up past the main cottage and spring-fed rock quarry, to the seven-gabled inn. ☛ The grounds around the inn are reputed to have more species of evergreens than any other place in New England. There are lovely trails for hiking, jogging, or cross-country skiing, depending on the season.

How to get there: Midway between Bennington and Manchester, the inn is one-half mile west of Arlington on Route 313. Turn onto River Road, cross the river, and go up the hill until you come to the inn.

∽

E: *Jim's stoneware studio in the barn displays his work and his wife's. I was fascinated watching him throwing pots on the wheel.*

Greenhurst Inn
Bethel, Vermont
05032

Innkeepers: Lyle and Barbara Wolf
Telephone: 802-234-9474
Rooms: 12, 7 with private bath.
Rates: $40 to $80, double occupancy, EPB.
Facilities: Open all year. Dinner only by advance reservations. Other restaurants nearby. BYOB. Tennis courts. Downhill and cross-country skiing, fishing, hiking, and golfing nearby. American Express, MasterCard, and Visa accepted.

The Greenhurst Inn was built in 1891. The Wolfs have restored it so beautifully that it is now listed on the National Register of Historic Places. There are eight unusually beautiful fireplaces throughout the inn.

As you enter the inn, you are in a huge foyer with one of the fireplaces and a very interesting staircase. Photographs that are for sale hang on the walls up the staircase. Lyle does the framing himself, and very well I might add. He gave me a beautifully mounted shell.

The inn's library has three thousand volumes; ☛ each guest room has a selection. The rooms are decorated with antiques and loving care. Every effort is made to ensure your comfort.

Perrier in every room, mints on the pillows, thick and thirsty towels, electric blankets, and Martha Washington bedspreads. A game cupboard in the north parlor is at your disposal and you are invited to make use of the television and piano in the south parlor. This was said so well in the Wolfs' brochure that I just stole it.

However, the brochure does not say that after dinner Lyle plays the piano while everyone sings. This is a nice touch. The south parlor is a wonderful room to sit in and watch a football game; it is so cozy and comfortable.

A unique touch are the Wolfs' well-done walking and driving tours. They have little brochures that are fun to read and very informative.

This inn is beautifully furnished, clean as a whistle, and well run. Go and enjoy.

How to get there: From I–89 take Exit 3. Go west on Route 107. The inn is in 3 miles on your left. From Rutland, go east on Route 4, north on Route 100, and east on Route 107.

*

E: *A really interesting zebra finch, called Edwin, and two dachsunds, Muffin and Mopsie, are at the inn.*

> *A country inn piled high with snow*
> *is a cheery fortress against the cold.*

The Black Bear Inn
Bolton Valley, Vermont
05477

Innkeepers: Sue and Phil McKinnis
Telephone: 802-434-2126
Rooms: 20, all with private bath and color television.
Rates: $39 to $89, double occupancy, EP.
Facilities: Closed mid-April to mid-May and November to mid-December. Breakfast, dinner, bar, lounge. Heated swimming pool, cross-country skiing, hiking. Tennis, fishing, downhill skiing, and golfing nearby. MasterCard and Visa accepted.

Four miles up twisting, curving Bolton Valley Road you come across this contemporary country inn, nestled in the mountainside as if it had been here forever. Once inside, you are greeted by the warmth of a woodburning stove and the aroma of freshly baked breads and muffins that fills the air.

Sue is the chef, and she does wonderful things with all foods. Everything is homemade. You could stay here for two weeks and not be served the same thing twice, and that even includes Sue's breads and muffins. The entrees, just to give you an idea, include fillet of beef with three-mustard sauce, or marinated roast duck with dried figs in red wine, or scrumptious salmon and other seafood. Sue always prepares a special, and up here it is just that.

The rooms are well appointed, with color televisions, good beds, and lovely balconies where in summer you may sit and smell the good clean air and enjoy the views. They are spectacular this far up in the mountains.

In summer the grounds are covered with wildflowers. The heated pool beckons you, comfortable lawn furniture is all around, and the beautiful high blue skies are yours to enjoy. The inn's fifty-four miles of cross-country ski trails make good paths for a hike and you may also borrow a canoe. Tennis is a short stroll away.

☛ Phil, an avid fly fisherman, conducts guided tours of the mountain streams. He knows where to find that trout.

How to get there: Coming west on I–89, take Exit 10 at Stowe-Waterbury. Turn left, then turn right onto Route 2 and follow it 7 miles. Turn right onto Bolton Valley Road in Bolton where I–89 passes over Route 2. The inn is in 4 miles.

✀

E: My kind of innkeepers who take in stray cats. They have Bruin, Be Scotch, and C-J. They must be good people.

The Inn at Long Last
Chester, Vermont
05143

Innkeepers: Jack, Paul, and Ami Coleman
Telephone: 802-875-2444
Rooms: 32, all with private bath.
Rates: $75 to $95 per person, MAP.
Facilities: Closed in April. Full breakfast, dinner, Sunday brunch, bar,
    lounge. Gift shop. Pool, tennis courts. Fishing in the stream and
    skiing nearby. All major credit cards accepted.

    Jack is a very different kind of innkeeper. There really is very
little that the man hasn't done in his former life. Talk to him and
you will see what I mean. His son Paul and daughter-in-law Ami
complete the inn team.

    The library lounge is lined with books. Many are about things
Jack has done, such as being an inmate in prisons or working in
the New York sanitation department so he could write about
them. The topper is that he was president of Haverford College
and most recently was head of the Edna McConnell Clark foundation, a $340-million charitable fund in New York City.

    This was the Chester Inn. It still sits on the village green, but
it has been 🖐 beautifully restored. Take the rooms, for example.
No two are alike, and each one is named for someone or some-

thing in Jack's past life, or for people he has admired. The Fair Winds Farm Room has a wood shovel and pick on the wall. The Connecticut River room has a photo of Steamboat Dock. They really are nice rooms. The ☞ porch on the second floor runs the width of the inn. A 110-year-old sleigh is out here. It was Ami's grandfather's.

Napery in the dining room changes with the seasons. This is a nice touch. A magnificent ☞ back bar with mirrors, which is twelve feet long and ten feet high, graces the dining room. It is a rare beauty. The food is exciting and the menu changes every night. Soups are unusual, such as Curried Apple and White Wine Soup and Chilled Strawberry Soup. Or perhaps you'd like to order Country Lamb Pâté with Lingonberry Sauce? You won't be sorry. One night you may find on the menu Norwegian salmon fillet, broiled and served with a creamy sorrel sauce. Another night might be Bluefin tuna steaks, marinated and grilled, served with avocado butter. These are just a sample of what they have. Desserts like ☞ blueberry pandowdy or black raspberry sherbet are sure to get me back.

How to get there: From I–91 take Exit 6. Watch for Chester signs and the inn is on the green.

✻

E: *I'm fascinated by this interesting innkeeper and his family. The brochure in itself is worth sending for.*

olive Metcalf

Mountain Top Inn
Chittenden, Vermont
05737

Innkeeper: Bill Wolfe
Telephone: 802-483-2311
Rooms: 35, all with private bath; 6 cottage units.
Rates: $70 to $135, per person, double occupancy, MAP.
Facilities: Open all year. Breakfast, lunch, dinner, bar, lounge. Heated pool, tennis, lawn games, pitch 'n putt with full-size greens, game room, horseback riding, sauna, whirlpool, exercise room, cross-country skiing, horse-drawn sleigh rides. Downhill skiing nearby. All major credit cards accepted.

In the 1870s the Mountain Top property was part of the Long family's turnip farm. In 1940 William Barstow, an engineer and philanthropist from New York, bought the farm and converted the barn into a wayside tavern as a hobby for his wife. The year 1945 brought William Wolfe to Chittenden. He fell in love with the place and Mountain Top Inn was born. His son, Bill, is now the innkeeper.

The inn is just beautiful with views that no money can buy. At a 2,000-foot elevation the inn overlooks Mountain Top Lake, which is surrounded by fantastic mountains. When you enter the inn you are in a very inviting living area with a large fireplace.

Ahead of you is the view and a spectacular 🖝 two-story glass-enclosed staircase that leads to the "Charlie James" cocktail lounge, presided over by a regal fox, and the dining room. The food served here is superb, beginning with appetizers like scallops sautéed with chutney and Dijon mustard, and Seviche. One entree that I love here is New England Seafood and Biscuits—lobster, salmon, and scallops simmered in a hearty, creamy stew and served over homemade biscuits. The broiler provides a few interesting items as well.

The rooms, most overlooking the lake and mountains, are large and luxuriously furnished. All have spacious baths. A nice touch is your bed turned down at night with a maple sugar candy on the pillow.

The inn has an excellent ski touring program. With over a thousand acres to ski on at an elevation of 2000 feet, the 🖝 views are awesome. The sugar house, a wooden structure, is well located near several of the inn's ski touring trails. It has been turned into a ski-warming hut where skiers in the spring have the added bonus of watching the 🖝 sap boiling-down process firsthand. There are two other warming huts on the property. The inn has a ski shop with instructors and all the latest equipment. Ice skating and toboggans also are fun, and downhill skiing is nearby at Pico and Killington.

Summer brings walking or hiking through the lovely countryside, and in fall the color show of the trees is breathtaking.

How to get there: From Rutland, head north on Route 7. Pass the power station, turn right on Chittenden Road, and follow it into Chittenden. Follow the signs up to the inn.

ॐ

E: 🖝 *Sleighs drawn by draft horses are a wonderful yester-year experience.*

The Craftsbury Inn
Craftsbury, Vermont
05826

Innkeepers: John and Susan McCarthy
Telephone: 802-586-2848
Rooms: 10, 6 with private bath.
Rates: $85 to $120, double occupancy, MAP. EP rates available.
Facilities: Open all year. Breakfast, dinner, bar. Cross-country skiing.
  Canoeing, swimming, fishing, horseback riding, tennis, and golfing
  nearby. MasterCard and Visa accepted.

The inn is a lovingly restored Greek Revival house that was
built circa 1850. The little town of Craftsbury, said by *The Boston
Globe* to be Vermont's most remarkable hill-town, was founded in
1788 by Colonel Ebenezer Crafts and lies in what is called the
Northeast Kingdom. The population today is something less than
700, and that includes Craftsbury, East Craftsbury, and
Craftsbury Common.

One year I arrived here on a chilly day in the middle of June
and was greeted by a lovely 🔥 fire in the television room. Boy,
did it feel good! Speaking of fireplaces, the one in the living room
is the original fireplace that warmed the first post office in Montpelier, Vermont's capital.

The rooms here are filled with antique wicker, and the beds

have handsome heirloom quilts. Fresh paint and paper have made this lovely old inn even nicer.

 All ice creams, breads, and pastries are prepared here. They also make their own stocks, and this does make a difference in the taste of food.

American-French cooking is how they describe their menu. Susan is a trained professional chef. The fresh duck and veal come from a local source so they know exactly what they are buying. Cornish game hen with green peppercorns is but one of the luscious items served. There are three entrees to choose from. John is the breakfast chef, and he is a whiz at blueberry pancakes, eggs Benedict, and more. They have their own vegetable garden to ensure freshness, and they sell very good Craftsbury honey.

There is much to do in this area. The McCarthys have put in a cross-country ski trail that is connected to the Craftsbury Sports Center. In the summer, you can rent a canoe, swim in nearby lakes, fish, horseback ride, play tennis, or play golf at Vermont's oldest course in Greensboro where the greens are fenced to prevent intrusion of the grazing cattle. Throughout July and August the Craftsbury Chamber Players perform every Thursday evening. Come and enjoy.

How to get there: Take I–91 to St. Johnsbury, pick up Route 2 west, and at West Danville take Route 15 to Hardwick. Follow Route 14 north to Craftsbury. The inn is on the right, across from the general store.

E: *John hails from Allentown, Pennsylvania, where I was raised. Small world.*

Olive Metcalf

The Inn on the Common
Craftsbury Common, Vermont
05827

Innkeepers: Penny and Michael Schmitt
Telephone: 802-586-9619
Rooms: 17, all with private bath; 5 with a fireplace or wood stove; all located in 3 buildings.
Rates: $75 to $95, per person, double occupancy, MAP.
Facilities: Open all year. Food and drinks for house guests only. Heated swimming pool, clay tennis court, English croquet. Boating and cross-country skiing nearby. Ski touring and ski packages available. MasterCard and Visa accepted.

It is a long way up here, but it's worth every mile you travel to be a guest of the Schmitts.

There are three buildings that make up the inn. The north annex is on the common with a lovely picket fence around it. All of its rooms are beautifully appointed. The wallpapers are ☛ Scalamandre reproduction from a South Carolina historic collection. The sheets throughout the inn are brand new and Marimekko. There's a very unusual sofa, an English knoll; try and figure how the arms go down. Two of the bedrooms in the north annex have a fireplace. One of the bathrooms has such a cute, tiny bathtub. There's a lovely canopy bed in one room. In the main house itself there are three new luxurious rooms and Penny loves to show them off.

Across the street is the south annex. The guest lounge has a fireplace, comfy sofas, a large television, and Betamax. There's a library of over 200 films on tape so even in bad weather there is something to do. You can fix lunch, make tea, or whatever you wish in the guest kitchen. Two Jotul woodburning stoves keep the rooms warm and cozy.

In the main house is the dining room with a 🖛 glass wall overlooking the rose gardens. All the gardens are lovely. Penny has green hands as well as a faithful gardener. The dining room has the perfect atmosphere to savor the sumptuous food. Roast native lamb with sorrel sauce is one entree; veal stew in an orange-lemon sauce is another. Salads are so good. I never had a red pepper mousse before and it is delicious. Cocktail hour in the library is a fun, social time. Michael is bartender. He also selects the dinner wines from the superb wine cellar to complement the meal.

A staff of naturalists runs a sports complex near the inn. One hundred and forty acres include lake swimming, sculling, canoeing, cross-country skiing, nature walks, and bird watching. Come on up. There is something for everyone.

How to get there: Follow I–91 to St. Johnsbury, take Route 2 west, and at West Danville take Route 15 to Hardwick. Take Route 14 north to Craftsbury, and continue north into the common. The inn is on the left as you enter the village.

❀

E: *The solar-heated swimming pool has a little waterfall to let the water in. It disturbs nothing in its peaceful location behind the south annex. Sam, the inn dog, enjoys watching it.*

olive Metcalf

Dorset Inn
Dorset, Vermont
05251

Innkeepers: Sissy Hicks and Gretchen Schmidt
Telephone: 802-867-5500
Rooms: 36, all with private bath.
Rates: $70 single; $120, double occupancy; MAP.
Facilities: Open all year. Breakfast, lunch, dinner, bar. Wheelchair accessibility to dining room. Swimming pool. Golf and theater nearby. MasterCard and Visa accepted.

Built in 1796, this is the oldest inn in Vermont, and it has been continuously operated as an inn. Today, the inn has been ☞ completely restored and has been listed in the National Register of Historic Places. There are wide-board floors, and beautiful Vermont pine is around the fireplace in the living room.

While the inn has retained the feeling of the eighteenth century, it is modern in its conveniences. It has been completely insulated. The bathrooms have been redone, some of the rooms have been air conditioned, and firm mattresses have been purchased. The whole inn is clean and neat.

The breakfast and luncheon room has a lovely old ☞ lion fountain. I love the sound of the water. The bar-lounge is spacious. There is no crowding in this large and rambling inn.

Sissy Hicks presides over the kitchen and is a very well known lady. Some of the luncheon items are curried mussels and noodles on spinach, beef, and scallions with rice, and biscuit-crust apple and turkey pie. Sounds great! At dinner the appetizers are numerous. One is New England cheese chowder. Sissy's entrees are really different. Breast of chicken with pear and cider cream. Or veal medallions with a lime-ginger sauce. The breakfast menu is pure ambrosia. I like it here. I think you can tell.

The Dorset Field Club, sporting one of Vermont's oldest nine-hole golf courses, ☞ extends golf privileges to guests of the inn. If culture turns you on, the Southern Vermont Arts Center and the Dorset Playhouse will provide the comedy and drama of good theater.

How to get there: Leave I–91 at Brattleboro and go left on Route 30 to Dorset. Or take Route 7 to Manchester Center, and go north on Route 30.

✳

E: *The recently restored taproom has its own menu from Sunday through Thursday in the summer and every night in the winter. It's lovely in here.*

> *When you have but one night to spend*
> *which inn to choose is as difficult as*
> *the choice you had years ago at the*
> *penny candy counter, and equally rewarding.*

Olive Metcalf

Village Auberge
Dorset, Vermont
05251

Innkeepers: Helmut and Dorothy Stein
Telephone: 802-867-5715
Rooms: 4, all with private bath; 2 suites.
Rates: $40, double occupancy, EPB; $65, double occupancy, MAP.
Facilities: Closed in April and November to mid-December. Dining room closed on Mondays. Breakfast, dinner, bar. Tennis, golf, swimming, and skiing nearby. All major credit cards accepted.

This is an authentic Vermont country inn. Informal and relaxed is the style of the innkeepers, who have thought of everything to make your stay here comfortable.

The living room with its glowing fireplace and good couches and chairs is restful after a day of skiing or shopping. Guest rooms are warmly furnished with four-poster beds and antique dressers, and the suites are very spacious.

The dining room, which is done in shades of warm green, is just beautiful. It is highlighted by a tin ceiling and a broad bay window. The room seats only forty-five people. The stunning place plates are a floral pattern from Villeroy and Boch, and Botanica made in Luxembourg. Needless to say with such magnificent surroundings, the food served here is extravagant, with

156

hors d'oeuvres and potages such as terrine of pheasant, a fish pâté, or hot or cold ☞ cream of mustard soup. This was a first for me and very good. There are entrees like quenelles of scallops, fillet of salmon, or rack of lamb for two. A real favorite is ☞ Châteaubriand Flambe au Cognac et Poivres Verts, also for two. Ready for dessert? A pastry tray has an enticing variety of tarts, tortes, and pastries. Or you can order crème caramel, homemade sorbet, or homemade ice cream. What a way to go.

A lovely stained glass window separates the dining room from the bar. The bar is done in rich, warm wood, and is a real beauty.

The inn is only five miles north of Manchester, where there are shops for your every wish. Three downhill ski areas and cross-country skiing are all nearby, and the Dorset Playhouse is less than a walk around the block from the inn.

How to get there: Take I–91 north to Brattleboro, then take Route 30 to Manchester. At blinking lights take a right and an immediate left, which brings you back on Route 30 north. Go about 5½ miles north of Manchester. Look for the inn on your right.

෯

E: *To see this beautiful inn in the snow is a picture to remember.*

Olive Metcalf

The Waybury Inn
East Middlebury, Vermont
05740

Innkeepers: Kim and Peter Varty
Telephone: 802-388-4015
Rooms: 14, 11 with private bath.
Rates: $55 to $80, single; $75 to $100, double occupancy, EPB.
Facilities: Open all year. Dinner, Sunday brunch, bar, lounge. Swimming, fishing, hiking, and skiing nearby. MasterCard and Visa accepted.

The Waybury Inn was built in 1810 as a stagecoach stop at the base of the Green Mountains. Known as the Glen House, the inn provided rooms for women workers at the local glass factory for many years.

Guest accommodations today have very comfortable double, twin, or king-sized beds. They have ☞ lovely Bombay fans on the ceilings, and all are carpeted, except one room that has the original stencils on the wood floor. There are nice ☞ fluffy towels. The whole inn is spotlessly clean.

Throughout the inn are hand-hewn beams, pine wide-board floors, and friendly fireplaces. The Waybury Pub is a fun place that is available for small parties. There are two fireplaces down here. The pub is used by the Middlebury Artists Association for the display of their art works. This is a nice touch.

Table napery is lovely, and so is the way the wine is displayed. The menu is very extensive and different. On the cover it reads: "The Waybury Inn stands as a symbol of tradition in country inns. Recognized as a National Historic Place, the Waybury Inn has delivered comfortable lodging and fine meals to travelers since 1810." Nine appetizers are listed. A real favorite of mine is ☛ Seviche. This is fresh bay scallops in citrus juices. I like a restaurant that offers roast leg of lamb, sliced thick or thin, your choice. Curried lamb is also offered. Vegetable crepe is another dish I have not seen elsewhere. The desserts are homemade and the wine list is very impressive.

How to get there: The inn is located 29 miles north of Rutland, Vermont, on Route 125 in East Middlebury.

❋

E: *Take a swim in the local swimming hole, a natural gorge in the rocky river that splashes nearby.*

If I ever find an inn that bakes fresh macaroons daily,
I shall rent a room for a hundred years.

Olive Metcalf

Blueberry Hill
Goshen, Vermont
05733

Innkeeper: Tony Clark
Telephone: 802-247-6735 or 802-247-6535
Rooms: 8, all with private bath.
Rates: In summer, $65-$85; in winter, $85; double occupancy, MAP.
Facilities: Closed April and November. Breakfast, packed lunch is available, dinner. BYOB. Cross-country skiing, swimming, fishing. MasterCard and Visa accepted.

The inn is a cross-country skier's dream come true. It is nestled at the foot of Romance Mountain in the Green Mountain National Forest and is surrounded by good clean air and well-groomed snowy trails. From the inn brochure I quote: "The Blueberry Hill Ski Touring Center, across from the inn, devotes itself to cross-country skiers of all 🖝 ages and abilities. Inside the fully equipped Ski Center are retail and rental departments, a waxing area, repair shop, and an expert staff to see that you are skiing better with less effort. Upstairs you can relax, make friends, and share the day's events in our lounge with its large windows, comfortable seating, and old wood stove. Surrounding the Ski Center are seventy-five kilometers of both challenging and moderate terrain. A loop around Hogback, a race to Silver Lake, or just making tracks in a snow world all your own . . . the activities never cease—from seminars, waxing clinics, night and guided tours, to the sixty-kilometer American Ski Marathon."

In the summer the ski trails are used for hiking, walking, or running. There are a pond for swimming and streams and lakes for fishing.

The inn is a restored 1813 farmhouse. Dinner is served family style in a lovely, candlelit dining room. There are four courses served in an unhurried, comfortable way. While I was here dinner included such delicious things as cold cantaloupe soup, scallion bread, broiled lamb chops with mint butter, stir-fried asparagus, lemon meringue tarts, and homemade ice creams. Tony's son made strawberry ice cream, and it was so good. Breakfasts are served in the greenhouse just off the kitchen. It is full of glorious plants. Three of the guest rooms are out here, just beyond the greenhouse.

There are plenty of books to read, and the rooms are comfortable with many antiques, quilts, and hot water bottles on the backs of the doors. Honest, they are there.

How to get there: From Rutland take Route 7 north to Brandon, then Route 73 east for 6 miles. Turn left at the inn's sign, and follow the signs up the mountain on a dirt road to the inn.

❈

E: *Their upside-down gardens hanging from the ceiling beams are a colorful and imaginative use of straw flowers, and the brick patio overlooking Dutton Brook is so restful and nice.*

olive Metcalf

The Old Tavern
Grafton, Vermont
05146

Innkeeper: Richard Ernst
Telephone: 802-843-2231
Rooms: 35, all with private bath, in 7 houses.
Rates: $50 to $105, single or double occupancy, EP.
Facilities: Closed in April, and on Christmas Eve and Christmas Day.
Breakfast for houseguests only, lunch, dinner, bar, television in lounge, parking, elevator. Swimming, tennis, nature walks. No credit cards accepted.

If you're looking for perfection in a country inn, go to a charming Vermont village called Grafton and you'll find The Old Tavern. It has been operated as an inn since 1801. Since 1965, when the inn was purchased by the Windham Foundation, it has been restored and is now one of those superb New England inns we are all seeking.

When you turn your car off pounding interstate highways to the tree-shaded route that winds to this quaint village, you step back in time. The loveliest of the old, combined with the comfort of the new, makes this an unbeatable inn. No grinding motors can disturb your slumber when you are in ☞ the best beds in all New England. The sheets and towels are the finest money can buy, and there are extra pillows and blankets in each room. The spacious rooms are filled with antiques, all in mint condition.

There is no "organized activity" at the Old Tavern. 🖛 The swimming pool is a natural pond, cool and refreshing. There are tennis courts nearby, and marked trails in the woods for walkers. This is the place to calm your spirits and recharge your batteries.

The cocktail barn is charming, connected to the inn by a covered walk. There are flowers everywhere, hanging in baskets, in flower boxes, and on various tables in the gracious public rooms. The food is excellent, with unusual soups, varied entrees, all cooked well, and served by pleasant waitresses.

🖛 Up the street a bit there is a six box stall stable that will accommodate guest horses, plus a four-bay carriage shed, if you care to bring your own carriage. All this for the exclusive use of Old Tavern guests.

How to get there: From I–91 take Exit 5 at Bellows Falls. As you come down the exit ramp, watch for Route 121, which you'll take to the inn.

E: *The houses across the street that are also part of the inn are enchanting.*

Highland Lodge
Greensboro, Vermont
05841

Innkeepers: Willie and David Smith
Telephone: 802-533-2647
Rooms: 11, all with private bath; 11 cottages.
Rates: $90 to $115, double occupancy, MAP.
Facilities: Closed April 1 to May 25, and after foliage season to mid-December. Breakfast, lunch, dinner. Beer and wine license only, setups are available. Parking. Swimming, boating, tennis. Golfing and horseback riding nearby. MasterCard and Visa accepted.

When the snow starts falling up here, it has to be one of the most beautiful places in the world. And you can bet that it's popular with cross-country skiers. There is a complete ski touring center with daily instruction, ski shop (sales, rentals, and repairs), guided tours, marked trails, and skier's lunch. All this is at an altitude of 1500 feet, where there are miles of ski touring through the wonderful scenery.

Winter isn't the only fun time of year to be here. Caspian Lake, with the lodge's own beach house, is just across the road for swimming, canoeing, and sailing. Fishing is good in June and September until mid-October for salmon, lake trout, rainbow trout, and perch. Tennis, golf, and riding are available for those so inclined.

Any inn that sends its chef to ☛ France to train for the kitchen surely gets my nod. The food has always been outstanding here and now it is even better. The menu is inventive and they have their great grilled ☛ Black Angus sirloin steaks to prove it. I love the dessert menu. They have great names, and taste equally great. Ishkabibble is a brownie topped with ice cream and homemade hot fudge. Forgotten Dessert is a meringue with ice cream and strawberries. It's nice to find these old favorites on a menu.

☛ Children are welcome here. A play lady comes in for the four-to-nine set when there are enough children. Baby sitters are available. The playroom offers amusement for kids of all ages, and the playhouse has a supervised play program for youngsters. With the children happily occupied, the lounges and library remain free and quiet for you.

This is the place to get away from it all. The views and utter peace are so wonderful, they are hard to describe. Come and enjoy.

How to get there: Greensboro is 35 miles northeast of Montpelier. Take I–91 to St. Johnsbury and follow U.S. 2 west to West Danville. Continue west on Vermont 15, to intersection with Vermont 16 about two miles east of Hardwick. Turn north on 16 to East Hardwick and follow signs west to Greensboro, at the south end of Caspian Lake. Highland Lodge is at the north end of lake on the road to East Craftsbury.

E: *The herb garden is a nice thing for any chef to have.*

olive Metcalf

Three Mountain Inn
Jamaica, Vermont
05343

Innkeepers: Charles and Elaine Murray
Telephone: 802-874-4140
Rooms: 17, all with private bath, in 3 buildings.
Rates: $60 to $75, per person, MAP.
Facilities: Closed April to June 15, except for special fishing weekends, and November except for Thanksgiving. Breakfast, dinner, pub, lounge. Swimming pool, cross-country skiing. Downhill skiing, tennis, golfing, fishing, and horseback riding nearby. No credit cards accepted.

The inn is well named, since it is within a few minutes of Stratton, Bromley, and Magic Mountains. Mount Snow is also within easy range. Skiers should love this location. Cross-country buffs will find a multitude of trails beginning at the inn's doorstep, including a ☞ dramatic trail along the long defunct West River Railroad bed. Tennis is available both indoors and out at nearby Stratton. Horseback riding is superb on lovely trails in the area, or go swimming in the inn's own beautifully landscaped pool.

This small, authentic country inn was built in the 1780s. The living room has a large, roaring fireplace, complete with an original Dutch oven. The floors and walls are of wide, planked pine, and there are plenty of comfortable chairs. A picture window offers views of the Green Mountains to complete the scene.

A cozy lounge and bar area make you feel very comfortable for sitting back to enjoy good conversation and a before or after dinner drink. 🖝 A good wine selection is at hand.

The rooms are tastefully decorated. One room has a four-poster, king-sized bed in it. Another has a private balcony overlooking the swimming pool and garden. A charming 🖝 Hansel and Gretel cottage also is available.

The inn was featured several years ago in 🖝 *Gourmet* magazine, so you can safely guess that the food served in the lovely dining rooms is good—served by candlelight, of course. Dinners are carefully prepared to order and the menu changes frequently to bring you the most seasonal foods available. Cucumber soup is excellent. They have locally smoked fish, broiled trout, and the crisp hash brown potatoes are yummy. 🖝 Strawberry shortcake is always in demand. Elaine also does wonders with berry pies. Be sure to order a piece.

How to get there: Follow I–91 to Brattleboro and take the second exit to Route 30, to Jamaica.

∽

E: *There are guided tours for fly fishermen on the West and Battenkill rivers. Write for these package deals, and remember you will eat what you catch.*

Jay Village Inn
Jay, Vermont
05859

Innkeepers: Bob and Jane Angliss
Telephone: 802-988-2643
Rooms: 16, 9 with private bath; 1 chalet.
Rates: In winter, $52, per person, double occupancy, MAP, includes gratuities. Rest of year, $25, per person, double occupancy, EP.
Facilities: Closed last week of April and first week of May. Breakfast, dinner, bar. Television in lounge. Trout brook, swimming pool. Golf and tennis nearby. Cross-country and downhill skiing 3 miles away. MasterCard and Visa accepted.

When you get to Jay you are nearly in Canada, so this makes the Jay Village Inn my most northern Vermont inn. Nestled at the foot of Jay Peak, this is a delightful country inn. Come any time of the year and enjoy the fireplace lounge and bar. It is noted for its après-ski especially, but it's equally pleasurable any season. Sip ☛ a hot buttered rum and enjoy the flaming fire. They have a player piano and some great old songs. Do any of you remember "The Teddy Bear's Picnic"? It is here.

They serve an ample breakfast up here in the hills. Pancakes, eggs any way you can imagine, French toast, and of course, real Vermont maple syrup. Breads are freshly baked every day. Deep-fried vegetables served with a tangy dipping sauce are a superb dinner appetizer. Lightly fried clam strips and Charleston chicken, honey-coated and deep-fried, are two of the dinner entrees. My favorite is still the House Special, a seven-rib rack of baby lamb, roasted to order. It doesn't come any better. For dessert their warm apple crisp gets my nod. It is served with dollops of cream. It may be a long way up here, but boy, you'll eat well.

If you are a skier you must know that Jay Peak has one of the longest, most dependable ski seasons in the East. The aerial tramway is a "trip," and there are exciting trails for every level of skiing, beginner to expert.

For other seasons there are two golf courses in the vicinity, and if you are a hiker you are close to the Long Trail. A relaxing summer day can be spent by the inn's pool that has a nice carpet-covered deck.

The dining room has been redecorated with crisp beige linens and nice curtains. The guest rooms all have good mattresses so you will sleep well.

How to get there: Take I–91 to Exit 26. Take Route 5 north to Route 14 north to Route 100, a total of 8 miles. Go left here for 6 miles to Route 101, then right for 3 miles to Route 242. Go left on Route 242 for one mile to the inn.

✳

E: *An independent spirit and a loveable dog is Barney, the Saint Bernard.*

Mountain Meadows Lodge
Killington, Vermont
05751

Innkeepers: Bill and Joanne Stevens
Telephone: 802-775-1010
Rooms: 15, 12 with private bath.
Rates: In winter, $42 to $48, per person, MAP. Lower rates in summer.
Facilities: Closed in May. Breakfast and dinner for house guests. BYOB.
  Television, game room. Hiking, swimming, boating, fishing. Cross-
  country and downhill skiing nearby. MasterCard and Visa accepted.

It was here that I met Bear, a mostly red setter, who had just come off the Appalachian Trail carrying his own backpack. True, I swear. If you are hiking inn-to-inn this is the southernmost inn and a good place to start.

The inn is very casual and relaxed and overlooks 110 acres of lovely Kent Lake. The lake is stocked with 🐟 rainbow trout and largemouth bass. There are boats and canoes for your pleasure. You can swim either in the lake or in the inn's pool.

Vermont home-style cooking at its very best is featured. The inn has a BYOB bar and a game room.

The rooms are fully carpeted and comfortable as sin, but the place to really relax is the large living room, which has a big

170

fireplace and lots of windows overlooking the lake. The view is lovely.

The inn has ☞ the largest ski touring center in the area, and for you more daring types, Killington and Pico Peak alpine areas are but minutes away.

How to get there: The inn is 10 miles east of Rutland, just off Route 4. Follow Route 4 from Rutland for 12 miles, and at Thundering Brook Road you will come to the inn's sign. Turn left. The inn is ¼ mile beyond.

❧

E: *Susqua is the gentle inn dog with only three paws and Cori is a golden retriever.*

If all inns were alike they simply would not be inns.

olive Metcalf

The Vermont Inn
Killington, Vermont
05751

Innkeepers: Alan and Judy Carmasin
Telephone: 802-773-9847
Rooms: 16, 12 with private bath.
Rates: In summer, $35 to $60, per room, EPB; in winter, $40 to $60, per person, MAP.
Facilities: Closed in May. Restaurant closed Mondays. Dinner, bar. Television, game room, sauna, hot tub, pool, tennis, lawn games. Gondola ride, summer theater, Norman Rockwell Museum, farmers' market, and skiing nearby. American Express, MasterCard, and Visa accepted.

You may be greeted at the door of this friendly red house by a companionable Labrador named Tammy. Judy and Alan are always here, and a nicer young couple you'll have to travel a long way to find.

The Vermont Inn is well known locally for the fine food served in the lovely dining room. As a matter of fact, the restaurant was ☛ awarded the Silver Spoon Award two years in a row. Just a sample of the food is tenderloin of pork, so different, sautéed with fresh mushrooms and flavored in sherry wine with cream. Steak teriyaki is excellent, as is their good selection of fish dishes.

There is also a children's menu, a true help for the traveling family.

The inn's guests are a mixed bag. You'll run into young professional people from Boston or New York, a grandparent or two, families, anyone from honeymooners to golden oldies. Alan has cultivated ☛ a fine wine cellar to enhance the good food.

When the Carmasins took over the inn they redecorated all the rooms. Floors were recarpeted or painstakingly restored to the original wood. What a labor of love! They have purchased attractive queen-sized four-poster beds for four rooms.

This old house has sturdy underpinnings. Some of the original beams still have the bark on them, and how the rocks of the foundation were ever put in place I cannot imagine. Everything was changed around, the old dining room became a lounge to make the inn cosier, so take advantage of the beautiful view of Killington, Pico, and Little Killington, straight ahead across the valley. There also is a room with a view that houses a hot tub, exercise machines, and lots of plants. It's a beauty and is ideal for anyone who wants to unwind after a day on the slopes or hiking.

Tammy's "Instructions to Guests" on how she is to be treated should be on the *must* list for every inn dog. They are tacked up at the desk. Drop in and read them, then stay awhile.

How to get there: The inn is 6 miles east of Rutland, via Route 4. It is also 4 miles west of the intersection of Route 4 and Route 100 north (Killington Access Road).

❦

E: *There is a secluded stream, so quiet, just right for meditating, or, if you are brave, to put a foot in.*

Nordic Inn
Landgrove, Vermont
05148

Innkeepers: Tom and Judy Acton
Telephone: 802-824-6444
Rooms: 5, 3 with private bath.
Rates: $53 to $70, per person, MAP.
Facilities: Closed end of March to Memorial Day weekend. Breakfast,
    lunch, dinner, Sunday brunch, bar, lounge. Cross-country skiing,
    ski shop, hiking. Golf, tennis, horseback riding, and downhill skiing
    nearby. MasterCard and Visa accepted.

I think it's nice to be able to go to an inn and have almost
everything you want right there, so you do not have to go running
around in your car.

This inn has ☞ twenty kilometers of groomed and marked
trails through the Green Mountain National Forest. The varied
terrain takes you through a winter wonderland, from stands of
towering red pine, over beaver ponds, through meadows, and
even past an old Colonial cemetery on a hilltop. There
are ☞ guided backpack tours from the inn, and, of course,
downhill skiing is nearby at Bromley, Magic, and my personal
favorite, Stratton. To make it even nicer for you, there is a ski
shop right here with plenty of instructors, so come on up.

174

At other times of the year you can hike the trails or go fishing. Nearby are horseback riding, golf, and tennis. Summer theater is handy in Dorset and Weston.

The bar and lounge area has a large stone fireplace; very cozy on a snowy day. There are tables and chairs as well as a nice bar in here. The solarium is lovely. Imagine having some of their delicious food and watching the snow fall or the ski school in action. A very, very relaxing place to be.

The food is glorious, dinner or brunch. They serve dishes like a superb seafood salad, Mussels Provençale, veal and chicken done in special ways, and ☞ broiled loin lamb chops served with a Dijon mustard, ginger, and rosemary sauce.

The bar has a special drink, Hot Glögg, containing vodka, cognac, red wine, slivered almonds, raisins, and cinnamon. Wow!

How to get there: The inn is between Bromley and Londonderry on Route 11, 14 miles east of Manchester.

༄

E: *Sissy, the inn cat, has the most unusual amber-cinnamon eyes I have ever seen on a cat. She shares the inn with Red, a golden retriever.*

The Village Inn
Landgrove, Vermont
05148

Innkeepers: Jay and Kathy Snyder; Elsie and Don Snyder
Telephone: 802-824-6673
Rooms: 20, 16 with private bath.
Rates: In winter, $35 to $60, per person, double occupancy, MAP; in summer, $40 to $63, per room, EPB.
Facilities: Closed April 1 to May 22, and October 20 to mid-December. Dinner, except on Wednesdays in summer. Pool, tennis, pitch-and-putt, bumper pool, Ping-Pong, volleyball, cross-country skiing. Downhill skiing nearby. MasterCard and Visa accepted.

   This is a family-run inn that welcomes families. ☞ Yes, that does mean you can bring your children. They will be well entertained, and so will you. Indoors is a fun game room, and outside are play things, a heated swimming pool, two Plexipave tennis courts, and a four-hole pitch-and-putt golf facility. A hike through the National Forest is unbelievably scenic and summer theater is nearby.
   Winter means snow, and there is plenty of it. It's only a short hop by car to Bromley, Stratton, Snow Valley, Magic Mountain, or Okemo. Cross-country skiing begins at the inn's door, or try your skills at snowshoeing or ice skating. After a long day revive

yourself in the whirlpool spa, and then enjoy the fireside warmth in the Rafter Room lounge. As the Snyders say, the lounge's provocatively supine couch is the ideal relaxation!

The architectural style of the inn is peculiar to Vermont, with one building added onto another building. It turns out to be charming. The first part was built in 1810. It has been an inn since 1939. The rooms are spick and span, spacious, and very comfortable. The common rooms, dining room, and just everything about this quiet spot are relaxing. And the Snyders, who are cordial and welcoming innkeepers, make you want to return year after year.

How to get there: Via I–91, use Exit 6 at Rockingham. Take Route 103 to Chester, then Route 11 to Londonderry. Continue past the shopping center for approximately a half mile, and turn right on Landgrove Road. Go 4 miles to the Village of Landgrove. Bear left after crossing the bridge and continue one mile to the inn, on your right.

From Manchester, take Route 11 past Bromley Ski Area, and turn left into Peru Village. At the fork in Peru bear left and continue 4 miles through the National Forest to the crossroads in Landgrove. Turn left toward Weston, and the inn will be on your right.

E: *From horse-drawn sleigh rides in winter to the blueberry pancakes, this is a nice place to be.*

Olive Metcalf

The Highland House
Londonderry, Vermont
05148

Innkeepers: Virginia and Jeff Morgan
Telephone: 802-824-3019
Rooms: 13, plus 4 suites, 15 with private bath, in 2 buildings.
Rates: $50 to $70, double occupancy, EPB. In fall foliage season, add 10
   percent.
Facilities: Closed Thanksgiving week, last two weeks in April, and the
   first week in May. Full breakfast, dinner Wednesday through Sun-
   day. Beer and wine license. Heated swimming pool, all-weather
   tennis court. Skiing, fishing, golf, and horseback riding nearby.
   MasterCard and Visa accepted.

The Highland House has really grown. There is a wonderful
new addition in the back. It has a living room with a fireplace that
is just lovely. The suites are out here, but no matter where you
put your head, you'll have a good night's sleep in this very quiet
inn.

The ☛ heated swimming pool was built up on a hill. There
are great views from here. The tennis court is also a nice addition
to the property.

There is much to do here, no matter what season of the year
you come. Trout fishing, golf, and horseback riding are nearby.

Go picnicking and hiking in the Green Mountain National Forest. Weston is close by, and its summer playhouse is fun. Fall foliage is spectacular throughout the area, or you can sit right here and watch the inn's 150-year-old maples turn colors. Winter brings cross-country skiing in the area, and downhill at Bromley, Magic, Stratton, or Okemo. All are 🖝 within twenty minutes of the inn.

The dining room is charming and the food is glorious. Among the appetizers are marinated artichoke hearts and mushroom caps stuffed with seafood and baked. Hats off to the chef for the crisp and perfect 🖝 slow-roasted duckling served with orange or fresh ginger sauce. (It is available only on Fridays and Saturdays.) Another winner is the chef's drunken chicken, boneless chicken breast sautéed and stuffed with Vermont mild cheddar cheese and baked with sherry. 🖝 Fettucine Alfredo is always delicious, and good fish entrees are offered. You should give this inn a try.

How to get there: Take Exit 2 from I–91 at Brattleboro. Take Route 30 north to Route 100, and the inn is just north of town on Route 100.

E: *The grounds are just beautiful.*

> *Insomnia is almost a blessing if you are in an inn
> within easy earshot of a country church bell.*

Olive Metcalf

Rabbit Hill Inn
Lower Waterford, Vermont
05848

Innkeepers: Eric and Beryl Charlton and son Paul
Telephone: 802-748-5168
Rooms: 20, all with private bath.
Rates: $45 to $90, double occupancy, EP.
Facilities: Closed four weeks in early spring and after foliage season to mid-December. Breakfast, dinner, bar. Cross-country skiing, trout fishing. MasterCard and Visa accepted.

In 1834 Rabbit Hill became an inn to service the new and very active trade route from Portland to the interior of New England and Montreal. It is said that as many as a hundred teams a day would ply the road by the inn, carrying produce, Fairbank scales, and maple syrup to the coast, and bringing back spices, molasses, textiles, and general merchandise. The inn's brochure describes the past so well.

Bedrooms are large and comfortable. Some have fireplaces, canopy beds, and chaise lounges. A pair of twin beds has very unusual carved headboards. There are stencils on the walls. All these things make for a very attractive inn. All rooms face east with a view of the Presidential Range. The porch on the second floor is a special spot to just sit, rock, and look. A nice sitting area is also up here with a full library. Please, when you take a book from this inn, send it back when you are finished. The inn also has a lovely living room, with double couches in front of the fireplace. An old organ is in here.

The dining room has wide floorboards and a Franklin-type wood stove. Whether you're eating breakfast or dinner in here, it is going to be excellent. Freshly squeezed orange juice and seasonal fresh fruit are a good way to start your day. Enjoy ☞ fresh fruit pancakes, French toast made with ☞ homemade oatmeal bread, or try Finnan Haddie. Dinner appetizers of stuffed mushrooms are done a bit differently from others I've had, and are very good. Entrees include roast duckling, curried chicken, and a marvelous seafood pie in puff pastry. Top it all off with Meringue Glaze or their homemade pies.

How to get there: Take Route 2 east from St. Johnsbury and turn right onto Route 18. Or coming from Route 5, take Route 135 east to Lower Waterford.

༝

E: *Good fishing for brook or rainbow trout and bass. Sailing above Moore Dam. Canoeing in the Connecticut River. There's much to do up here.*

> *"Venite ad me ownes qui stomacho laboratoratis*
> *et ego restaurabus vos."*
> *"Come to me all whose stomachs cry out in anguish*
> *and I shall restore you."*

The Governor's Inn
Ludlow, Vermont
05149

Innkeepers: Charlie and Deedy Marble
Telephone: 802-228-8830
Rooms: 8, all with private bath.
Rates: $75, per person, double occupancy, MAP.
Facilities: Closed in April. Breakfast, dinner, afternoon tea. Picnic hampers available for lunch. Bar. Skiing, boating, fishing, and numerous historical attractions nearby. All major credit cards accepted.

Deedy is the chef and she really does justice to the title. All the ☞ food is prepared each day for that day. She does not buy any prepackaged portion-control type foods and there is no microwave oven. Breakfast may feature the Governor's Special Breakfast Puff or Charlie's nearly world famous ☞ Rum Raisin French Toast. In the picnic hamper for lunch you may find the Governor's Braised Quail, or cucumber and dill butter sandwiches with Pacific smoked salmon. Sounds so nice and tastes so great by the side of a bubbling brook or any other spot in this marvelous countryside.

Dinner is a grand six-course affair. I do not care for bluefish, but if I did, I'd surely have it here. It's flambéed with gin! Salads are different. One I like is ☞ Strawberry Chardonnay with

Champagne. The after-dinner coffees and Victorian tea are also special.

The inn's "Collection of Recipes" includes several that you may find in your picnic basket. "P.M. Magazine" and *Vermont Life* have discovered the inn. It's no wonder, because both Charlie and Deedy are graduates of the Roger Vergé Gourmet Cooking School.

I think you get the message. The food is excellent.

The dining room where you enjoy this good food has restful blue tablecloths and a beautiful collection of ornate tea cups, added to quite often by contented guests. The parlor has a magnificent 1895 marbleized slate corner fireplace, a real work of art. The governor of Vermont who lived here surely had a beautiful home.

The bedrooms are so attractive, with lovely wallpapers. The beds have all new linen and a flannel top sheet to boot. There's one brass bed over one hundred years old.

How to get there: Take Exit 6 north from I–91 and follow Route 103 west to Ludlow. The inn is at 86 Main Street.

✳

E: *Miniature cordials in your room are a nice touch.*

The Okemo Inn
Ludlow, Vermont
05149

Innkeepers: Rhinard and Toni Parry
Telephone: 802-228-8834
Rooms: 12, 10 with private bath, some with brass beds.
Rates: $60 per person, double occupancy, MAP. Five-day ski and golf
packages available.
Facilities: Open all year. Breakfast, dinner, liquor license. Fireplaces in
public rooms. Swimming pool, sauna, cross-country ski trails.
Downhill skiing and golfing nearby. All major credit cards accepted.

The Okemo Inn is the oldest established country inn in the
Ludlow area. Built in 1810, it has been lovingly restored into the
country inn it is today. It is practically at the foot of Okemo
Mountain, which it was named for.

Needless to say, skiing, both alpine and cross-country, is a
popular pastime for guests of the inn. In addition, golfers have
found the inn to be a nice home base for nearby Fox Run. The
inn has some interesting package plans for holidays, so do call
and inquire about them.

☛ A good deal of care goes into this inn. There are flowers
everywhere and the grounds are lovely. Toni is a whiz with stencils, as you will see when you visit. The rooms are decorated with

warmth, good beds, and antiques, and are very clean. A collection of "necessary china" for bedroom use in times bygone is displayed on the bookshelf in the second floor hall. It's a wonder. They have installed a ☛ fully automatic state-approved fire detection system throughout the inn. This is a real plus.

☛ Meals are served family style. This is always a nice change. There are homemade soups and tasty tossed salads. Roast beef with oven-roasted potatoes and tender carrots in a delicate sauce is one example of a typical dinner. Do get there some special weekend for their old-fashioned barbecue. It contains everything you could desire.

The inn has a liquor license and the lounge has a working fireplace and color television. There is a large ☛ sauna for tired muscles or just because. In warm weather the inn's own private pool is lovely. There is an abundance of things to do in this area and the innkeepers are happy to help you plan your day.

How to get there: Take Exit 6 north from I–91, and follow Route 103 to Ludlow. The inn is located one mile from Okemo Mountain public transportation, which includes Vermont Transit buses and Amtrak trains to Bellows Falls, and 25 miles from Springfield or Rutland Airports.

৵৽

E: *A little dog named Chevas is here to greet you.*

A night at an inn adds a tinge to the coming day
that cannot be described, only enjoyed.

Birch Hill Inn
Manchester, Vermont
05254

Innkeepers: Pat and Jim Lee
Telephone: 802-362-2761
Rooms: 5, all with private bath, plus a cottage for summer only.
Rates: $50 to $60; per person, double occupancy, MAP.
Facilities: Closed late October to December 26, and April 15 to May 15.
  Breakfast, dinner every day except Wednesdays and Sundays. Beer
  and wine license, wine served with dinner. BYOB for other alcoholic
  beverages. Children over 6 are welcome. No pets. Fishing, swim-
  ming, cross-country skiing, hiking. Golf and alpine skiing nearby.
  No credit cards honored, but personal checks accepted.

At one time Birch Hill was a horse farm. Now it is a lovely
inn and about as perfect as a small country inn can be. Located
on a beautiful country road, it has a meadow with 🖝 beefalo
roaming and picture-perfect views. There are clumps of birch
trees, which were planted in 1917. Pat's family has lived here
since then.

A 🖝 stocked trout pond is on the grounds, or you fishermen
can go cast your lines in the Mettawee and Battenkill rivers. The
inn also has a nice swimming pool, which is great for exercise or
relaxation on a warm summer day, and I have been told there is

a huge rock quarry nearby that is great for swimming. Downtown Manchester has the Equinox Golf Club, which has a beauty of a course. There are all sorts of things to do in this area. Shopping is a must. Boy, I sure do have a good time while I'm here.

Alpine skiing is at two nearby courses, Bromley and Magic Mountain. Cross-country is right at the door of the inn and the trails are uncrowded and suitable for all abilities. Nice for hiking in the summer, too.

The guest rooms are lovely, comfortable, and afford views of either mountains or farm and pond. One has a fireplace. Books and flowers are in all of the rooms. This is a nice touch. There is a cottage for summer use only, which is perfect for a family or honeymooners.

One entree is served at dinner. The beefalo, which is raised right here, is a real treat. It is tender and  lower than beef in calories and cholesterol. Good soups and fresh vegetables are perfect accompaniments to the meal. This is all served at a lovely oval table. It's so nice when the innkeepers dine with their guests, as the Lees do here.

The living room has a library, fireplace, record player, piano, a lovely old spinning wheel, and an eighteenth-century grandfather clock. This is quite an inn.

How to get there: Go north on Route 7. Just past Equinox House is a fork in the road. Take the left side of the fork. This is West Road. In a few miles on the right is the inn. Or, from Route 30 going toward Dorset, turn left on West Road.

🌸

E: *A guest refrigerator to keep your own mixers, soda, or whatever, and a pair of golden retrievers, Abby and Megan, add the perfect finishing touches.*

Olive Metcalf

The Inn at Manchester
Manchester, Vermont
05254

Innkeepers: Harriet and Stan Rosenberg
Telephone: 802-362-1793
Rooms: 20, 16 with private bath.
Rates: $50 to $75, per room, EPB.
Facilities: Open all year. Breakfast, dinner, beer and wine license. Swimming pool. Skiing, golf, tennis, and theater nearby. American Express, MasterCard, and Visa accepted.

Lush greenery in the bay window of the living room is the sight that greets you when you walk in the front door of this inn. The many fireplaces surrounded by restful sitting areas, the numerous good antiques, and the dining room with ☛ Tiffany lamps add up to a warm country inn atmosphere. The antique Champion oak stove is the focal point in the game room, which is an ideal spot to unwind after a day on the ski slopes. Here you can watch television, or play games or cards at a card table. A good library is in here also.

The guest rooms are spotless and so very nice. ☛ Sheets, comforters, dust ruffles, and towels are color coordinated, and the beds are perfect for a good night's sleep. The carriage house has recently been renovated. It is luscious. Each room has its own private bath, and is individually decorated with coordinating sheets, comforters, towels, and antiques. There are Tiffany-style lamps, queen-sized beds, cast-iron and brass beds, and a beauty in cherry. Attractive artwork hangs throughout. All very nice indeed.

The food is homemade, even the breads. ☞ Apple pancakes with local maple syrup can start anyone's day right. Fragrant soups, creamy desserts, and vegetables from their organic gardens are just some of the many good things you can expect to find here. Meals are served family style. The menu changes daily and beer and wine are available.

The inn is conveniently located in the heart of just about everything, with skiing, downhill and cross-country, only minutes away. Summer brings great antiquing, summer theater, specialty craft shops, and boutiques. Golf and tennis are within walking distance of the front door.

How to get there: The inn is approximately 22 miles north of Bennington, Vermont, on Route 7. It is on the left.

∽

E: *The in-ground swimming pool is in a lovely meadow between the carriage house and the creek.*

The style is the inn itself.

Olive Metcalf

The Reluctant Panther
Manchester Village, Vermont
05254

Innkeepers: Edward and Loretta Friihauf
Telephone: 802-362-2568
Rooms: 13 rooms and suites, all with private bath and television; 8 with fireplace; in 2 buildings.
Rates: $70 to $200, double occupancy, EP.
Facilities: Closed mid-April to Memorial Day, and November to mid-December. Breakfast, dinner, bar, lounge. Elevator. No pets. No children. Golf, tennis, hiking, and skiing nearby. American Express, MasterCard, and Visa accepted.

The inn is mauve on the outside and a good bit of lavender and wine colors are inside. These are colors I love and, believe me, the inn is hard to miss with its yellow shutters. There are marble sidewalks and beautifully manicured gardens and lawns.

The rooms are unique. In some rooms the carpets ☛ go right up the walls. In others there are mad wallpapers. One has loving owls, and the newer lavender room has the wildest paper ever, and in extremely good taste. ☛ Six of these delightful bedrooms have a fireplace. There is nothing more restful than a crackling fire in your own room.

A very nice touch is a tiny elevator for those who have problems with stairs.

Ed and Loretta have acquired the Corner House, the building right next door, giving the inn a yard of over two acres. The Mary Porter Suite has a fireplace in the bathroom. Honest, I would not tell a fib. Whirlpool tubs are in the bathrooms and all the suites are sumptuous, as we have grown to expect from Ed and Loretta. A half bottle of wine and glasses in each room are a thoughtful touch.

The greenhouse for dining makes a perfect atmosphere for the fine food served here. The menu is a five-course prix-fixe dinner. There are four selections for the first course. Peach Sparkle is divine; half of an Elberta peach under Brut champagne. The salmon mousse is also different. The second course is soup. Two cold and two hot. The third course is salad with a choice of homemade dressing. The entree is the fourth course. Some are brace of quail, baked in a special wine sauce, or smoked pork, and, of course, Loretta has daily specials. The fifth course is the dessert. All are made right here. The coffee is also special and super fresh. They grind their own coffee beans, a small amount at a time.

Start your day, as I did, with Ed's concoction the Panther Blossom—grapefruit, orange, tomato, cranberry, and prune juices. Tastes great!

The bar-lounge area is nice and comfortable and watched over by a large bear. He's "lit" at night. How about that.

How to get there: As you approach Manchester from the south on Route 7 keep an eye on the left and soon the Reluctant Panther will pop into view.

E: *I love their letter to former guests, which begins, "Dear Panther Alumni."*

The Village Country Inn
Manchester Village, Vermont
05254

Innkeepers: Jay and Ann Degen
Telephone: 802-362-1792
Rooms: 30 rooms and suites, all with private bath.
Rates: $65 to $95, double occupancy, EPB. MAP rates on request.
Facilities: Open all year. Full breakfast, dinner, bar, lounge. Swimming
    pool, tennis. Golfing and skiing nearby. MasterCard and Visa ac-
    cepted.

Located in the heart of Manchester, this inn was known as
the Worthy Inn for many years. Now it has a new name and a
new look to go along with it. Today it is a lovely French country
inn done in shades of mauve, celery, and ecru, and stunning
inside and out. Ann was a ☛ professional interior decorator and
the inn reflects her expertise. Mauve is a color I adore.

The boutique is the French Rabbit, with well-dressed rabbits
to greet you. ☛ Ann has wonderful taste, and the boutique is full
of very nice things.

Tavern in the Green is the name for the bar and lounge. It
has an upright piano and ☛ nice people who play and sing. One
night I stayed here a playwright was in this room with a marvel-

192

ous selection of music and songs. What an unexpected treat. A door from here leads out to the swimming pool and gardens.

There is a large fieldstone fireplace dating back to 1889 in the living room with comfortable couches and chairs around it. Tables are provided for all sorts of games.

The rooms are magnificent and each one is different. They are done in ice cream colors. One pair of twins has matching canopies. Lace, plush carpets, down pillows, and nice things on dressers and tables give the rooms an elegant atmosphere. Good towels are such an important feature to inn guests and, needless to say, they are here.

Dining is a joy. The dining room is lovely and the food is glorious. Chilled tomato bisque with dill is excellent. Salads aren't run of the mill, and entrees are creative. Grilled loin of lamb with rosemary and juniper sauce, and medallions of veal with wild mushrooms, shallots, and Madeira in a natural veal sauce are just two of the selections. I chose crème brûlée for dessert. It was grand. Freshly made bread pudding with apples and hazelnuts captivated my dinner companion. Very good indeed. Breakfast is a full one, with many choices.

The Village Carriage Company comes to the inn with coachmen decked out in top hats and tails and horse and carriage. The inn has package plans for using the carriage, such as a champagne picnic in the carriage.

How to get there: Coming north on historic Route 7A you will find the inn on your left right in Manchester Village.

❋

E: *This is a beautiful inn carefully watched over by Tiffany, a little Yorkie, and Cinnamon, the inn cat.*

The Four in Hand
Marlboro, Vermont
05344

Innkeepers: Peter and Sheila Kane
Telephone: 802-254-2894
Rooms: 8, all with private bath.
Rates: $55, double occupancy, continental breakfast included.
Facilities: Closed in April. Lunch in season, dinner, pub. Skiing nearby.
   MasterCard and Visa accepted.

Traveling west on Route 9 you come around a corner and on the right-hand side, set back from the road, you'll find The Four in Hand. Peter and Sheila, such energetic people, have done a wonderful job of remodeling this inn.

The rooms, all doubles, are fresh and comfortable. The owners have developed a delightful common room where you can have coffee, read a paper, or just chat with other guests.

Peter is the chef. He's as good at creating fine meals as he is at innkeeping. Some of his entrees are scallops of veal with wild mushrooms or breast of chicken with mustard sauce. His cold poached salmon is an enticing summer dish. So is the cold lobster. Terrine of chocolate is a house special for dessert, and absolutely unforgettable for a chocoholic like me. The crème brûlée is also excellent.

The wine cellar is a beauty. 🖝 The Backdoor Pub is a treat, great for relaxing after skiing in front of a roaring fire. Sheila is the bartender and she has the honor of being called 🖝 the best martini maker on the mountain. All is here from a good hot toddy or just about anything else you wish to drink, to burgers, chili, and hot dogs. Local entertainment is on Fridays, and during the school year there are films on Thursday evenings.

This is a nice family venture.

How to get there: From I–91 take Exit 2 at Brattleboro, then Route 9 west to Marlboro. The inn is on the right.

∽

E: *The cat is named Jiggs, an orange cat. Orange cats are always good inn cats.*

> *The snow could pile as deep as a mountain*
> *with no worry for me, for I was in the tavern*
> *of a friendly country inn.*

Olive Metcalf

Longwood Inn
Marlboro, Vermont
05344

Innkeepers: Tom and Janet Durkin
Telephone: 802-257-1545
Rooms: 15, 13 with private bath; 4 with fireplace and one with Jacuzzi.
Rates: $75 to $125, double occupancy, EPB. $125 to $175, double occupancy, MAP.
Facilities: Open all year. Closed Christmas Eve and Christmas Day. Breakfast, lunch during music festival and foliage season, Sunday brunch. Dinner daily in season and Thursday through Sunday out of season. Bar. Music and skiing nearby. MasterCard and Visa accepted.

The copper lanterns at the door of this over 200-year-old inn are magnificent. The inn has served many uses over its life; a dairy farm known as Five Maples when milk was eight cents a quart, a halfway house, a college dormitory, the site of a local theater, and now a lovely country inn. In the summer there is still live theater in the old red barn, a step across the yard from the house. In nearby Marlboro is the ☞ world-renowned music festival each summer.

Any time of year is a good time to come to the Longwood. In winter you can ski downhill or cross-country close by. Bring your bicycle in the other seasons, or rent a horse and see this pretty area from the ease of a saddle.

The most important ingredient to good living found at Longwood's restaurant is the restful luxury of dining at leisure. The menu invites you to partake of homemade soups, fresh vegetables, or a Caesar salad made at your table. Fish is a specialty of the house prepared in an almost endless variety of ways. Good garlicky shrimp is a favorite of mine. Desserts are delectable: coupes aux marrons or mousse au chocolat. Breakfasts are pure New England with homemade muffins and Wilhelmina blueberry pancakes with pure maple syrup. Sound good? Come on up and try it.

How to get there: From I–91 take Exit 2 at Brattleboro. Take Route 9 west to Marlboro. The inn is on the right.

✳

E: *Barnaby, the inn cat, really runs the inn with an iron paw.*

> *The groaning breakfast board*
> *of a good inn always makes it difficult*
> *to remember the word "diet."*

Red Clover Inn
Mendon, Vermont
05701

Innkeepers: Mary and Elliot Schwartz
Telephone: 802-775-2290
Rooms: 15, 11 with private bath.
Rates: $45 to $60, per person, double occupancy, MAP.
Facilities: Open all year. Breakfast, dinner, bar. Television, swimming
    pool. Downhill and cross-country skiing nearby. American Express,
    MasterCard, and Visa accepted.

In the center of Vermont, just five miles east of Rutland, is
a flower of a country inn. The red clover is the state flower of
Vermont. The inn is the former summer home of General John
Woodward, and was built around 1840.

This is beautiful, peaceful country, and not far away there
are antique shops, outlet stores, and areas for cross-country and
downhill skiing. From June to October a 🐾 Farmers' Market is
open every Wednesday and Saturday with produce and preserves,
local crafts, and musical talent. A bike ride on some of the back
roads around here is lots of fun.

The inn is very comfortable. The living room has cozy chairs
and couches. Curl up in front of a fire with a good book or a
friend! The pub is adjacent to the living room and will provide

you with your favorite drink. The rooms are beautifully appointed and restful, just what you expect in a good inn.

There are three dining rooms and the food that comes out of the kitchen is divine. Some of the chef's creations are chilled curried zucchini soup, smoked rainbow trout, and entrees such as Poached Sockeye Salmon with Béarnaise Sauce, Veal Scallopini, and broiled loin lamb chops served with a special hollandaise and seasoned with Dijon mustard, dry white wine, fresh ground pepper, and herbs. Desserts are glorious. Try ☛ Rhubarb Crisp. Breakfasts are not ho-hum either. Do come up here and enjoy. Dinner is by candlelight, of course.

How to get there: Take Route 4 east from Rutland, and the inn is on the right, down narrow Woodward Road.

ভৈ

E: *The converted carriage house is the Plum Tree House, sur-rounded by plum trees, so ☛ the chef serves his duckling with brandied plum sauce. Oh my.*

Middlebury Inn
Middlebury, Vermont
05753

Innkeepers: Frank and Jane Emanuel
Telephone: 802-388-4961
Rooms: 73, 65 with private bath, air conditioning, color cable television, and telephone.
Rates: $60 to $80, EP.
Facilities: Open all year. Breakfast, lunch, dinner, bar. Parking. Elevator, gift shop. Skiing, swimming, golfing, fishing, boating, and museums nearby.

There has been an inn standing at this same location since 1788. There have been some changes, due to fire and the inroads of time, but the present brick building, known as the Addison House, was constructed in 1827. One hundred years later, when the Middlebury Hotel Company took over, extensive repairs were made, and in 1977 Frank and Jane Emanuel became the innkeepers. Their efforts to restore the inn to its former elegance have been aided by a grant from the Vermont Historic Preservation Division.

The inn has an excellent central location in the delightful town where Middlebury College is situated. There are many his-

200

toric buildings, museums, and shops to visit in the town, and all around is an abundance of outdoor activities.

The Addison House has a delightful veranda and a really large lobby. 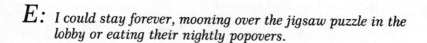 The dining room is beautiful, and the food that is served here is delicious. The elegant candlelit buffets shouldn't be missed, from the served appetizer and sherbet courses to the finishing touch of a fingerbowl. The Morgan Room Tavern and Terrace offers excellent liquid refreshment, including the inn's own "Candied Apple." Upstairs the wide halls wander and dip, up one step and down three, wide enough for those ladies of long ago to have maneuvered their hoopskirts with grace.

Additional rooms are in adjacent buildings, or wings off the original building. The Jonathan Carver Wing was constructed in 1897, and the Thomas Hagar House, which was built in 1816, is now attached to the Addison House. The Porter Mansion, built in 1825, has five handsome guest rooms, several fireplaces of rare black marble, and a lovely curving staircase in the front parlor. More contemporary-style rooms are found in the Governor Weeks House and the Emma Willard House. The East Wing has been completely and beautifully refurbished.

Whatever type of room you need, you'll find a wide variety of good choices here.

How to get there: Go up Route 7, and you run right into Middlebury. The inn is in the middle of town.

❁

E: *I could stay forever, mooning over the jigsaw puzzle in the lobby or eating their nightly popovers.*

The Middletown Springs Inn
Middletown Springs, Vermont
05757

Innkeepers: Jane and Steve Sax
Telephone: 802-235-2198
Rooms: 10, 7 with private bath.
Rates: $110 to $120. double occupancy, EPB.
Facilities: Open all year. Breakfast, dinner, full license. Skiing, hiking, biking, golfing, fishing, swimming, and canoeing nearby. MasterCard and Visa accepted.

The approach to this lovely old Victorian inn on the village green is quiet and peaceful. The white wicker on the front porch adds just the perfect accent to this stately building.

The windows throughout the inn are almost floor to ceiling. A beautiful ☛ curved staircase takes you upstairs to the spacious bedrooms, which are filled with antiques. I slept in a lovely sleigh bed in the honeymoon suite. The inn provides ☛ robes for the rooms that share baths. This is a nice touch if you have forgotten to bring yours.

There are two high-ceilinged dining rooms. The rug in one of them is as old as the inn (1880) and really in great shape. Some of the furniture is massive and could be used only in a large home such as this. The library is unique, with a woodburning stove and a revolving fan hanging from the ceiling. The music room has an old grand piano. Please go and play—the innkeepers would love you to.

One entree is served each evening. Chicken Cordon Bleu, Baked Stuffed Haddock, and Beef Victorian (similar to stew, only it's better) are some of the dishes they make. Tomatoes with cognac is a vegetable dish I like. The carrot soup is excellent.

Behind the inn is the carriage house, built in 1840. It has three guest rooms with a shared bath. Nice for a large party of friends.

How to get there: From Manchester, Vermont, take Route 30 north to Pawlet to Route 133 north to Middletown Springs. The inn is at the junction of Routes 133 and 140.

E: *The upstairs sitting area and small library are very quiet and cozy.*

> *Where else, in all good conscience,*
> *could I stay but at a country inn.*

olive Metcalf

Zack's on the Rocks
Montgomery Center, Vermont
05471

Innkeepers: "Zack" and Gussie Zachadnyk
Telephone: 802-326-4500
Rooms: 1 cottage, sleeps two.
Rates: $70 per night, EP.
Facilities: Open all year. Closed Mondays and Christmas Day. Dinner by
    reservations only, bar. MasterCard and Visa accepted.

    After you finally find Zack's you really will not believe what
you see. His cottage home and restaurant are literally hanging on
the rocks over an incredible valley.
    This is my smallest inn. A cottage that sleeps two has a living
room, dining ell, kitchen, two fireplaces, a bedroom, and a *wow*
of a bathroom with a sunken tub. Even if you cannot stay here,
stay in town and come up here to eat Zack's food. It is 🖝 fantastic,
and so are he and Gussie, his wife.
    Zack's is so unique that it is almost impossible to describe.
When you approach the door of his restaurant you will find it is
locked. Ring the sleigh bells, and the door will be opened by
Zack. He will be in a wondrous costume and the 🖝 performance
begins. I will tell you no more except about the food. The menu
is printed on a brown paper bag, which is in beautiful contrast to

his restaurant and Gussie's bar. Zack does all of the cooking. He is the most inventive chef and innkeeper I have had the pleasure to meet. The dining room has to be seen to be believed.

And Gussie's bar is something special. It has an organ with a full grand piano top built over it. This is my first organ bar. The room has a stone fireplace and is done pub style but with a flair. The bar has five stools, but to go with it is the best stocked back-bar in Vermont. To top it all the inn plays music from the forties. What a pleasant sound.

The inn dog is Gypsy, the largest German shepherd north of the Mason-Dixon line, and probably below as well. Pyewacket is a noisy Siamese cat who runs the inn and Zack.

Reservations here are an absolute must.

How to get there: Going north from Stowe on Route 100, turn left on Route 118 at Eden. When you reach Montgomery Center, turn right on Route 58. The inn is up the hill on the left, after the road becomes dirt.

E: *Zack's cottage is called Fore-the-Rocks. The private home is called Off-the-Rocks, and the inn is called On-the-Rocks. Gussie's bar is After-the-Rocks. Lots of rocks up here.*

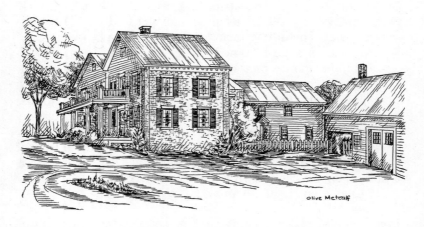

olive Metcalf

Black Lantern Inn
Montgomery Village, Vermont
05470

Innkeepers: Rita and Allan Kalsmith
Telephone: 802-326-4507
Rooms: 11, 9 with private bath; 1 suite.
Rates: In winter, $50 to $75, per person, double occupancy, MAP; in summer, $40 to $75, double occupancy, EP.
Facilities: Closed first two weeks in May. Breakfast, dinner every day in winter and weekends only in summer and fall. Bar. Parking. Television in lounge, fireplace in sitting room. Cross-country skiing. Downhill skiing, fishing, swimming, golfing, and tennis nearby. All major credit cards accepted.

When you get to Montgomery Village you are nearly in Canada, perhaps six or seven miles from the border. This is a quiet Vermont village, and the Black Lantern has been nicely restored by its hard-working owners. Whether you come in the snow for a skiing vacation, or on a green summer day, there is a warm welcome at this friendly inn. It is also surprising to encounter a rather ☛ sophisticated menu in this out-of-the-way corner of the world.

You can ski at Jay Peak, where there are fifty miles of trails for every kind of skier, outright novice to expert. Not too far away, over the border, there are four Canadian mountains, and ski-week tickets are available. Cross-country skiing starts at the inn door, and is undoubtedly the best way to see beautiful Vermont in the winter.

Summer brings the joy of outdoor life. Fishing, swimming, golfing, tennis, and hiking are all very near. You've heard about those country auctions, haven't you? Or would you rather spend the day browsing through antique shops? Whatever you choose to do, there will be a superbly quiet night to catch up on your sleep. The inn's guest accommodations are very comfortable, and the three-room suite is a joy. It has a fireplace and a Jacuzzi. This is heaven.

The double-peaked roof on this nice, old, 1803 farmhouse covers a typical north-country inn. Small, friendly, and just a little bit different.

How to get there: Go north from Stowe on Route 100, and turn left on Route 118 at Eden. This will take you into Montgomery Center. Continue down the main street and out of town, and before too long you will reach Montgomery Village and the inn. From I–89 in Burlington, turn right at St. Albans onto Route 105, toward Enosburg Falls. Pick up Route 118 at East Berkshire, and follow it to Montgomery Village and the inn.

✻

E: *Blazer, a handsome golden retriever, is the inn dog.*

Olive Metcalf

Camel's Hump View Farm
Moretown, Vermont
05660

Innkeepers: Jerry and Wilma Maynard
Telephone: 802-496-3614
Rooms: 8, one with private bath.
Rates: $21 to $25, per person, EPB. $30 to $35, per person, MAP.
Facilities: Open all year. Breakfast, dinner by reservation. BYOB. Game
    room. Fishing in Mad River. Skiing nearby. No credit cards ac-
    cepted.

The inn is an 1831 farmhouse, complete with lots of animals. A herd of ☛ white-faced Hereford cows wanders along the
banks of the Mad River out back of the inn. They are so friendly,
they will come when you call them. There are also a pig and
Missy, a Sheltie dog.

Wilma has a large garden. She cans strawberries, raspberries,
and blueberries, so the meals feature ☛ homegrown vegetables
and fruits all year. They also have their own chickens and you
cannot get fresher eggs. Wilma bakes all her own breads and
desserts. One entree is served each night. Homemade soup or
fresh fruit cocktail starts your dinner. The entree may be pork
chops in a sweet and sour sauce, or baked ham, or an Italian dish,
with salad and dessert.

208

The rooms are very clean and neat. There are bunk rooms for skiers. In the evening, find a book to read or play bumper pool or Ping-Pong in the game room. You also can sit in the living room and enjoy the sight and sound of the interesting fountain.

The Mad River flows by the inn and is wonderful for you fishermen. There are three ski areas nearby, Sugarbush, Sugarbush North, and Mad River Glen. Camel's Hump is on the list of inns involved in hiking and bicycling from inn to inn. There are short trails through this farm country. This I would love to do.

How to get there: Take Exit 9 off I–89 and go left on Route 100B. The inn is on your left.

≈

E: *Maybe I could take a friendly cow for a walk.*

Were it not for a night's rest in a country inn tomorrow would be but another day.

olive Metcalf

The Four Columns Inn
Newfane, Vermont
05345

Innkeepers: Jacques and Sandy Allembert
Telephone: 802-365-7713
Rooms: 13 rooms, 3 suites, all with private bath and air conditioning; 2 with fireplace.
Rates: $65 to $100, double occupancy, continental breakfast included. Ski packages available.
Facilities: Inn closed in April and November 1 to Thanksgiving. Restaurant closed Tuesdays. Dinner, jacket required. Sunday brunch all year, Saturday brunch May through October. Bar. Swimming pool. Hiking, ice skating, and skiing nearby. MasterCard and Visa accepted.

The inn is located on the most photographed town common in Vermont. The area is just beautiful and so is the inn. Sandy and Jacques are truly marvelous innkeepers. They are friendly and so is their staff.

The rooms are full of antiques. The Victorian Room has a brass bed. Another room has a canopy bed with a lace top, and four-poster beds are in others. Handmade rag rugs are all over and 🐖 plants in your room are a wonderful touch. Big towels and good pillows and mattresses; all these things make up a fine inn. The third floor suite has a lovely porch with wicker furniture facing the common. A nice place to sit and watch the world go by.

The inn has nice living rooms where you can gather to visit with other guests, read, watch television, or just relax. The dining room with a fireplace has blue and white napery. A beautiful armoire is used to display the superb wines served here.

The inn was given three well-deserved stars in the Mobil Travel Guide for its food and rooms. Jacques managed several restaurants in New York City before becoming an innkeeper. He always gave his diners the very best and he continues to do just that here in Newfane. Chef Gregory was a protégé of the former owner, who was a fine chef himself, and he stayed on with the Allemberts. He is inventive and loves to use local fare. He buys Vermont raised milk-fed veal and does his own butchering. I've had the veal here and it is heavenly. One of the chef's appetizers is charred raw tenderloin with cayenne mayonnaise, which is oh, so good. One dinner offering is boned, sliced double breast of duck with a rhubarb and radish sauce. You can't miss with food like this. The dessert cart is sinful. How do you choose between white or chocolate mousse?

The lounge has a pewter bar, which is very unusual. A piano is in here, plus plants and more country charm than you can shake a stick at. Do I like it here? Just wish I lived closer.

How to get there: The inn is 220 miles from New York and 100 miles from Boston. Take Exit 2 from I–91 at Brattleboro to Route 30 north. The inn is in Newfane, 100 yards off Route 30 on your left.

✳

E: *Max is a big, beautiful German shepherd who watches over a wonderful set of twin boys, especially at the inn's lovely swimming pool. Down at the stream is a hammock waiting for you.*

Old Newfane Inn
Newfane, Vermont
05345

Innkeepers: Eric and Gundy Weindl
Telephone: 802-365-4427
Rooms: 10, 8 with private bath.
Rates: $65 to $90, double occupancy, continental breakfast included.
Facilities: Closed April to mid-May, late October to mid-December, and
on Mondays. Lunch in summer and fall, dinner, bar. Parking. Ski-
ing nearby. No pets. No credit cards accepted.

The inn is well named, for old it is, 1787 to be exact. It has
been carefully kept, however, and the weary traveler will find
great comfort and fabulous food.

Almost all the rooms have twin beds. The rooms are large
and tastefully furnished. Gundy has beautiful taste in her decorating. There is an informal bar and lounge, and the dining room
has tables with pink cloths over white ones. Very effective. There
is a huge brick wall with fireplace in the dining room that gives
a wonderful feeling of warmth and good cheer. The ☛ floors
here are polished to a turn and beyond. And not just run-of-the-
mill glassware for the inn. ☛ The drinks I had before lunch
were served in crystal.

Eric is a fine chef. His soups are a bit different and very

212

good. I have tried both the cold strawberry and creamed water-cress. Loved them both. By the way, I hate calves' liver, but Eric asked me to try his. What magic he performed I do not know, but I ate every bite. Veal is king here. Eric butchers his own, so he gets the exact cuts he wants. Of course, the menu also has sea-food, lamb, fowl, and fine steaks. The dessert menu reads like poetry from the flaming suzette and jubilee to a fabulous om-elette surprise. There are also some cream pies that demand that you do not even think of calories.

How to get there: Take Exit 2 from I–91 in Brattleboro, and follow Route 30 north. The inn is on Route 30, on the left in Newfane.

꙳

E: *Gundy arranges pillows on the beds just beautifully.*

> *"Come away, O human child!*
> *To the waters and the wild*
> *With a faery hand in hand . . ."*
> —William Butler Yeats

Olive Metcalf

The Inn at Norwich
Norwich, Vermont
05055

Innkeeper: David McDonald
Telephone: 802-649-1143
Rooms: 26, all with private bath; 2 suites with kitchen facilities; television and phone in all rooms.
Rates: $60 to $96, double occupancy, EP.
Facilities: Open all year. Breakfast, lunch, dinner, Sunday brunch, bar. Swimming, canoeing, golfing, and skiing nearby. MasterCard and Visa accepted.

Right on the sign for the inn it says, "Since 1797," and it is truly said, because travelers up the beautiful Connecticut River Valley have been finding a warm welcome at this grand old house ever since. It is just a mile away from Dartmouth College, and alumni, skiers, tourists, and commercial travelers find a special homelike atmosphere here that is dignified but a lot of fun.

The friendly bar and lounge area is named ☛ the Jasper Murdock Tavern, after the inn's first owner. The dining rooms are lovely, with good napery and comfortable Thomasville chairs. The big bow window in the main dining room is a delight, but I still love to eat on the flower-filled porch. It's a nice place to watch the snow in winter.

The food is glorious. Sunday brunch has a new one on me: ☞ Pojarski. Come and see what it is. Lunch has some different items, such as Ham Salad in Puff Pastry or Veal Strips Béarnaise, and then on to dinner. Ambrosia. One appetizer is Baked Brie with Almonds. Nice and different. The ☞ roast duck is completely boned, a real treat. The desserts are wonderful. The wine list is one of the most extensive I have seen.

The rooms have very good beds and mattresses. There are canopied beds and some iron and brass beds. All are beautiful.

How to get there: Take Exit 13 from Route I–91. Go west a bit less than a mile to the center of town. The inn is on your left.

❋

E: *You can come to Norwich by air, car, bus, or rail, or walk if you must, but do come.*

Choose your inn, and enter in the world of relaxation.

olive Metcalf

Johnny Seesaw's
Peru, Vermont
05152

Innkeepers: Gary and Nancy Okun
Telephone: 802-824-5533
Rooms: 30, all with private bath; cottages with fireplaces.
Rates: In summer, $19 to $31, per person, EPB; in winter, $35 to $68, per person, MAP.
Facilities: Closed end of skiing to Memorial Day, and end of foliage until Thanksgiving. Breakfast, dinner, liquor license. Parking. Television, game room, swimming, tennis. Skiing, hunting, golfing, horseback riding, and fishing nearby. MasterCard and Visa accepted.

Skiing Magazine says this inn has the best Yankee cuisine in New England. The food is good, ☛ tasty country food prepared with imagination, featuring home-baked bread and homemade soup. Val is the fine lady chef who turns out all this fine fare.

The inn has a unique character, mostly because of the guests who keep coming back. It is set 2,000 feet up, on Bromley Mountain. The sixty-five-by-twenty-five-foot pool, marble-rimmed, is a great summer gathering place, and the tennis court is always ready. There are six nearby golf courses, and riding is offered at the Ox Bow Ranch near Weston.

For the many skiers who come to Vermont, Bromley's five

chairlifts and GLM Ski School are right next door. Stratton and Magic Mountains, the Viking Ski Touring Center, and Wild Wings X-C, are but a few minutes away.

For fishermen and hunters, or those who wish to take up the sport, the Orvis Fly-Fishing and Wing Shooting Schools in nearby Manchester have classes. The sportsman classes are held twice weekly, in three-day sessions through October, and participants may stay at the inn. The nearby towns boast many attractive and interesting shops.

How to get there: The inn is 220 miles from New York, 150 from Boston. From Route 7 take Route 30 right at Manchester Depot. The inn is 10 miles east, on Vermont Route 11. From I–91, follow Exit 6 to Route 103 to Chester. The inn is 20 miles west, on Vermont Route 11.

E: 🖝 *The circular fireplace in the lounge really attracts me, to say nothing of the cushioned platform along one side of the room. Argus, the inn dog, will keep you company here.*

*Cats, birds, flowers, and dogs
in companionate confusion are to be found
where hospitality has bested the world of commerce.*

Wiley Inn
Peru, Vermont
05152

Innkeepers: Toni and Patrick Smith
Telephone: 802-824-6600
Rooms: 17, 9 with private bath.
Rates: In winter, $85 to $100, double occupancy, MAP. Rest of year, $45 to $60, double occupancy, EPB.
Facilities: Open all year. Breakfast, dinner. BYOB. Game room, heated swimming pool. Hiking, horseback riding, fishing, skiing, and Alpine Slide nearby. MasterCard and Visa accepted.

The Wiley Inn is an attractive inn in a nice area of Vermont. Toni and Patrick are friendly and pleasant innkeepers who do a good job of making their guests feel right at home.

Two of the guest rooms have fireplaces. The Bromley Room has wonderful photographs of the mountain. The game room is full of fun things to do. The ☛ player piano has tons of rolls to play. There's a real, old-fashioned ☛ juke box that has only music of the forties, and that's nice. Lots of games and magazines are here for you to enjoy.

There is a plaque in the game room that I just love. It reads:

Oh how I wish I could foresee
What is about to happen to me
For here I am about to descend
I pray the Lord I do not upend.
—The Skier's Prayer

This is a BYOB inn; however, the set-ups are here for you. There is another fireplace in the dining room. This surely feels good on a cold night.

No matter what season, there are things to do at the Wiley Inn. In the summer, swim in the inn's heated pool. The Long and Appalachian trails are nearby; so are horseback riding, fishing in the Battenkill River, and the Alpine Slide at Bromley. In spring, watch the maple sugaring to see how the syrup is made. Fall, the foliage is king, and in winter there are Bromley, Stratton, and Magic Mountain for you downhill skiers. Cross-country ski-touring centers are within minutes. Go and enjoy.

How to get there: From I–91, take Exit 6 to Route 103 to Chester, Vermont. Go left onto Route 11 and the inn is 20 miles west in Peru.

E: *A cat called Kitty and a black Labrador retriever called Tessie are never in your way.*

The Pittsfield Inn
Pittsfield, Vermont
05762

Innkeeper: Tom Yennerell
Telephone: 802-746-8943
Rooms: 10, 6 with private bath.
Rates: $40 to $49, per person, double occupancy, MAP.
Facilities: Closed mid-April to mid-May. Breakfast, dinner, bar, lounge.
   Tennis, racquetball, swimming, golfing, horseback riding, skiing, and theater nearby. MasterCard and Visa accepted.

Tom is the ambitious and nice innkeeper of an inn and tavern that have been here since 1835. The town is small with a one-room post office and a bandstand on the village green, but within minutes there are tennis, racquetball, swimming, golfing, horseback riding, rivers for fishing, and summer theater. In winter there is downhill skiing at Killington or Pico ski areas, as well as ski touring and cross-country skiing. ☛ This inn is a pleasant home base for anything you care to do.

The inn's combination living room, bar and lounge has a woodburning stove, an upright piano—just waiting for you to play—and lots of games. The bar is of ☛ antique marble.

Guest rooms are warmly decorated with bright wallpapers, interesting antiques, and quilts on the comfortable beds. Some rooms are small and some are large. One is in my colors, lavender and white. They are all very clean.

The dining room is bright and airy. The food is good. Tortellini, an appetizer that I really like, is on the menu. It is a beef-filled pasta in a light pesto sauce. Another nice way to start a meal is with the potato skins with melted Swiss cheese. Entrees that beckon are Beef Wellington and Roast Long Island Duckling. The house special is lean loin of pork, butterflied and stuffed with homemade sausage, and glazed with an onion and sage gravy. Linguine Alfredo is always good. Desserts are freshly made each day.

The Tweed and White rivers are close by, so come on up all you fishermen. They are full of trout and salmon. Ski touring is close by, and so are downhill and cross-country skiing. The inn is part of an inn-to-inn hiking system. You also can bike or ski from inn to inn. This is fun to do.

How to get there: The inn is 20 miles northeast of Rutland. Take Route 4 east and Route 100 north to the village of Pittsfield. The inn is right on the green.

E: *I truly am a chocoholic, and the chef made me* *chocolate covered strawberries surrounded by Bavarian cream and with whipped cream on the top sprinkled with blueberries. What a way to live.*

olive Metcalf

Stonebridge Inn of Poultney
Poultney, Vermont
05764

Innkeepers: Lenore Lyons and Jane Davidson
Telephone: 802-287-9849
Rooms: 5, 2 with private bath.
Rates: $64 to $84, double occupancy, EPB.
Facilities: Open all year. Full breakfast, dinner every night except Monday. Service bar. No children under 10. Downhill and cross-country skiing, boating, swimming, fishing, hunting, and golf nearby. MasterCard and Visa accepted.

When you reach Poultney, you are almost in New York state, and here you will find this very nice country inn. The house was built in 1808 by Thomas Ashley for his daughter on land he acquired in a 1761 crown grant. This beautiful example of Greek Revival architecture was a private residence for 176 years until Lenore and Jane bought it in 1983. After a lot of hard work, they turned it into the lovely inn it is today.

There is a piano in the living room and guests are always encouraged to play it. A ☞ library is available for quiet reading or perhaps a game of chess. Four of the guest rooms have canopy beds. All have color-coordinated sheets and towels. The staircase up to the rooms is a beautiful curved one.

222

Dinner is served on Wedgwood china. All the food is freshly prepared. Soups and pastas are ☞ made from scratch in the inn's kitchen and their ☞ steak tartare is a real winner. One-quarter pound of prime beef tenderloin is ground just for your order, seasoned with capers and onion, and served with dark pumpernickel slices. Oh my. Why does this have to be so far from my home? They also serve Caesar salad the way it was originally, without ☞ anchovies. Ladies, I take my hat off to you for that one. Another different salad is grapefruit and radishes with romaine lettuce, tossed with oil and grapefruit dressing. Nice and inventive. Their rack of baby lamb, which I adored, has four ribs with an herb and garlic dressing. This is truly marvelous food.

How to get there: From Rutland take Route 4 west. Turn south on Route 30 and turn left. The inn is there. Or come up Route 30 to Route 140 and turn right. The inn is at 3 Beaman Street.

∽

E: *Naturally, all the pastries are homemade and worth a trip from anywhere.*

I have enjoyed the hospitality of a good inn and am ready for the day ahead.

olive Metcalf

The Golden Stage Inn
Proctorsville, Vermont
05153

Innkeepers: Kirsten Murphy and Marcel Perret
Telephone: 802-226-7744
Rooms: 10, 6 with private bath.
Rates: $60 to $65, per person, double occupancy, MAP.
Facilities: Closed April and November. Breakfast, dinner, full license. Swimming pool. Bike tours. Hiking, skiing, Alpine Slide, and gondola rides nearby. American Express, MasterCard, and Visa accepted, but personal checks preferred.

The Golden Stage Inn still is known locally as the Skinner place, for Otis, the actor, and his daughter Cornelia Otis Skinner, the author. The house was built over 200 years ago, shortly after Vermont's founding. It was once a stagecoach stop, and is reputed to have been a stop on the underground railway.

When you drive in you immediately notice the rockers on the porch and the abundance of flowers that surround the inn. It's very pretty in the summertime. Sit and rock on the porch and enjoy the breathtaking views of the Black River Valley and Okemo Mountain.

One of the rooms has its own little porch. There are lovely quilts, some antiques, and lots of books. The living room with its cozy fireplace is very comfortable after a day of doing your own thing. There are all sorts of games and puzzles. Maybe all you want to do is sit and knit or read or play with Mischa and Natasha, the inn cats. This inn is a nice place to do it.

Marcel is Swiss, and the delicious food he cooks reflects his Swiss background. Veal and mushrooms with a wine sauce and pork tenderloin in a mustard cream sauce are just two of his good entrees. Kirsten is the baker. She makes a chocolate walnut torte that would make a chocolate lover swoon. Croissants on Sunday morning are a heavenly way to start the day. The inn also has a huge vegetable and herb garden, so necessary to their good cooking.

Four acres of rolling lawns, beautiful gardens, and trees are just what you need for a picnic, a long walk, or for being alone. Surrounding this haven of loveliness are thousands of acres of forests to hike in and four mountains noted for their good skiing. They are Okemo Mountain, Mount Ascutney, Bromley (fun in summer, too, with its exciting Alpine Slide down the mountain), and Killington Peak, which has year-round gondola rides, the longest in the United States. Killington often has the longest ski season in the East.

☞ Biking from inn to inn is another way to see this wonderful country. While you bike to the next inn, a support van transfers your luggage. This is my idea of neat.

How to get there: Take Route 103 north out of Chester and just before you get to Ludlow you will see the Golden Stage Inn. From I–91 take Exit 8 onto Route 131 west to Proctorsville.

*

E: ☞ *A cookie jar that is never empty. Nice.*

Olive Metcalf

Okemo Lantern Lodge
Proctorsville, Vermont
05153

Innkeepers: Charles and Joanie Racicot
Telephone: 802-226-7770
Rooms: 9, 2 with private bath.
Rates: $60 to $65, per person, MAP.
Facilities: Closed April and November. Breakfast, dinner, beer and wine
   license. Golf, tennis, bicycling, skiing, and skating nearby. All major
   credit cards accepted.

The inn was built in the early 1800s. It is a lovely Victorian
with natural butternut woodwork and original stained glass windows.

In the living room is an exquisite old pump organ. This room
is all comfort, with armchairs, couches, a crackling fire to warm
your toes, and an ☞ enticing chaise lounge in front of a sunny
window.

Bedrooms are cheerful, clean, and neat. Furnishings include
a bit of wicker, antiques, and canopy beds. Would you like
a ☞ champagne breakfast in bed? Just ask.

Heavenly aromas are always coming from the kitchen,
whether they are from the freshly baked bread, freshly perked
coffee, or bacon sizzling on the grill. And I hear Charles is

getting 🖝 rave reviews for his butterflied leg of lamb cooked to perfection on the grill. Box lunches are available for hikers.

There are lovely cut flowers inside the inn from the flowers that grow all over the beautiful property. You just know that a lot of care goes into this inn.

There is so much to do in this area all year. Spring is the time to watch the maple sugaring or just go fishing in one of the well-stocked lakes or streams. In summer golf, tennis, hiking, and bicycling are close at hand. Fall is foliage and cider. Winter brings skiing and skating, or you could also curl up with a good book by the fire.

How to get there: Take I–91 to Exit 6 in Bellows Falls. Go north on Route 103 to its junction with Route 131 and turn right. The inn is on the left in a quarter of a mile.

∞

E: *Tumble in the Rumble, as it says in their brochure. In good weather a ride in the 🖝 rumble seat of a 1935 Plymouth complete with a raccoon coat on the driver and assorted appropriate coats for the guests is my kind of fun.*

Spring flowers add the final brush strokes
at the edges of the granite walk
to the inn's front stoop.

Olive Metcalf

Parker House Inn
Quechee, Vermont
05059

Innkeepers: Barry and Claire Snyder; owner, Roger Nicolas
Telephone: 802-295-6077
Rooms: 4, all with private bath.
Rates: $75 to $120, double occupancy, EPB.
Facilities: Closed for two weeks in spring and fall. Restaurant closed on
Wednesdays. Breakfast, dinner, full license. Downhill and cross-
country skiing, hot air ballooning nearby. MasterCard and Visa ac-
cepted.

The Parker House Inn and French Restaurant are owned by
Roger Nicolas, who also owns the Home Hill Inn and French
Restaurant in Plainfield, New Hampshire. They are both superb.
In 1857 Joseph C. Parker, state senator, businessman, and
mill owner, built the Parker House for his family and personal
lavish entertaining. Today the rooms are named after ☛ the
original Parkers. They all are grand. They are furnished with
beautiful antiques, wonderful beds, and comfortable upholstered
chairs and couches. The white and brass beds are so beautiful.
In remodeling the inn, walls were uncovered in the foyer,
and the ☛ original stenciling on the plaster was still there. The

stencil was restored by a local artisan, Tony DeGeorge, and is truly lovely. It is so nice to find such treasures in these old houses.

There are three lovely dining rooms. One overlooks the Ottauquechee River. The napery, in burgundy and white colors, is very warm and rich. The porch, which also 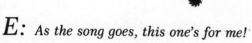 overlooks the river, is used for summer dining. Wherever you dine, you'll love the wonderful French food that is served here. Want some ideas? 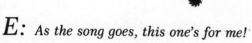 Tenderloin of New Zealand venison, Châteaubriand with pesto sauce, chicken breast sautéed with wild mushrooms, mousse of Nantucket scallops with lobster sauce, milk-fed veal, and on and on. For dessert, try 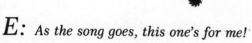 white chocolate mousse surrounded by dark chocolate and a raspberry sauce, or poached pears. And you should see the wonderful things Claire does with puff pastry! Breakfasts feature 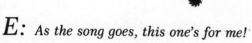 croissants, blueberry muffins, homemade jams and jellies, and fresh-squeezed juice.

This is a lovely inn. Wonderful food, great innkeepers, and an unbeatable location. Simon Pearce, an Irish glassblower, is next door. In summer there are hot air balloon rides and winter brings skiing, alpine and cross-country.

How to get there: Take Exit 1 off I–89 north. Turn left on Route 4 for 4 miles, crossing the Quechee Gorge. Turn right at the flashing traffic light. Cross over the covered bridge and turn left. The inn is on the left.

❀

E: *As the song goes, this one's for me!*

olive Metcalf

The Quechee Inn
Quechee, Vermont
05059

Innkeeper: Michael Maderia
Telephone: 802-295-3133
Rooms: 23, all with private bath and television.
Rates: $126 to $186, double occupancy, MAP.
Facilities: Open all year. Breakfast, dinner, lounge, full license. Cross-country skiing learning center, fly fishing lessons, bicycles and canoes to rent, downhill skiing, golf, tennis, squash, swimming, boating, fishing, and hiking. American Express, MasterCard, and Visa accepted.

The first time I saw and heard Quechee Gorge I was standing on the bridge that spans it. Now I know another way to see this remarkable quirk of nature. The inn is but one-half mile from it, and ☞ the innkeepers will show you how to see it from an unusual angle.

Quechee Inn was a private home from 1793 until 1976. Beautifully converted to an inn, it reflects the care the innkeepers give it. Some of the rooms have the largest ☞ four-poster, king-sized beds I have ever seen, and others have comfortable twins. Seven more guest rooms, in the wing off the original building, have picture windows overlooking the meadow and lake. All rooms are equipped with color cable television.

There are lovely stencils in the dining room and a beautiful awning over the porch. Adjoining the dining room is a small library and conference room wired for audio-visual equipment. It's a real treat to be able to have a business meeting at a place like this. The living room has an abundance of comfortable chairs and couches, a piano, color television, books, and a fireplace. One feels at home here any season of the year.

Breakfast is a sumptuous buffet. Everything is delicious. Dinner is equally good. They include avocado with boursin cheese and melon with prosciutto among their appetizers. I chose duckling with three citrus sauce—tangy orange, lemon, and lime, and delectable—for my entree. My friend Arthur had pork with apricots and almonds. I tried it, of course, and oh boy, was it good. There are several chef's specials in addition to a great menu.

The inn guests have full club privileges at the Quechee Club. The golf courses are breathtakingly scenic and are great tests of golf. If you do intend to play, let the inn know when you call for reservations so they can arrange a tee-off time for you. You may also play tennis and squash here.

How to get there: From I–91 take Route 89 north to Exit 1. Go west on Route 4 for 1.2 miles, then right on Club House Road for one mile to the inn.

*

E: *Old-fashioned New England dining with homemade breads, sticky buns, and regional specials such as trout and venison make a visit here a must.*

Saxtons River Inn
Saxtons River, Vermont
05154

Innkeeper: Averill Campbell Larsen
Telephone: 802-869-2110
Rooms: 19, 11 with private bath; 2 suites.
Rates: $35 to $65, double occupancy, continental breakfast included.
Facilities: Closed in March. Dinner every day except Tuesday, Sunday
    brunch, bar. Antiquing, skiing, golfing, canoeing, music, museums,
    and theater nearby. No credit cards honored, but personal checks
    accepted.

Blessings on the Campbell family, and especially on Averill Campbell Larsen, who was responsible for renovating this turn-of-the-century inn and revitalizing the little village of Saxtons River. I've been saying this a long time and I still mean it.

Cross the wide front porch and come through the gracious front door. To the right is a little breakfast room, to the left, the ☛ copper bar. Straight ahead is the dining room. Tiffany chandeliers light the flower-bedecked tables, and some of the freshest, most original food is brought out from the spick-and-span kitchen to please even the most particular diner.

The menu changes, of course, with what is fresh and good in season. If you are really not hungry you can have ☛ soup, salad, and bread for a most nominal price. If you are starving, begin with soup—how about some West African Peanut Soup?—or Mushrooms Maison or Picadilla, wheat tortillas filled with hot sausages, olives, spices, tomatoes, and cheddar cheese. Then go on to a main course of Chicken Satay with an Indonesian Peanut Sauce, Szechuan Shrimp, or Spanakopeta, a spinach and feta cheese pie. But be sure to save room for dessert. They are all appallingly good, and are outlawed by every diet club in the country.

☛ The guest rooms are spectacular, handsomely decorated with a combination of old furniture and crisp new fabrics. Your innkeeper has traveled around the world and knows what is needed for creature comforts, including pleasant places to read, with lights in the right places. She has slept in every one of her guest rooms, an acid test, and she has her own aerie at the top of the tower, five stories above the world of Saxtons River.

How to get there: From I–91 take either Exit 5 or 6 at Bellows Falls. Pick up Route 5, and proceed to Route 121. Saxtons River is on Route 121, and the inn is on Main Street in the center of town.

E: *I love to read in bed, and this is the most comfortable place for doing it.*

clive Metcalf

Rowell's Inn
Simonsville, Vermont
05143

Innkeepers: Lee and Beth Davis
Telephone: 802-875-3658
Rooms: 5, all with private bath.
Rates: $100 to $120, double occupancy, MAP.
Facilities: Closed three weeks in April and first two weeks of November. Full breakfast, dinner, beer and wine license. BYOB for other alcoholic beverages. Summer antique shop. Skiing, fishing, hiking, summer theater, and more nearby. MasterCard and Visa accepted.

Built in 1820 as a stagecoach stop, this inn has served many purposes over the years. It was a post office and general store, and then in 1900 F. A. Rowell came along, purchased it, and it became Rowell's Inn. He put in the ☞ elegant tin ceilings, ☞ cherry and maple planked dining room floors, central heating, and indoor plumbing. The brochure says during the mid-1900s the inn was a preferred luncheon stop on the "Ideal Tour" between Manchester, Vermont, and the White Mountains for a hearty fare of trout and chicken. Today the inn is on the National Register of Historic Places.

Rowell's tavern is a BYOB pub for guests only. There are an old checkers table, shoeshine chair, and icebox, an upright piano, and a woodburning stove. Now where else but a country inn would you find a room such as this?

One entree is offered each night at the five-course dinner. Some examples are beef tenderloin, roast leg of lamb, veal marsala, or chicken. Pan-fried trout is a house specialty. This course is preceded by appetizers like mushroom strudel, hot cream soups, and salad such as fresh greens with oranges and grapes and a delicious homemade dressing. Dessert may be apple pie or chocolate mousse or another dreamy thing. All this good eating is served in a nice dining room or a sunporch decorated with plants.

Three of the lovely rooms have sinks and two have working fireplaces. Some brass beds, quilts, and hooked rugs add to the tasteful decor of the rooms.

Close at hand you'll find hiking, golf, tennis, biking, trail riding, and fishing for trout in streams. The area provides summer theatre, great shopping, and antiquing. All this plus—as you'd expect in a good Vermont country inn—alpine and cross-country skiing.

How to get there: The inn is on Route 11, 7 miles west of Chester.

❈

E: *An antique shop connected to the inn is open from June through October. It is watched over by Muffy, the inn dog.*

Olive Metcalf

The Londonderry Inn
South Londonderry, Vermont
05155

Innkeepers: Jim and Jean Cavanagh
Telephone: 802-824-5226
Rooms: 25, 20 with private bath.
Rates: $29 to $65, EPB.
Facilities: Inn open all year. Restaurant closed late October to mid-
  December, and April to mid-June. Dinner, bar. Pool tables, Ping-
  Pong, swimming. Skiing, horseback riding, and hiking nearby. No
  credit cards honored, but personal checks accepted.

The inn sits high on a hill overlooking the village of South
Londonderry. It is central to three big ski areas, Bromley, Magic
Mountain, and Stratton.

In summer there is a large good swimming pool. Nearby
they have horseback riding, hiking, and bicycle trails. Any time
of the year there is pool to be played on the inn's two 🖝 vintage
pool tables. In addition, there are many comfortable places to
relax, read a book, do needlepoint, or just enjoy a blazing fire on
the hearth.

The inn dates back to 1826 when it was a farmhouse. The
rooms have twin, double, and king-sized beds with 🖝 down
comforters, 🖝 down pillows, and large thirsty towels. Jean also

puts 🖙 fresh flowers in the rooms. These little touches are far too often overlooked by innkeepers.

The inn has a nice lounge and a service bar off the living room, so you can be comfortable by the fire before dinner with your favorite cocktail in hand. The menu changes nightly, but always includes four to eight entrees served with fresh vegetables, four or five appetizers, at least one homemade soup, and great desserts.

Honey is the inn dog you will love.

How to get there: Take Exit 2 from I–91 at Brattleboro, and follow Route 30 north to Rawsonville. Then take Route 100 to South Londonderry. The inn is on your left.

∽

E: *The dessert names are really creative, FBI Cake, Orient Express Torte, and Hungarian Rhapsody.*

> *If you have never been drawn shivering*
> *from the warmth of a good bed*
> *by the sizzling lure of bacon on the grill,*
> *you have never been in a country inn.*

The Inn at South Newfane
South Newfane, Vermont
05351

Innkeepers: Connie, Herb, and Lisa Borst
Telephone: 802-348-7191
Rooms: 6, all with private bath.
Rates: $55 to $88, per person, double occupancy, MAP.
Facilities: Closed in April. Full breakfast, dinner, fully licensed. No
    children under 12. A pond for swimming or skating. Skiing nearby.
    No credit cards honored, but personal checks accepted.

The entrance to the inn is the Great Room. It is a huge square room done in several shades of gold—very impressive. The living room is elegant comfort, with a fireplace and a table for cards or games. It is a nice room for quiet conversation. Off this room is a ☛ porch overlooking the lawns and pond, with rockers and chairs and utter peace. The pond is wonderful in all seasons, providing ice skating in the winter and swimming in the summer. The lounge, called the Map Room by guests, has a fireplace. This room also leads out to the porch and yard.

The bedrooms here are individually decorated in period-appointed comfort. They have ☛ extra pillows, fluffy comforters, and patchwork quilts. There are four rooms with queen-sized beds and two rooms with twins.

238

The dining room is lovely. White napery, gleaming crystal, candles, and soft lighting set the stage for daughter Lisa, the inn's chef and a graduate of the Culinary Institute of America. Lisa's menus are varied and imaginative and change with the season. Everything is made from scratch, including the breads, pastries, and desserts. (Her father's hand is in this department.) All the soups, salad dressings, and mayonnaise are made daily. Lisa established an airmail order system that supplies her with red-tailed venison from New Zealand, Arctic pheasant from Sweden, and exotic mushrooms from the West Coast. Then she prepares such entrees as escargots in pastry cases with garlic, cream, and mushrooms; and curried lamb, garnished with peanuts, raisins, and coconut. Besides these you'll find fresh fish and a special of the day. Oh my, then one has to pick from the dessert tray.

How to get there: Take Exit 2 off I–91 into Brattleboro. From Brattleboro center, proceed north on Route 30 for 9 miles. You will see the inn's sign on the right. Turn left (west) and continue for 2 miles through Williamsville. Go over the covered bridge, and drive another 1¼ miles to the inn.

✳

E: *This is a beautiful part of the world, topped off with good food, nice innkeepers, an inventive chef, and two marvelous cats, Gumby and Mocha.*

The Hartness House
Springfield, Vermont
05156

Innkeeper: Tom Spaulding
Telephone: 802-885-2115
Rooms: 44, all with private bath, air conditioning, telephone, and television.
Rates: $55 to $58, double occupancy, EP.
Facilities: Open all year. Breakfast, lunch Monday through Friday, dinner Monday through Saturday. No food on Sunday. Bar and lounge. Swimming pool, tennis. Cross-country and downhill skiing nearby. All major credit cards accepted.

Because the inn had its start as the home of James Hartness, a one-time governor of Vermont, it has much to offer. ☛ A private forest for walking, a clay tennis court, and most important a ☛ 600x turret telescope that has to be seen to be believed. It stands on top of five underground rooms, which are connected to the inn by a 240-foot tunnel built in 1910. There are a library, workshop, study, lounging room, and lavatory. It is soundproof, cool in summer, warm in winter, and all under the front lawn of the inn. Do go and see; it is truly amazing.

You can relax with a good book on the deck overlooking the ☛ heated swimming pool. For more strenuous exercise there is a 🖝 lighted clay tennis court. The surrounding area offers skiing and pleasant roads for driving through the countryside. There is everything here for an overnight or an extended stay.

The guest rooms are cozy. They are tastefully done with period wallpapers and charm. Some are furnished with antiques. There is a grand staircase to the second floor. It does not take much imagination to envision a bride making a descent on a staircase such as this.

Dining is as elegant for breakfast as it is for lunch or dinner. Lunch selections include good salads, sandwiches, and hot entrees. Choose from dinner entrees like rack of lamb, Veal Piccata, or Veal Marsala. There is much more, followed by a daily selection of sweets. A very good wine cellar helps add the finishing touch to the meal.

How to get there: From the police booth in downtown Springfield, go up Summer Hill, starting at the light. Keep going up the hill as it curves around to the left until it levels off (a cemetery is on the right) at the five-street intersection. Bear left on Orchard Street. The inn is 300 yards ahead of you.

൙

E: *Although James Hartness was something of a recluse and needed absolute quiet, he married a lovely butterfly of a lady. Do visit the house they created together.*

Butternut Inn
Stowe, Vermont
05672

Innkeepers: Jim and Deborah Wimberly
Telephone: 802-253-4277
Rooms: 18, all with private bath.
Rates: $26, summer; $40, fall; per person, double occupancy, EPB. In winter, $48 to $60, per person, double occupancy, MAP.
Facilities: Closed mid-April to mid-May, and November to mid-December. Breakfast, dinner, afternoon tea. BYOB. Heated swimming pool. Skiing nearby. MasterCard and Visa accepted.

Through the red door and into a charming country inn, this is Butternut, located partway up a mountain road ☞ with a wonderful view of Mount Mansfield. It really does not matter what season you arrive, as they are all spectacular. Stowe is the ski capital of the East for downhill skiing, and there is excellent cross-country skiing as well. In the fall the mountains look as if they have been painted. In the summer the inn has a ☞ solar-heated swimming pool, and there's a lovely mountain stream babbling along nearby.

The inn has a family room with a good library, Ping-Pong, pool table, and board games. Next to it is an unlicensed bar, so bring what you want, and a beautifully carved piano. Hopefully there is one in every crowd who can play. The dining room is beyond, cozily warmed by a potbelly stove. Lovely stained glass Tiffany lamps hang over the tables. All in all this is an inn with most everything.

Food is served family style, with one entree each evening. Everything is homemade and so good. Deborah is the chef. There is a fine salad bar, something I really do like. Afternoon tea is served with Deborah's yummy butternut cookies.

The rooms are delightful. On the third floor are large family rooms, and everywhere the inn is very clean. There are hand-made and carved sleigh beds and bear heads. You'll find many carved things in the inn, all done right here by a very handy man.

How to get there: From Stowe take Route 108 to the inn on the left.

❀

E: *Breakfast is served poolside in the summer and by the fire-side in the dining room in the winter.*

Charda
Stowe, Vermont
05672

Innkeepers: Karl and Joan Jokinen
Telephone: 802-253-4598
Rooms: 11, all with private bath.
Rates: In summer, $35 to $60, double occupancy, EP; in winter, $28 to
$35, per person, EPB.
Facilities: Open all year. Breakfast, dinner, bar. Skiing. All major credit
cards accepted.

Charda looks just like it belongs in the Alps. It has such a
splendid view of Mount Mansfield and Spruce Peak.

The rooms have always been ☛ clean and comfortable, but
Joan has really spruced them up for eye appeal. Bright colors add
such a lot. The old barn that was turned into rooms is charming.

The dining room is lovely, and there's a small bar in its
center with great espresso and cappuccino machines to turn out
heavenly coffees. The menu is a joy. Steak, of course, and pork
and duck. ☛ Braised Hungarian beef goulash, served with
homemade spaetzle, is a winner, and so is Szekely goulash,
Transylvania style—pork pieces baked with sauerkraut. The appetizers are also very gourmet; small stuffed cabbages, Hungarian stuffed mushrooms, and many more. The dessert list is

yummy: Black Forest cherry torte, apple strudel, peach melba, and, of course, ☛ they have Palacsinta.

There's a heavenly porch that is used for breakfast and cocktails in season. What a view!

How to get there: Take I–89 to Route 100 and go north. The inn is on the left, north of Stowe.

๑๕๐

E: *They have a motto: A guest arrives, but a friend returns.*

> *Innkeeping takes twenty-five hours*
> *of every twenty-four, but done right*
> *it makes a wonderful life.*

Edson Hill Manor
Stowe, Vermont
05672

Innkeepers: Larry Heath, Jr., and Anita Heath
Telephone: 802-253-7371 or 802-253-9797
Rooms: 11, 5 with private bath, in the manor; 6, with 2 baths, in the annex; 8, all with private bath, in the carriage house.
Rates: $45 to $95, per person, MAP; higher on holidays.
Facilities: Open all year. Breakfast, lunch in winter only, dinner, fully licensed bar, après-ski lounge. Pool, fishing, horseback riding and instruction, cross-country skiing with rentals and instruction. Ice skating and golf at Stowe Country Club nearby. All major credit cards accepted.

Here you are, halfway between Stowe and Mount Mansfield, 1500 feet above the hubble-bubble of that lively village of Stowe that is growing every year. Here is truly luxurious living, in a house that was built in 1939 for a family that loved to ski and ride.
☞ The swimming pool here is beautiful. It won an award from Paddock Pools of California. The stocked trout pond is a must for anglers, and you can use the inn's boat. How nice to go catch a fish and have it for your breakfast. When the snow comes, ☞ the stables turn into a cross-country ski center, so there you are, practically taking off from the inn door.

This attractive house has been run as an inn since 1953, and there are still homelike touches. The pine-paneled living room has an aura of quiet elegance that reflects the feeling of gracious living all too often missing from our busy lives.

Downstairs are bar and lounge. A skier's lunch is served here. Hot soup of the day, chef's salad, hot chili, and good sandwiches. A special on cold days is hot mulled cider. Dinner, from the homemade soups to the desserts, is just dandy. The raw vegetable selection with a maple curry dip is a nice change. Veal is prepared differently every day; what a grand versatile meat this is. Their baked stuffed scrod has a delicate crabmeat stuffing and a lobster-based sauce. Yum.

The inn has very nice guest accommodations. The eight rooms in the carriage house have beamed ceilings, brick fireplaces, and private baths.

This is a beautiful inn. Many of the paintings were done by ☛ Effie Juraine Martin Heath, the grandmother of the family. The view is spectacular, and Bow, the inn's golden retriever, is a must-see beauty.

A note of particular interest to all you moviegoers is that Edson Hill Manor was the winter filming location for Alan Alda's "The Four Seasons."

How to get there: Take Route 108 north from Stowe 4.9 miles, turn right on Edson Hill Road, and follow the signs uphill to the Manor.

E: *The old delft tiles around many of the fireplaces are so appealing. Look closely at the living room curtains. Somebody shopped hard for that material.*

Foxfire Inn
Stowe, Vermont
05672

Innkeepers: Irene and Art Segreto
Telephone: 802-253-4887
Rooms: 5, all with private bath.
Rates: $50 to $65, double occupancy, EPB.
Facilities: Open all year. Breakfast, dinner, bar. Parking. Swimming
    pool. Downhill and cross-country skiing, fishing, skating, and hik-
    ing nearby. American Express, MasterCard, and Visa accepted.

The Segretos want to welcome old and new friends, and
there are myriads of them, to their inn. The house is more than
150 years old and has been restored to easy comfort by these
enthusiastic innkeepers. And there is so much to do here, from
the finest skiing in the East to great lounging by the pool.

There is a beautiful inn dog, Coby, a "formerly white"
Samoyed who smiles his secret smile to greet you. Irene says he
is just impossible to keep clean, but he did not look that dingy to
me. Could be the contrast with the snow.

Irene has created a 🐾 garden room that is a great spot for
breakfast and dinner. It is all white lattice with loads of hanging
plants. This is a gazebo to end them all.

The best Italian kitchen in New England may seem a bit

misplaced so far north in Vermont, but it is here. Taste, and you will agree. The tomato sauce is an old family recipe brought over from Naples. And do try things like Baked Broccoli, which is a combination of tomato sauce, ricotta cheese, and broccoli. There are seven different and delicious veal dishes. Boneless breast of chicken is prepared five ways, and the Eggplant Parmigiana has a special place in my heart. Shrimp Marinara I can still taste. As the front of the menu says, here you discover "The Italian Art of Eating."

And when you can push yourself away from the table, you have Stowe at your door, with antiques, shops, skiing, skating, walking, hiking, fishing, and more.

How to get there: Take I–89 to Route 100 north into Stowe. The inn is on the right, 1½ miles north of town.

❋

E: *Pass me another tortoni, please. I am settled in for the season.*

> *A cricket on the hearth of a country inn*
> *is music beyond the angels.*

Olive Metcalf

Green Mountain Inn
Stowe, Vermont
05672

Innkeeper: Diane Gergely
Telephone: 802-253-7301
Rooms: 57, all with private bath, color television, and telephone.
Rates: $58 to $105, single; $68 to $115, double occupancy; EP. Higher
rates in fall and during Christmas.
Facilities: Open all year. Breakfast, lunch, dinner, lounge. Beauty shop,
gift shop, health club with sauna, whirlpool, massage, and exercise
machines. Racquetball and complete health program. Skiing, heated
swimming pool. All major credit cards accepted.

This lovely inn turned 150 years old in 1983, and to properly
celebrate the event, ☞ it was completely restored. There are period wallpapers, paints, and stencils, smoke alarms and sprinkler
systems, and a handcrafted reproduction furniture line, named
after the inn by the manufacturer.
☞ The Health Club is fantastic. What a place! It has everything you could want in it. Massage, sauna, whirlpool—such
luxury. Inquire about the inn's complete health package, which
includes diet. If the Health Club isn't for you, there's a ☞ heated
outdoor swimming pool with a sun terrace, a glorious spot on a
summer day.

The Whip is the lounge area, which provides a casual setting for the food that is served all day. A beautiful, huge fireplace is along one wall, and the beer tap is the most unusual I've seen. It is colorful ceramic and serves three different beers.

The dining room is charming. At lunch the chicken salad plate was beautifully served and delicious. Dinner was even better. Everyone who works here makes you feel right at home.

After you've had an active day on the ski slopes, the public rooms are a great place to relax. The library has a chess set at the ready. The connecting parlor with a roaring fire in the fireplace has the daily newspapers, including the *New York Times*.

The guest rooms have twin beds or canopy-covered queen-size beds, with comfortable mattresses. All are well appointed, with lots of towels and extra pillows.

This inn really has everything.

How to get there: Take I-89 to Route 100 north into Stowe. The inn is at the intersection of Routes 100 and 108.

✳

E: *This is the ski capital of the East. How nice to relax in this lovely country inn.*

Olive Metcalf

Ten Acres Lodge
Stowe, Vermont
05672

Innkeepers: Dave and Libby Helprin; Bob Howd, general manager
Telephone: 802-253-7638
Rooms: 17, all with private bath, in 2 buildings; 2 guest cottages.
Rates: In summer, $50 to $80; in fall and winter, $65 to $105; double
occupancy, EPB. Guest cottages higher.
Facilities: Closed April to mid-June and early November to December
20. Breakfast, dinner, bar. Pets in cottages only. Swimming pool,
tennis court, cross-country skiing. Downhill skiing nearby. All major credit cards accepted.

The living rooms at Ten Acres Lodge are the most inviting
and comfortable these bones have enjoyed in many a mile. You
find soft couches and chairs, large fireplaces, ☞ bookcases full
of good reading, and windows that look out on sheer beauty year
round. In summer, dairy cows graze in the rolling farm fields
across the road, and in winter, cross-country ski trails crisscross
the hillside. Around the inn are maples more than one hundred
years old that provide lazy New England shade.

The dining rooms are beautifully appointed from the poppy-
colored wallpapers to the napery. The food is thoughtfully prepared. The ☞ menu changes every night. There are things for

252

starters like fresh artichokes and scallops with saffron mayonnaise or garlic sausage with roasted red peppers. And this I love, fried brie with apples. The menu has a variety of fish, veal, steak, and lamb entrees, all skillfully cooked by the chef. AAA has just awarded the inn a four-diamond rating.

The very comfortable guest rooms are carpeted and pine-paneled or wallpapered with pine trim. The beds are queens and doubles, covered with lovely homemade spreads. The guest cottages have their own kitchens, working fireplaces, and terraces that look out at all the wonderful scenery that surrounds Stowe.

The inn has a neat bar and a game room all set for a game of backgammon, chess, or checkers. Outside, you are in the ski capital of the East. The mountains are just beautiful. Go and enjoy.

How to get there: From Route 100 north in Stowe, turn left at the three-way stop onto Route 108. Proceed approximately 3 miles, then bear left onto Luce Hill Road. Ten Acres is located in approximately ½ mile, on the left.

‍

E: *Hill House, a new addition to the inn, has eight deluxe rooms with cable television, telephone, fireplace, and deck or patio. It is really nice.*

Tucker Hill Lodge
Waitsfield, Vermont
05673

Innkeepers: Emily and Zeke Church
Telephone: 802-496-3983
Rooms: 20, 14 with private bath.
Rates: $54 to $67, per person, double occupancy, MAP.
Facilities: Open all year. Dinner served in season. Sunday brunch only
through October, cross-country lunches, bar. Swimming pool, ski
touring center. Fishing, tennis, and golf nearby. All major credit
cards accepted.

You will find Tucker Hill Lodge nestled on a wooded ridge
overlooking the road that winds up to the Mad River Glen Ski
area. This is Route 17, and it is one of the most spectacular roads
I have found in many a country mile.

Flowers are the first thing you see as you arrive at the inn.
They are everywhere and are glorious.

Rooms here are not fancy, but clean and comfortable. You
will find antiques and fresh flowers and handmade quilts on the
beds. The living room is pine paneled with a fieldstone fireplace.

Food is the name of the game here. The inn won the coveted
1985 Vermont Restauranteur of the year and is one of a few that
was awarded four diamonds by AAA. The innkeepers grow their

254

own herbs and vegetables, smoke their own meats, and make their own jams and jellies and vinegars.

Are you ready for this? ☞ Fresh homemade ravioli with a filling that is too good to try to put into words, and broiled Long Island oysters are two of the dinner appetizers. Soups—Shrimp Bisque, ☞ Smoked Vermont Duck Soup, or ☞ Sweet Red Pepper and Goat Cheese Soup. Wow! Do you want to hear about the entrees? Baked Red Snapper in Pastry. Sautéed Pork Medallions with Raspberries. Sautéed Black Angus Tenderloin of Beef. Grilled Center-Cut Vermont Lamb Chops. Believe me, the list of these tempting entrees goes on and on. This is some menu. Eight or more fancy coffees are offered along with mind-boggling desserts like Black Currant Cheesecake with Blueberries, ☞ Fresh Peach Brandy Tart, and Fresh Fruit Tart.

Breakfast and lunch are served outside by the pool and so are cocktails in season. In cool weather a neat lounge is a fun spot, decorated with antique farm and kitchen tools.

There is a lot doing up here. A ski touring center is right here at the inn. In addition, there is a Robert Trent Jones golf course nearby, plus swimming, tennis, fishing, and more. Or you can just relax in this lovely inn. Do remember to pat Blue, the inn dog.

How to get there: Turn west off Route 100 onto Route 17 in Waitsfield in the Mad River Valley. Go 1½ miles west; the sign for the lodge will be on your left.

❋

E: *I cannot think of a nicer place to sit than on the deck, under the trees, sipping something long and cool.*

The Waitsfield Inn
Waitsfeld, Vermont
05673

Innkeepers: Judy and Bill Knapp
Telephone: 802-496-3979
Rooms: 14, all with private bath.
Rates: $55 to $75, per person, double occupancy, MAP.
Facilities: Closed from end of ski season until the end of May. Full
   breakfast, dinner, Sunday brunch, bar, lounge. Tennis and ice skat-
   ing. Cross-country and downhill skiing, sleigh rides, golf, and
   antiquing nearby. All major credit cards accepted.

   The inn sits in the beautiful Mad River Valley in the middle
of the Green Mountains. Within ten minutes is a choice of 🖛 one
hundred ski runs of all degrees of challenge. There are plenty of
cross-country ski areas and sleigh rides as well. Skating under
the lights in the inn's own backyard also is nice. In fall the leaves
are like a painting on the mountain, and during spring and summer bicycling, golf, tennis, and more are all nearby. I can vouch
for the 🖛 antique shop next door. I bought a beautiful copper
coffee warmer set there.
   The dining rooms are small and very inviting. The cuisine is
continental with traditional favorites. All food preparation, including the baking, goes on right in the inn's own kitchen. Veg-

etables are fresh and cooked to order. Shellfish Supreme is a wonderful appetizer and all the soups are homemade. ☛ Roast duck with raspberries is my idea of heaven. Eggplant-pecan curry is a rare treat, and so are the Colorado brook trout, vegetable tempura, and veal and chicken dishes. Get the idea? The food is excellent. And as they say, "Save room for one of the homemade desserts." You'll be glad you did. For the crowning touch, order their expresso or cappuccino (regular coffee, of course, is also available). Sunday brunch has some real winners. Chicken pot pie, seafood crepes, eggs any style, pancakes, French toast, and the list goes on. Breakfast is glorious. I'll tell no more about the food, so come on up.

The lounge has a big fireplace, piano, plenty of games and books and wonderful sitting areas of good couches and chairs. There is also a very small lounge with a fireplace. You can really relax in this lovely inn.

All of the guest rooms are beautifully furnished with antiques and quilts. Some of the rooms have ☛ lofts for children. This is a very nice feature for the traveling family.

*How to get there:*The inn is on Route 100, 15 minutes south of Exit 9 off I–89.

❧

E: *A cup of mulled cider in either lounge would be a nice way to end a day.*

To find a good inn as darkness glowers on the horizon, there is no treasure to match it.

olive Metcalf

The Inn at
Thatcher Brook Falls
Waterbury, Vermont
05676

Innkeepers: Mark and Mary O'Neil
Telephone: 802-244-5911
Rooms: 13, all with private bath, some with television.
Rates: $64 to $79, double occupancy, EPB.
Facilities: Open all year. Full breakfast, dinner, bar and lounge. Canoe-
  ing, biking, hiking. Golf and tennis nearby. Cross-country ski area
  from door. All major credit cards accepted.

This is a lovely Victorian inn. It was, as Mark says,
a ☞ Victorian fixer-upper when they purchased it, so they pro-
ceeded to restore the old place. The project was not only challenging, frustrating, exciting, and expensive, but also, they say,
at times it was quite humorous. Now that it is complete, they look
back, feel rewarded, and say, "It was all worthwhile." It is a
charming inn. I love porches, and this one has a ☞ gazebo built
in.

The rooms are colorful, neat, and clean. One has a canopy
bed. The shower curtains are remarkably lovely. ☞ Mary has
done the decorating and has done it well. Cordials are left in your

room for you to enjoy. A sitting area, well equipped with books and games, is up by the rooms.

There are three dining rooms and a lovely deck with umbrellas. The tables are lovely with restful pink napery and darker, complementary napkins. A full Vermont country breakfast is served here, as is dinner. One appetizer that is a favorite of the innkeepers is delicate smoked fish served on a Vermont cheddar cheese scone. Soup du jour is prepared daily to reflect the Vermont weather. Entrees include Vermont rack of lamb, veal done differently every day, the fish of the day, and steaks. Prime rib is served weekends only. I love finding prime rib on inn menus, as it is so good. Leave room for Bailey's famous Black Bottom Cheesecake.

Across the street behind the old Colby mansion are two sets of beautiful waterfalls.

How to get there: The inn is ¼ mile north of I–89 on Route 100, the road to Stowe.

E: *Bailey's Tavern is named after the inn dog. It's lovely with a fireplace and library.*

> *"The righteous minds of innkeepers*
> *Induce them now and then,*
> *To crack a bottle with a friend*
> *Or treat unmoneyed men."*
> —G. K. Chesterton

The Inn at Weathersfield
Weathersfield, Vermont
05151

Innkeepers: Mary Louise and Ron Thorburn
Telephone: 802-263-9217
Rooms: 10, all with private bath; 2 suites.
Rates: $65 per person, double occupancy, MAP plus tea.
Facilities: Open all year. Breakfast, afternoon tea, dinner, tavern. Horse and carriage stalls. Tennis, sauna, pool table, Ping-Pong, TV and VCR with movies, exercise equipment. No children under 8. All major credit cards accepted.

This beautiful old inn was built circa 1776 and has a wonderful history. At one point during the Civil War it was an important stop on the Underground Railroad, hiding slaves en route to Canada. The inn is set well back from the road. Your rest is assured.

Everything that Mary Louise and Ron do to improve this lovely inn is done with class and lots of care. In the new wing are five redone rooms with sensational ☞ old bathtubs. These are real honest-to-goodness Victorian bathrooms. There are Rumford fireplaces in all of these rooms and in a lot of the other rooms as well. Each suite has two rooms and can hold four people. All the rooms are beautiful with fresh flowers, fresh fruit, canopy beds, and feather pillows.

Over the years Ron has built an extensive and good wine cellar. The tavern is handsome and so is the greenhouse dining area. Mary Louise found some old stencils to use and her quilt collection is a beauty.

The food is imaginative and different. Cider jelly is made nearby and used in some cooking. I never had had it before, so I bought some and used it as a baste on lamb chops at home. Delicious! Chicken Weathersfield is just one of Mary Louise's recipes that does wonderful things with boneless breast of chicken. The inn has many mulberry trees from which the owners make a sweet and sour mulberry sauce, one use for which is on stuffed pork chops.

Daughter Heather and husband, Jack, are potters. Their fine work is used in the inn, and certain pieces are for sale here.

There is a horse and carriage that will take you to the old swimming hole. The area here is full of berries. In winter you may go for a sleigh ride. All of this and a beautiful country inn.

How to get there: Exit 7 from I–91. Take Route 106 north to Perkinsville. About one-half mile short of the village you will find the inn on your left, set well back from the road.

❃

E: *A wassail cup is served from a cauldron in the keeping room fireplace. High tea is a special I love along with a gaggle of inn dogs known as "Mom's Moldy Muppets."*

Olive Metcalf

Deerhill Inn
West Dover, Vermont
05356

Innkeepers: Eileen and Ron Armonath
Telephone: 802-464-3100
Rooms: 17, 16 with private bath.
Rates: $130 to $150, double occupancy, MAP.
Facilities: Closed Easter to Memorial Day. Breakfast, dinner, lounge, full license. No pets. Not recommended for small children. Swimming pool, tennis. Golfing and skiing nearby. All major credit cards accepted.

The setting for the Deerhill Inn is perfect. Surrounded by lovely maple and fruit trees, it is perched on a hill with views of the countryside's beautiful mountains and lush meadows. It is nice and quiet up here. This is good country for hiking or cross-country skiing. Nearby are Mount Snow, Carinthia, and Haystack for downhill skiing. In summer you're sure to enjoy the inn's swimming pool and tennis court. The Mount Snow eighteen-hole golf course is close at hand.

There are several large living areas with ☛ fireplaces and comfortable furniture. There also is a small, well-stocked library. The ☛ views of Mount Snow from any place in this lovely inn are beautiful and so tranquil.

262

The guest rooms are clean, bright, and handsomely furnished. There's a choice of twin, double, queen, and king beds, and there are four lovely canopy beds. All very restful.

I love romantic dining, and here at the Deerhill it is by candlelight with attractive pink and white napery. The food has a touch of Europe blended with the best of Vermont. The escargots are served with garlic and herbs under puff pastry in a ramekin. I love garlic, and these escargots are good. The fresh sole with lime butter is nice and different. So is the duck that has a date and port sauce. And it is rare to have rack of lamb for one person. A really nice touch.

How to get there: Take Route 9 to Wilmington; turn north onto Route 100 at the traffic light and continue to West Dover village. Pass the church and post office; at the antique store turn right onto Valley View Road. The inn is 300 yards up the road on the right-hand side.

✳

E: *Eating my way through New England is fun with food like this.*

A glass of good whiskey
before an open fire in a good inn
is an unspoken toast to life
as it should be lived.

The Inn at Sawmill Farm
West Dover, Vermont
05356

Innkeepers: Rodney, Ione, Brill, and Luz Williams
Telephone: 802-464-8131
Rooms: 11 rooms, all with private bath, in the inn; 10 cottage rooms, all with private bath and fireplace.
Rates: $160 to $220, double occupancy, MAP. In foliage season and between Christmas and New Year's Day, $10 higher.
Facilities: Closed the Sunday after Thanksgiving to mid-December. Breakfast, dinner, bar, lounge. Swimming pool, tennis court, trout and two bass fishing ponds. No pets. No children under 10. No credit cards accepted.

The Williams have transformed an old Vermont barn into the gayest, warmest, most attractive inn that I have seen in many a country mile. Ione is a professional decorator and Rod is a noted architect, which makes for a wonderful marriage of talents for just a perfect inn. The Williams' son, Brill, runs the kitchen and he does a superb job of it. Brill's lovely wife, Luz, is in charge of the inn's gift shop, and she has filled it with beautiful things, some from her ☞ native land, Colombia.

The inn's copper collection is extensive. The ☞ over-sized fireplace in the living room is surrounded with it and there's a huge copper-topped coffee table that's a beauty. They also have a handsome brass telescope on a tripod for your viewing of Mount Snow. A most incredible bar of solid copper also lives here. This is in the Pot Belly Lounge.

Accommodations are very different, with some Victorian rooms, some done in Chippendale, and all with the flavor of New England at its best. The cottage rooms have fireplaces. The accommodations upstairs in Spring House have a living room with fireplace, bedroom, and bath in the most glorious colors imaginable. I was in Farm House and my room was done in the softest pastels, with a king-sized bed and a lovely dressing room and bath. They are all color coordinated with thick towels and extra pillows. ☞ Little boxes of Godiva chocolates are in each room. A very nice touch.

Dinner is beyond belief. Brill is a fine chef. There are twelve appetizers. ☞ Coquille of Crabmeat Imperial under glass was my choice. Brill's wife, Luz, who joined me for dinner, had thinly sliced raw sirloin of beef with shallot and mustard sauce. Of course I tasted some of hers. Outstanding. The soups are inventive and good. One entree is Medallions of Pork Tenderloin with cognac, cream, and walnuts. There are many more. They are perfectly complemented by wines from Brill's impressive wine cellar. Desserts are all homemade. Breakfast also is special. Fresh orange juice and homemade tomato juice are just starters. The staff who serve all these goodies are very courteous.

How to get there: Take I–91 to Exit 2 in Brattleboro. Take Route 9 west to Wilmington, and then follow Route 100 north 6 miles to West Dover.

༄

E: *The inn makes a specialty of special times. Do try to get up here for Christmas. It's something you will never forget.*

Olive Metcalf

Snow Den Inn
West Dover, Vermont
05356

Innkeepers: Marjorie and Andrew Trautwein
Telephone: 802-464-9355 or 464-5852
Rooms: 8, all with private bath.
Rates: $50 to $90, per person, double occupancy, EPB. On holidays ten
 percent higher.
Facilities: Closed in May. Full breakfast, dinner in winter, BYOB.
 Downhill and cross-country skiing, golf, tennis, swimming, boating,
 and music festival nearby. American Express, MasterCard, and Visa
 accepted.

    Snow Den Inn was built in 1885 by John Davis, who used
lumber that he worked in his waterwheel mill. It was a family
home until 1952 when it was converted to an inn.
    Snow Den is a good name for an inn up here in snow coun-
try. There is so much to keep you busy and happy in this area.
The inn is two miles from Mount Snow, and two minutes from
the Mount Snow Golf Course and Country Club. ☛ Facilities at
the club are available to guests at Snow Den. The Marlboro Music Festival is nearby, and so are summer playhouses, craft shows,
and fairs. Cross-country skiing is only minutes away, and the

Stratton, Magic, and Bromley ski areas are forty-five minutes away.

The inn is informal and comfortable. The den is large, and has a fireplace and a picture window that overlooks Mount Snow. This is a good place to relax after a busy day. The bedrooms are large. ☞ Five of them have color television and fireplace. On a blustery winter night this is heaven.

The dining room is attractive. Breakfast and dinner are served in here in the winter. The rest of the year, when no dinner is served in the inn, you'll find that many fine restaurants are nearby.

How to get there: Follow Route 100 from Wilmington to West Dover. The inn is on your right in the middle of the village.

❋

E: *This area has a lot going for it, and the inn is located well— not too far from the action.*

> *"Does the road wind uphill all the way?*
> *Yes, to the very end.*
> *Will the day's journey take the whole day long?*
> *From morn to night, my friend."*
> —Christina Rossetti

West Dover Inn
West Dover, Vermont
05356

Innkeepers: Donald and Madeline Mitchell
Telephone: 802-464-5207
Rooms: 10, plus 1 suite, all with private bath and television.
Rates: $60 to $100, double occupancy, EPB. Suite higher.
Facilities: Closed first two weeks in May and two weeks after Labor Day. Dining room closed from Memorial Day to June 15. Breakfast, dinner every day but Wednesday, bar. No children under 8. Skiing, hiking, golfing, swimming, and more nearby. All major credit cards accepted.

The Mitchells are to be complimented for restoring this fine old inn. An inn since 1846, it became the site of the town offices and had many changes before 1889, when the first addition was completed. It was known as the Green Mountain Inn until 1955.

Rooms are newly redecorated and have hand-sewn quilts and antiques. The suite is lovely. It has a ☛ fireplace in the sitting room, a queen-sized bed, and ☛ a Jacuzzi in the spacious bathroom. The magnificent old organ in the parlor is a dream. Henry and Iodine are the inn cats. I love their names. Smoky is the inn dog.

The Capstone is the restaurant. I've known the chef for a

number of years and, believe me, he is good. He prepares appetizers like shrimp scampi, herring in mustard sauce, and soups such as Bavarian Dumpling Soup. It is super. One entree I really like and don't see often enough on menus is pot roast. Shrimp Papillon en Cajun is shrimp broiled in a fine blend of Cajun spices. Frogs legs provençale and braised lamb shanks are excellent. I could go on, but I believe you get the message. The food is memorable.

The inn's location is a perfect base for whatever you care to do—swimming, sunning, leaf peeping, skiing, hiking, shopping, and much more. You could also come here to just relax and enjoy.

How to get there: Take Exit 2 for I-91 at Brattleboro, Vermont, then take Route 9 west to Route 100 north. In West Dover you will find the inn on your right in the village.

❇

E: *Tableside service is nice. Tournedos au Poivre, or Fettucine Alfredo and Caesar Salad, which are prepared for two.*

Let us escape for a day, or better a week,
and hide away in a country inn.

olive Metcalf

The Inn at Weston
Weston, Vermont
05161

Innkeepers: Jeanne and Bob Wilder
Telephone: 802-824-5804
Rooms: 13, 7 with private bath.
Rates: $49 to $64, per person, double occupancy, MAP. EPB rates available.
Facilities: Closed two weeks in April. Dining room closed Wednesdays, except in foliage season. Breakfast, dinner, Sunday brunch, bar. Television in game room. Wheelchair ramp available for dining room and one ground-floor bedroom. Cross-country skiing from inn door. Downhill skiing, hiking, summer theater, and museums nearby. No credit cards accepted.

Weston is a small Vermont village that has a lot going for it. The Weston Playhouse is the ☞ oldest professional summer theater in Vermont, and the building is a landmark too. At the Old Mill Museum you can watch craftsmen at work in authentic period workshops. The Vermont Country Store and the Weston Bowl Mill also are here. These, plus the lovely village green, are all within a pleasant stroll from the inn.

Built in 1848 as a farmhouse and converted to an inn in

270

1951, this is a lovely full service inn. Its pleasant tavern with a fireplace and a pub-style bar is very nice.

Rooms for the most part are small but adequate. There are sinks in the rooms that do not have baths. ☛ Quilts are on the beds. In the back of the house are two rooms that share a living room. The living room has a woodburning stove, nice chairs, and couches.

Pretty pink and white napery is used in the candlelit dining room. ☛ *Gourmet* magazine has written about the inn. That's a good indication of how memorable the food is. Pâté Maison is made right here. Other appetizers are Stuffed Artichoke Hearts with Sausage, Spinach, and Pignoli, and Scottish Smoked Salmon. Oh, it's hard to make a choice when everything is so tempting. Among the entrees I spotted Fruite de Mer en Papillote, which is fresh fish and shellfish baked in parchment, and oh, so good. The selection of fish in this entree changes. Cold poached salmon is served with a saffron-flavored mayonnaise and veal is deliciously different each day. All breads and desserts are made here.

How to get there: Off I-91, on Exit 6, take Route 103 to Chester. Follow Route 11 to Londonderry, and turn right on Route 100 to Weston. The inn is in the village.

∾

E: *Bogart is a golden retriever. He's the inn dog, of course.*

Windham Hill Inn
West Townshend, Vermont
05359

Innkeepers: Linda and Ken Busteed
Telephone: 802-874-4080
Rooms: 15, all with private bath.
Rates: $60 to $70, per person, double occupancy, MAP.
Facilities: Closed April and first half of November. Breakfast, dinner,
full license. All the activities of all seasons. MasterCard and Visa
accepted.

At Windham Hill Inn you are sitting on the top of the world.
It is beautiful up here. The West River Valley stretches as far as
the eye can see. Built originally about 1825, it was a working
dairy farm, and in 1962 was converted into an inn, which it has
remained.

The meals are memorable. Linda is the chef, and she makes
all her own 🐾 breads and desserts as well as her soups and
appetizers. In season all the vegetables are fresh, for most of
them come from the inn's gardens. Guests are given their choice
of dining with others at one of two large tables, or at tables for two
in the Frog Pond room. The pond is 🐾 spotlighted after dark.
Ken is the breakfast chef, and together this pair make a great
team.

272

The rooms are charming. Linda and Ken recently renovated the lovely old barn on the property to add five more guest rooms to the inn. They are very unusual, plus their views are spectacular. Two of the rooms in the house have their own balconies.

The living room is full of Victorian wicker and has a good New England wood stove. Off of this is a lovely balcony that overlooks the world. The whole inn feels like home. There are plants everywhere. I found a large stack of old *Life* magazines, something I love. They also have a well-stocked library.

The inn has its own Cross-Country Learning Center. Under the personal supervision of a professional ski instructor, the program is targeted for beginning to intermediate skiers. If downhill skiing is your preference, the inn is close to Stratton Mountain, Big Bromley, Magic Mountain, Mount Snow, and Maple Valley. A schuss-boomer's dream come true. The inn also has its own floodlit ice-skating pond, tobogganing, sledding, and snowshoeing.

As the innkeepers say, the inn continues to be one of the best kept secrets in Vermont.

How to get there: Take Exit 2 off I-91 in Brattleboro, then Route 30 for 21 miles to West Townshend. At the Country Store turn right, up the hill, onto Windham Road. Look for the inn's sign on the right in 1½ miles.

✳

E: *The peonies were in bloom. They have some in two colors. Another garden sight I have never seen before was their magnificent* Fringe tree. *And let us not forget Tober the cat and Peggy the dog.*

Brook Bound
Wilmington, Vermont
05363

Innkeeper: Jim McGovern
Telephone: 802-464-5267
Rooms: 14, 10 with private bath; 2 housekeeping chalets.
Rates: $55 to $70, double occupancy, EPB.
Facilities: Open all year. Breakfast only meal served. Dinner served at
the Hermitage nearby. BYOB. Recreation room, pool table, Ping-
Pong, swimming, tennis. Music and skiing nearby. No credit cards
accepted.

In the beautiful Green Mountains of southern Vermont, off
a country road in a lovely quiet setting with commanding views
of Haystack and Mount Snow, there is this warm and friendly inn
waiting to welcome you.

The grounds are spacious, and the 🖝 pool is heated. It sits
up above the inn with the tennis courts beyond. There are glorious big trees all over, and in the fall they are a sight to behold.

Breakfast is the only meal served at Brook Bound, but the
Hermitage, which is also owned by Jim McGovern, is nearby, and
a great spot to have some dinner. Setups are provided for your
drink at Brook Bound; and in the winter it all happens around a
neat fireplace. The inn has 🖝 a refrigerator especially for guests

274

to keep luncheon food and snacks or drinks. This is a nice thing to do.

Two chalets are close by. The smaller one holds up to six persons and the larger one can accommodate nine. You do your own cooking and housekeeping.

The inn is close to several ski areas for both downhill and cross-country skiing. There is so much to do in this area any season of the year that it would take pages just to list everything.

You are only twelve miles from the Marlboro Music Festival or the Brattleboro Music Center's Bach program. A real turn-on for a music lover.

How to get there: From Wilmington take Route 100 north and turn left on Cold Brook Road. Go 2.2 miles to the inn.

E: *Cross-country ski trails connect the Brook Bound to the Hermitage, so you can go right out the front door.*

A warming fire, a strong drink, a genial innkeeper . . . and winter is somewhere in the hills, but is not here.

Olive Metcalf

The Hermitage
Wilmington, Vermont
05363

Innkeeper: James McGovern
Telephone: 802-464-3759
Rooms: 15, all with private bath, 11 with fireplace.
Rates: $80 to $90, per person, double occupancy, MAP.
Facilities: Open all year. Breakfast, lunch in season, dinner. Accessible
   to wheelchairs. Sauna, wine cellar, game bird farm, trout pond,
   tennis, hiking, cross-country skiing from the door. All major credit
   cards accepted.

   High on a windy hill facing Haystack Mountain, you will
find a unique and heartwarming country inn, The Hermitage.
The owner is a man for all seasons who knows what he is doing.
He also has a certain charm, maybe it is the quick smile or a
fleeting twinkle as he says, ☞ "No piped-in music in *my* inn."
You might, though, find a classical guitarist some night, or someone at the piano in the lounge.
   Come in the very early spring, and you will find maple sugaring going full blast. There are four sugarhouses on the property, and Jim McGovern makes about 700 gallons of maple syrup
a year. In summer the big kettles are kept simmering, making
homemade jams and jellies. Along with this talent for making the

most of nature's bounty, Jim is an oenophile (wine lover), and has a 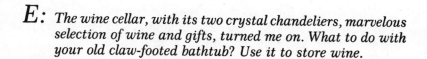 wine cellar with a stock of 30,000 bottles. You are never at a loss for the perfect wine to enjoy with this inn's first-rate food.

Dining at the Hermitage is truly gourmet and includes homegrown game and fresh vegetables. The dining rooms are lovely. The newest addition is the Delacroix Room named for Michael Delacroix whose paintings are featured throughout the inn. There's a fireplace to warm you while you enjoy some of Jim's wines.

Jim raises as many as sixty different species of game birds. Most of them, such as pheasant, partridge, duck, quail, turkey, and goose, are raised for gourmet dining. Jim also has show birds, brilliantly colored species of ducks and peacocks and a pair of black swans. He has an incubator for the eggs and I watched the babies breaking out of the eggs. Cognac and Burgundy, two friendly English setters (Jim also raises them), may come by to say hello, but they are likely to be distracted by a passing gaggle of geese that will fly off in a flurry of wings. Jim also has a large collection of decoys of every description on display and for sale.

The comfortable rooms, eleven with their own working fire-places, are furnished with antiques and, oh, those brass beds. In the carriage house you will even find a sauna.

How to get there: Take Route 9 to Wilmington, follow Route 100 north 2 miles to Coldbrook Road on the left. The Hermitage is 3 miles down Coldbrook Road.

E: *The wine cellar, with its two crystal chandeliers, marvelous selection of wine and gifts, turned me on. What to do with your old claw-footed bathtub? Use it to store wine.*

Nutmeg Inn
Wilmington, Vermont
05363

Innkeepers: Del and Charlotte Lawrence
Telephone: 802-464-3351
Rooms: 10, all with private bath; 1 suite.
Rates: $60 to $110; suite $125; double occupancy, EPB.
Facilities: Closed two weeks in April. Full breakfast, dinner for houseguests only. BYOB. Marlboro Music Festival, downhill and cross-country skiing nearby. MasterCard and Visa accepted.

The Nutmeg Inn was originally an Early American Vermont farmhouse with a connecting carriage house. In 1957 the house was remodeled and restored into a country inn.

The rooms at Nutmeg are quaint, cozy, and creatively decorated. The old-fashioned ☞ quilts are real beauties and the warm color schemes used make the rooms very inviting. I especially remember one charming king-sized bed.

The living room is rustic with a lovely fireplace made of stone. This is in the original carriage house. There are books and color cable television, or as the Lawrences say, come and meet old or new friends around our "bring your own cocktail bar." It is well equipped with an icemaker.

The dining room has a bow window and a wood stove. It is

very nice to sit here and look out at the snow falling on the lovely lawns. A full breakfast is served: Choice of eggs done any style, French toast, or pancakes are just a few possibilities of what you may find. At dinnertime it's fun to meet and dine with people from many different parts of the country. Dinner may be roast beef, or chicken in a tarragon cream wine sauce, or pork tenderloin with herb dressing. It is all beautifully served.

How to get there: The inn is on Route 9 in Wilmington, one mile west of the traffic light in town.

E: *Wilmington is a lovely area in southern Vermont, offering much to see and do. Marlboro Music Festival in summer, colorful leaves in fall, and skiing in winter.*

> *"There is nothing which has*
> *been contrived by man by which*
> *so much happiness is produced*
> *as by a good tavern or inn."*
> —Dr. Samuel Johnson

Olive Metcalf

Trails End
Wilmington, Vermont
05363

Innkeepers: Bill and Mary Kilburn
Telephone: 802-464-2727
Rooms: 20, all with private bath; 2 suites.
Rates: $25 to $50, per person, EPB.
Facilities: Closed in April and November. Breakfast, dinner, BYOB. Guest refrigerator and glasses. Cross-country skiing from the door, ice skating, swimming pool. Downhill skiing and Marlboro Music Festival nearby. No credit cards honored, but personal checks accepted.

Once you arrive at Trails End you would never know Route 100 is just a stone's throw away. The elevation is 1000 feet. There are miles and miles of untrampled nature walks and cross-country skiing trails right from the door. You'll find a manmade pond to skate on and open meadows to browse in. Utter peace surrounds you.

You enter the inn through a lounge area. Here are books, games, and 🖛 bumper pool. Another lounge area has a 🖛 fifteen-foot fieldstone fireplace and a cathedral ceiling. Floor-to-ceiling windows overlook the swimming pool and gardens. I can just see myself sitting up here on a cold winter night, snow outside and warm comfort inside.

The bedrooms range from small to large. All are cozy and clean. Two have fireplaces and refrigerators in them, and one also has a deck.

There are a few round tables in the dining area. This is a nice way to dine, because you can really get to know the other guests. Antique kerosene lamps provide the lighting. Dinner consists of four courses, served family style. A single entree is offered, such as Veal Marsala, pork loin with Madeira sauce, or a variety of chicken dishes. Cookouts are held during the summer, with steaks, corn on the cob, and watermelon. The kitchen here is really the heart of the inn. Hard cider and cookies are always available during the winter and cookies and lemonade in the summer—you cannot beat this.

The innkeepers tell me this is a popular place to stay for the Marlboro Music Festival. I can see why.

How to get there: From Wilmington go up Route 100. Across from Philip Davis's sign turn right. Then take the first right and go ⁹/₁₀ mile up the hill to the inn on your right.

E: *The flowers inside the inn come from the lovely gardens outside, which are looked over by Parker, the inn dog.*

Olive Metcalf

The White House
Wilmington, Vermont
05363

Innkeeper: Robert Grinold
Telephone: 802-464-2135
Rooms: 12, all with private bath, 2 with fireplace; 1 suite.
Rates: $75 to $90, per person, MAP.
Facilities: Open all year. Breakfast, dinner, Sunday brunch. Skier's lunch
    in winter. Bar, lounge, swimming pool inside and out, health spa
    with sauna, steamroom, whirlpool. Cross-country and downhill ski-
    ing nearby. Credit cards honored, but personal checks preferred.

You would expect an inn named The White House to be
elegant and, believe me, this one is. Built in 1914, the mansion
has much to offer.

The gallery on the main floor has an extremely unusual
wallpaper that was printed in Paris in 1912. There are high ceilings throughout the inn and the living room is large with a fireplace and beautifully covered (blue, of course) couches and
chairs. So nice to come back to after a day on the ski trails.

There are two dining rooms, both of which are very elegant,
and a small private dining room. The food served in
this ☛ three-star inn is superb, but would you expect anything
else in The White House? Here's just a sampling of what they

282

offer. There are nine appetizers, including brandied grapefruit and interesting soups. The one I liked best was shrimp stuffed mushrooms. Entrees are numerous and varied with always a special one or two. All are oh, so good and served with excellent salad and breads. Of course, all the desserts are homemade. I get hungry just writing about Bob's inn.

The grounds are sumptuous, with a lovely rose garden and fountain, and below this is a sixty-foot swimming pool. There's another small fountain outside the lounge, and from this delightful room you watch spectacular sunsets over the Green Mountains.

The health spa is what you need after a day of fun; exercise and massage room, sauna, whirlpool, steamroom, and showers. There's also an inside pool to relax in. Ah, what an inn.

How to get there: From Route I-91 take Route 9 to Wilmington. The inn is on your right just before you reach the town.

※

E: *Intrigue! Why did the original owner of the house put in a secret staircase? You will have to ask where it is.*

> *The warmth of a country inn*
> *can only be likened to*
> *a well-made down comforter.*

Olive Metcalf

Juniper Hill Inn
Windsor, Vermont
05089

Innkeepers: Jim and Krisha Pennino
Telephone: 802-674-5273
Rooms: 15, 10 with private bath.
Rates: $50 to $80, double occupancy, EPB.
Facilities: Closed first weekend of November until about December 20,
 plus March and April. Full breakfast, dinner. No children under 12.
 Downhill and cross-country skiing, swimming, and golf nearby. All
 major credit cards accepted.

This inn has been many things. Once it was known as a
summer White House, because former presidents Rutherford
Hayes, Benjamin Harrison, and Theodore Roosevelt were guests
of the original owners. It has also been a school, an inn, and then
a teaching and retreat facility for the Catholic Xaverian Brothers.
In 1980 it started a long restoration trek back to its original state-
liness. Four years later Jim and Krisha purchased it and did more
restoration work. Today it is simply lovely.

Large white columns lead into a thirty-by-forty oak paneled
entry hall that once displayed hunting trophies and was used as
a ballroom. It now is the main parlor and called The Great Room.
Two smaller parlors are provided for reading or quiet conversa-

tion. There is a ☛ beautiful grand staircase centered on a large Palladian window in a very private library wing.

Nearly all the rooms have been refurnished with the Penninos' personal collection of ☛ antiques acquired while they lived in Europe for four and a half years. Some rooms have marble sinks and one has a summer porch. Beds include a sleigh bed, brass beds, and four posters. They all afford you a very good night's sleep. As one guest put it, "Most comfortable bed I've slept in."

Jim and Krisha really care about furnishing the inn well. They have found the ☛ dining table that was originally in the house. It is a rare gem. The top alone weighs over a thousand pounds.

Jim is the breakfast chef, specializing in dishes like homemade apple pancakes or French toast. He also cooks eggs, of course. Dinner is Krisha's department. There are four courses, with one entree offered. She makes soups such as Vermont cheddar cheese or barley. Leg of lamb is prepared two different ways. Stuffed breast of veal and Rock Cornish hens with blackberry sauce are two other specialties. Krisha includes a variety of Greek foods on the menu. Now that's something not often found in New England inns! Homemade jams and desserts. Jim says Krisha makes a great pie crust. Come on up and see for yourself.

How to get there: From I-91 going south, take Exit 9. Go about 3 miles on Route 5 south to Juniper Hill Road, which is on the right. Go ½ mile up the hill to the driveway on the right.

∽

E: There's plenty of room in this very comfortable inn to roam about, and you're sure to like the nice innkeepers.

Olive Metcalf

Lincoln Covered Bridge Inn
Woodstock, Vermont
05091

Innkeepers: Phil and Pat DiPietro
Telephone: 802-457-3312
Rooms: 8, all with private bath.
Rates: $40 to $90, includes continental breakfast.
Facilities: Closed two weeks in April and all of November. Dinner, bar, lounge. No children under 8 or pets. TV room, games, and VCR for movies. Golf, fishing, cross-country and alpine skiing nearby. MasterCard and Visa accepted.

     Lincoln Bridge is the only known remaining wooden bridge of its kind and design left in America. Built in 1877 and renovated in 1947, it spans the Ottauquechee River. It is at one end of the inn's property.

     Five acres of land and this beautiful river are right here at the inn. A nice spot to go wading or fishing, so you fishermen should bring your lines and catch some fish. There is an old stone fireplace for cookouts and a picnic table with umbrellas and chairs, so do come and relax. In the wintertime it's snowmobiles and skiing that will keep you busy.

     The summer porch is the ski room in winter. There is a nice

living room with a TV and VCR with a library full of good movies. This is a great place to relax on a snowy winter night.

Accommodations are cozy in both the inn and the lovely carriage house. The queen- and king-sized beds are new and comfortable.

The dining room is done in cool greens. Pat is the baker and Phil is the chef. His cooking is Northern Italian style. Appetizers like this are served: Fettucine Cardinal, with their own lobster sauce, and Clams Posillipo, littlenecks steamed in a tangy tomato sauce. One marvelous entree is Cioppino—lobster tail, shrimp, clams, scallops, and mussels simmered in a fresh tangy tomato sauce served over a bed of linguine. Other entrees are veal done in many good ways and chicken that sounds superb. Steaks, chops, and pork all are delicious. Desserts made by Pat are excellent; she is so good at what she does.

How to get there: From I-91, take Exit 9 and follow Route 12 north to Route 4. The inn is on Route 4, three miles west of the village green in Woodstock.

✳

E: *Two tees on the grounds for golfers to practice is a nice extra.*

olive Metcalf

The Village Inn
Woodstock, Vermont
05091

Innkeepers: Kevin and Anita Clark
Telephone: 802-457-1255
Rooms: 8, 6 with private bath.
Rates: $45 to $85, double occupancy, EPB.
Facilities: Open all year. Full breakfast in winter, continental breakfast from Easter to Thanksgiving. Dinner, bar, lounge. Golf, tennis, skiing, swimming, boating, and shopping nearby. MasterCard and Visa accepted.

Woodstock is a beautiful area. The Village Inn is within walking distance of the lovely village green. Once this was a forty-acre estate on the Ottauquechee River. The Victorian mansion and carriage house, built in 1899, are all that remain of the estate.

Lots of charm and comfort are found in the bar. The very pretty ceilings are of carved tin, and there is a beautiful stained glass window. The room also has a nineteenth-century oak bar. Upstairs is a large common room with a porch, television, and games. And—this is a good thing to know—the inn has a fire alarm system.

Rooms are gracious, comfortable, and furnished nicely. Some

have marble sinks in them. One has a ☛ king-sized bed and a working fireplace.

I loved the romantic dining room, complete with a working fireplace, the original tin ceilings, and natural oak woodwork. A chef-owned inn is always a plus. The menus are enticing. Among the appetizers I saw chicken tempura, ☛ vegetable egg roll, and Fettucine Anita. I chose the stuffed baked potato skins, which were very good. ☛ Roast Vermont turkey is an entree that is too often forgotten on menus. Roast duck with a cognac and orange sauce has people coming back again and again. Roast lamb, roast prime ribs of beef . . . and the menu goes on. Desserts, well, all I'll say is that they're homemade and delicious.

Covered bridges, elegant shops, skiing, sleigh rides, golf, or tennis anyone? Go swimming or boating in one of the many lakes. Come on up and enjoy yourself.

How to get there: From I-91 take Route 89 north to Exit 1. Turn left into Woodstock. The inn is on the left.

❦

E: *This whole area and this lovely refurbished inn get my applause.*

> *I love all good inns, but secretly I have*
> *a rather special fondness if the boniface is fat.*

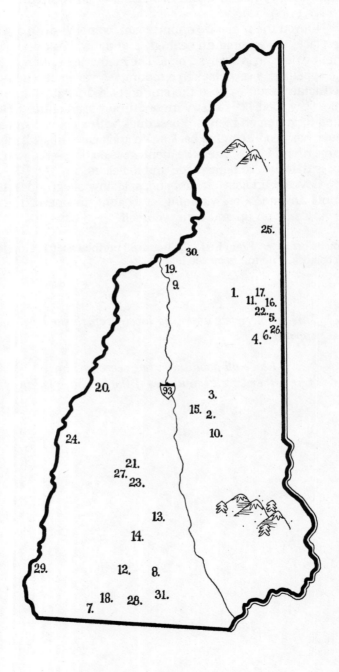

New Hampshire

The Nolchland Inn
Bartlett, New Hampshire
03812

Innkeepers: John and Pat Bernardin
Telephone: 603-374-6131
Rooms: 9, all with private bath; 4 suites
Rates: $52 to $72, per person, double occupancy, MAP.
Facilities: Open all year. Full breakfast, dinner, BYOB. Trout pond for
   fishing and ice skating. Hiking, skiing, swimming, canoeing, fish-
   ing, and bicycling nearby. All major credit cards accepted.

The inn was built in 1862 by·a wealthy Boston dentist,
Samuel Bemis. He used native granite and timber, and you can
bet that the construction of this building was some job.

☛ Seventeen fireplaces are in the inn, and all of the rooms
have working fireplaces. There are high ceilings and beautiful
mountain views. The dining room looks over the pond, which
is ☛ stocked with trout. Yes, you may catch your own. There's a
raised hearth fireplace in here that has a frame around it dating
back to 1790.

Pat is a gourmet chef. The menu changes daily, but always
offers a choice of three or four entrees. The soups are all homemade, like Curried Cream of Tomato Bisque and Cream of Fresh
Asparagus. An appetizer I loved was Leek, Onion, and Spinach

Tart. One entree Pat makes is Beef Wellington. Her Cajun-style Chicken is boned chicken baked on a bed of ham, pan-fried potatoes, and mushrooms, dressed with Béarnaise sauce and a touch of Cajun seasonings. Chocolate Raspberry Torte wins a star in my book. What a delightful combination of tastes.

There's so much to do in this area you may have a hard time deciding where to start. Hiking is by far the nicest you'll find almost anywhere. There are beautiful waterfalls and granite cliffs to scale. The Saco River is the place for swimming, fishing, or canoeing. Whitewater Class III and IV are here in the spring, so come on up with your canoe. Or bring your bicycle, as biking is fun here. Skiing of all kinds is very close by—or do you want to try snowshoeing? This is the place for it, or you can go ice skating on the inn's pond. If more sedentary activities suit your fancy, rocking chairs on the porch are ideal for reading and needlework.

How to get there: Follow Route 302 from North Conway to the inn. It is 20 miles north of North Conway.

❀

E: *Marcel and Reggie are a pair of white ducks, and the inn dog, a golden retriever, is Ruggs.*

Red Hill Inn
Center Harbor, New Hampshire
03226

Innkeepers: Rick Miller and Don Leavitt
Telephone: 603-279-7001
Rooms: 13, all with private bath; one cottage.
Rates: $65 to $100, double occupancy, EPB.
Facilities: Closed two weeks in April and all of November. Breakfast,
    lunch in season, dinner, Sunday brunch. TV and VCR, cross-country
    skiing, hiking. Sailboat rentals, swimming, tennis, and golf nearby.
    All major credit cards accepted.

    Traveling along Route 25B, you glance up a hill and sitting
there is this lovely old restored country inn. Not very long ago,
Rick and Don waded through waist-high snow to begin a project
that was destined to become a showplace of New Hampshire's
Lakes Region. What they had to do to make the inn what it is
today is just incredible. Their crew consisted of themselves plus
two others. Rick and Don alone sanded the floors of twenty-five
rooms.

    Oak paneling is in the living room. A huge bay window
affords you a view of Squam Lake and the Squam mountain
range, the foothills of the White Mountains. There is an immense
fireplace here that surely felt good one cool July night.

The rooms, all named after mountains, are different. Two of them have a sunroom and balcony, and ☞ three have their own fireplace. That same July night I lit a fire in the fireplace in my room; it felt and looked great. Most of the rooms are large and very comfortable, with grand views. During the inn's restoration they discovered ☞ nursery rhyme characters that had been painted on the walls and covered by panels. Of course they are here for you to see.

The dining rooms are lovely. Both have fireplaces and views, and the food that is served here is sumptuous. I had a garlic night—escargots, then garlic dressing on my salad, and finally the best ☞ shrimp scampi around. Of course I had to taste my dinner companion's lamb, and boy was it good. Sunday brunch's menu is ☞ unusually large. Something for everyone from lamb chops, omelettes, and eggs Benedict to cool salads. The luncheon menu is the same, just a joy—lobster salad, diet tuna salad, and on and on. The desserts at every meal are glorious. All are baked here. I had ☞ the best lemon meringue pie I've had in many a country mile.

There are more than 150 acres for cross-country skiing or hiking. It's a nice ten-minute walk down a hill and through the woods to the beach on Squam Lake. All this plus an inn cat named Kir, the innkeeper's collections, and utter peace. Do I like it here? You bet.

How to get there: Take Exit 23 off Route 93. Follow Route 104 east toward Meredith. At Route 3, go left, and follow Route 3 north about 4 miles to its junction with Route 25B. The inn is ⅛ mile off Route 3 at the corner of 25B and College Road.

❧

E: ☞ *The herb path is outside the sun porch–dining room. All hearty for the cold New Hampshire weather, all used in the kitchen, and so pretty to see.*

olive Metcalf

Corner House Inn
Center Sandwich, New Hampshire
03227

Innkeepers: Jane Kroeger and Don Brown
Telephone: 603-284-6219
Rooms: 4, 1 with private bath.
Rates: $50 to $60, double occupancy; EPB.
Facilities: Closed a few weeks in the spring and in the fall. Lunch, dinner, beer and wine license. Skiing and hiking nearby. American Express, MasterCard and Visa accepted.

This is a very interesting town. Different. The inn is centrally located so you can walk to everything. The ☛ New Hampshire League of Arts and Crafts is here as well as pottery shops, galleries, and museums. There are five major ski areas within a short driving range.

The inn has been operating as an inn for more than one hundred years. To keep pace with its history, the waitresses are in colorful period pinafores. The food they serve is excellent. The kitchen is famous for its ☛ crepes, and several different ones are prepared each day. I have tried a few and, wow, are they good. They also do fabulous things with soups. Another great inn specialty is ☛ dessert; apple crisp or apple pie stand out, and I dare you to eat just one of their cookies and not go back for more.

Of special note is the inn's house salad dressing. It is a buttermilk-dill combination. One of my party usually hates salad, but he ate it down to the last wisp of lettuce.

Roast duck is unusual. It is glazed with a variety of fruit sauces. And a new one on an old "inn creeper" like myself is Crab 'n Scallop Pie topped with puff pastry. Well, that tells enough about this good New Hampshire food.

The rooms are very comfortable. Bay windows in the living room, a spinning wheel, and plants give that touch of comfort you love in an inn. The carriage house is now the main dining room.

How to get there: Up I-93 to Exit 24, thence Route 3 to Route 113. Route 113 goes directly to Center Sandwich.

*

E: *Good inn animals are here. The cat is Anna and the dog, a golden retriever, is Cousteau.*

> *For one night at least*
> *let me escape from all those things*
> *the Puritans tell me I must face.*
> *Let me find a friendly inn.*

Stafford's in the Fields
Chocorua, New Hampshire
03817

Innkeepers: Ramona and Fred Stafford
Telephone: 603-323-7766
Rooms: 14, 8 with private bath; cottages.
Rates: $60 to $85, per person, double occupancy, MAP.
Facilities: Open all year. Breakfast, dinner, liquor license. Trail lunches
 available. No smoking dining room. Parking. No pets. Clay tennis
 court, cross-country skiing. All major credit cards accepted.

At the end of a quiet country lane sits a really lovely country
inn. It comes with a babbling brook, has forests at hand, and
overlooks some rolling fields. You will also find a barn with truly
unusual acoustics. ☞ Square dancing is fun here in the summertime.

Ramona Stafford likes to cook in a sort of French country
style with wine and herbs and spices and, best of all, with great
imagination: Pork Tenderloin with Prunes, and Stuffed Chicken
Breast with almonds and raisins. Most of Ramona's recipes are
included in the inn's own cookbook. How nice. Now we can try
to repeat some of her good cooking in our own homes.

Breakfast is the way to start your day. Omelettes are different, sour cream with green chives, mild country cheddar, or

cheddar and salsa. For Sunday brunch a real special is ☛ Eggs Hussard with Marchant du Vin. It translates to a wine merchant or a wine sauce in the vernacular. You could also try eggs Benedict or blueberry pancakes. You will not go wrong. Ramona serves well-balanced meals.

The inn is immensely comfortable with cross-country skiing right on the fields, and just utter peace. As Fred Stafford says, there is an inexhaustible supply of "nature things to do." Just sitting, watching the swallows swoop or a leaf spin slowly to the ground restores what you may have lost in the hustle and bustle of today's world.

Turn in the lane some snowy evening and see Stafford's glowing in the field, waiting to welcome you from a world well left behind.

How to get there: Take Route 16 north to Chocorua Village, then turn left onto Route 113 and travel one mile west to the inn. Or, from Route 93, take Exit 23 and travel east on Route 104 to Route 35, and then to Route 16. Proceed north to Route 16 to Chocorua Village.

❧

E: *Wolfie, a Belgian sheepdog, lives here.*

Darby Field Inn
Conway, New Hampshire
03818

Innkeepers: Marc and Marily Donaldson
Telephone: 603-447-2181
Rooms: 17, 13 with private bath, 2 with semiprivate bath; 1 suite.
Rates: $55 to $80, per person, double occupancy, MAP. Package plans
available.
Facilities: Open all year. Dining room closed March 30 to May 1. Break-
fast, dinner, bar. Television, library, swimming pool, skiing, hiking.
American Express, MasterCard, and Visa accepted.

Set high atop Bald Hill in New Hampshire's White Mountains with spectacular views of this wonderful country is Darby
Field Inn. Located 1,000 feet above Mount Washington Valley
and only three miles from Conway Village, the inn delights wan-
derers adventurous enough to leave the beaten path.

The inn borders the ☛ White Mountain National Forest
where guests are welcome to cross-country ski, snowshoe, hike,
or walk to nearby rivers, waterfalls, and lakes.

Rooms are charming, some with four-poster beds, patchwork quilts, and braided rugs. Most rooms have private baths,
and they are tucked away wherever space was available. How do
you feel about an L-shaped shower stall?

Downstairs the inn's huge ☛ cobblestone fireplace is the center for warm conversation. If you want a bit livelier time come into the pub, which sometimes features local singers.

Candlelit dinners begin with fine wine and a smashing sunset view up the valley. The food reflects the careful preparation of the chef. You'll always find a chef's special and fresh fish du jour. Whatever you order up here it will be excellent. Desserts are interesting. You must try Darby Cream Pie, quite different. The ☛ Irish Revolution will really end your day nicely.

Darby Field, a notorious Irishman, was the first white man to ascend Mount Washington. Had the inn been here in 1642, it is doubtful whether Mr. Field would ever have passed the pub.

How to get there: Turn on Bald Hill Road a half-mile south of the Kancamagus Highway on Route 16, then go one mile up the hill and turn right onto a dirt road. The inn is one mile beyond.

❋

E: *The inn dogs are Malamutes, Lupo and Chuska. Beautiful animals.*

A good innkeeper, a good cook,
and an affable barkeeper
are as standard in a country inn
as a fire engine in a fire house.

The Inn at Crystal Lake
Eaton Center, New Hampshire
03832

Innkeepers: Walter and Jacqueline Spink
Telephone: 603-447-2120
Rooms: 11, all with private bath.
Rates: $50 to $65, per person, double occupancy, MAP.
Facilities: Open all year. Full breakfast, dinner, bar, lounge. Skiing, swimming, hiking, and theater all nearby. All major credit cards accepted.

The inn was built in 1884 by Nathaniel G. Palmer and was known as the Palmer House until the Spinks bought it and completely remodeled it. Because of its commanding views of the lake, they renamed it The Inn at Crystal Lake. This is truly a Victorian inn.

You enter the inn on a ☛ marble floor with fossils embedded in it. While you're at the inn, make sure you examine Walter's fossil and rock collection, or ask him about the geology of the area. Fascinating. Walk through the Victorian parlor complete with a ☛ 237-year-old grandfather clock, mauve carpet, and Victorian fireplace and sofa. The next room is a lovely three-level dining room featuring ☛ Walter's metal sculptures. Part of the dining room is a Victorian greenhouse.

Walter is the chef. He has worked for some of the finest restaurants and inns. The emphasis is on unhurried, relaxed dining with a variety of international cuisine. Some things you may find are hot chicken liver salad or smoked salmon for starters; broiled lamb chops with honey or orange sauce, medallions of veal in mushroom sauce, poached salmon, or Dover sole for dinner entrees. The desserts are grand. Breakfast, a full country feast, features Jacqueline's ☛ warm Irish soda bread.

All of the rooms are named after gemstones. The beds are queens and doubles and have beautiful brass and iron headboards. The showers are ☛ nice and large.

A game and television room is tucked away in one area and a lounge and bar is in another area. This inn really roams about. The patio in back is brick, with tables in summer that are watched over by four inn cats, Dipsy, B. W., Stasha, and Chester.

How to get there: From I-95 take Route 16 to Conway. Turn right on Route 153 to Eaton Center and the inn.

⤲

E: *The balconies beckon me, and so does the porch with its wicker rockers and chairs.*

Fitzwilliam Inn
Fitzwilliam, New Hampshire
03447

Innkeepers: Charles and Barbara Wallace
Telephone: 603-585-9000
Rooms: 25, 12 with private bath.
Rates: $26 to $30, single; $30 to $35, double; EP.
Facilities: Open all year. Breakfast, lunch, dinner, bar. Television, sauna, swimming pool, cross-country skiing. All major credit cards accepted.

The Fitzwilliam Inn is still the same fine New England country inn that has been offering food, grog, and lodging to weary travelers since 1796. Now that's a long time.

The location of the inn makes it easy to get to, and since it is located ☛ 1200 feet above sea level, the air is crisp and clean. Once you are here there is much to see and do.

Go swimming in the inn's own pool, play shuffleboard, sit in the sauna, or do some cross-country skiing. Square dancing is offered on summer weekends and Sunday afternoon concerts are held during the winter. And in the evening the bar is a great little taproom where hot winter drinks are called Broken Legs.

The men's room is a must. It has a blackboard for graffiti and a great red rocking chair for relaxing. The patio or country dining room overlooks the pool and is wonderful for private parties.

Accommodations are varied and all are very comfortable. Your room is likely to have been decorated by a wonderfully talented lady who lives here. She does wonderful stencils. They all flow together from the walls, curtains, and onto the chairs and tables. She has even put stencils on the lampshades. They really are very beautiful. She also builds furniture. Do ask Charlie, Barbara, or their son to point out her work to you.

I think it's nice when an inn serves lunch, and this is a good one. Almost all the dinner entrees are ☞ broiled. This I like. There are three kinds of steaks, good lamb chops, salmon, and trout. For a change have the baked stuffed jumbo shrimp.

The ☞ people who work here are most pleasant and add to the ambience of the inn. This is a fun place to be.

How to get there: The inn is 205 miles from New York, 65 miles from Boston. Vermont Transit buses stop at the door. It is on Route 119, just west of the intersection of Route 12.

E: *Over the fireplace hangs this word puzzle. The Wallaces will have to unscramble it for you.*

> If the B mt put:
> If the B. putting:
> Don't put: over A - der
> You'd be an*it!

Olive Metcalf

The Inn at Crotched Mountain
Francestown, New Hampshire
03043

Innkeepers: John and Rose Perry
Telephone: 603-588-6840
Rooms: 14, 5 with private bath, 4 with fireplace.
Rates: $50 to $60, per person, double occupancy, MAP.
Facilities: Closed first three weeks in November. In winter, open only on weekends and holidays. Breakfast, dinner, bar. Tennis, swimming pool, cross-country skiing. Golfing, fishing, and summer theater nearby. No credit cards accepted.

This 150-year-old colonial house is located on the northern side of Crotched Mountain. There is a forty-mile view of the Piscataquog Valley, complete with spacious skies. Both innkeepers have gone to ☞ school to learn their trade, and what a charming house to practice it in. They are both pretty special themselves. Rose is from Singapore, and John is a Yankee.

Come and stay, there are many things to do. There are three golf courses in the nearby valley, fishing is great, and there is a wading pool for the young, as well as a thirty-by-sixty-foot pool for real swimmers. Two areas provide skiing, one at the front

door, and another down the road. Two clay tennis courts elimi-
nate that tiresome waiting for a playing area. And come evening
there are two summer theaters, one at Peterborough and another
in Milford.

There are two English cockers who live here, Kong and
Anan. Anan is Kong's daughter. There are numerous streams,
ponds, and lakes for fishing and mountains for hiking. Golf is
nearby. Come and enjoy this wonderful countryside with Kong
and Anan. They would love to have you.

How to get there: Take 101A from Nashua to Milford, Route 13 to New
Boston, and Route 136 to Francestown. Take Route 47 2½ miles, then
turn left onto Mountain Road. The inn is one mile up the road.

E: *Any house that has nine fireplaces needs a wood lot and a
man with a chain saw.* ☞ *Four of the bedrooms here have
a fireplace, so remember to request one when you reserve.*

*The register of a country inn
is a treasure of the names of good people.*

Olive Metcalf

Franconia Inn
Franconia, New Hampshire
03580

Innkeepers: Richard and Alec Morris
Telephone: 603-823-5542
Rooms: 32, 24 with private bath.
Rates: $50 to $75, double occupancy, EP. MAP rates also available.
Facilities: Closed April 1 to May 25, and mid-October to December 15
    Breakfast, dinner, bar, lounge. Swimming, four tennis courts, cross-
    country ski center, horseback riding, hot tub. Downhill skiing and
    soaring nearby. All major credit cards accepted.

This is an inn in the fine tradition of old New England hos-
telries. The rooms are simple and comfortable. Many of the rooms
connect with a bath, an ideal situation when you bring youngsters, and this is an inn that welcomes children. Never a dull
moment any season of the year. While the children play Ping-
Pong or watch a movie, you can relax in 🖝 the lounge and listen
to selected classical and popular music by the glow of the fireplace.

A card room and a library are here for your enjoyment, as is
a screened porch overlooking the pool and the mountains. And
they have something a bit unique, a game room for children, no
adults allowed. Another entertainment for you is horseback riding.

308

There are ☞ trail rides through Ham Branch stream and around the hay fields.

The living room is paneled with old oak and, with the fireplace, is very warm and cozy. A lovely candlelit dining room, with pink and white napery, serves glorious food. The chef has treated escargots in an innovative way. They are marinated, baked in butter, garlic, and ☞ Ouzo, and sealed in a puff pastry shell. Superb! Bouillabaisse à la Provençale is really a winner, and so is Spicy Ginger and Soy Sauce Sauté. A vegetarian pastry is delightful for vegetarians. ☞ Breakfast in bed? It's here, if you wish, complete with a pitcher of mimosas. I could stay forever.

There are sixty-five miles of cross-country trails right at hand, and they also have facilities so that you can ski from inn to inn on connecting trails. Downhill skiing is but ten miles away. Do come and enjoy.

How to get there: Take I-91 north to the Wells River-Woodsville Exit. Go right on Route 302 to Lisbon, New Hampshire. A few miles past Lisbon, go right on Route 117 to Franconia. Crossing the bridge into town, go right to the Exxon station. There, take another right to Route 116, and you're 2 miles to the inn. Or, if you have a single-engine plane, the inn has its own F.A.A.-listed airfield with a 3,000-foot-long runway.

༻

E: ☞ *Horse-drawn sleigh rides in this beautiful winter wonderland are my idea of heaven.*

Olive Metcalf

The Horse and Hound
Franconia, New Hampshire
03580

Innkeepers: Betty and Bob Larson; managers, Bob and Eric Larson
Telephone: 603-823-5501
Rooms: 10, 6 with private bath.
Rates: $45 to $75, double occupancy, EPB.
Facilities: Closed a few weeks in April and November. Dinner. Skiing,
    soaring, biking, hiking. MasterCard and Visa accepted.

The Horse and Hound is located at the base of Cannon
Mountain just north of Franconia Notch. Tucker Brook rushes
down from the top of the mountain just past the edge of the inn's
property. In winter you can set off from the door of the inn on
your cross-country skis. In other seasons, ☛ bicycling is a big
thing here at the inn. There is a seven-mile circle for you to try.
Should be fun up here in these beautiful mountains.

You also can go soaring in a plane or just take an airplane
ride. What a way to enjoy the fall foliage. I did it once in a
helicopter and it was sublime.

There are three fireplaces to warm you whether you are in
the living room or the dining rooms. The library lounge
has ☛ lots of books that are well organized in categories such as
bike books, children's books, and classics. There is music in here

310

also. They play a lot of old and new jazz and classical jazz; this is such a fine sound.

Comfortable accommodations are here. The rooms are bright and airy and have lovely views.

The menu is good and the food is excellent. Under appetizers, the Chef's Seafood Bisque is good. I like the Chef's Fancy; he comes up with interesting ideas. I also like a veal du jour where the waiter explains the day's choice. There are several beef entrees and all are tender. The lamb, as they say about their double lamb chops, is doubly delicious. It's also nice to be able to order roast Tom Turkey with all the fixings any time of the year. Too often turkey is served only on the holidays. The desserts and pastries all are made here and are so good.

How to get there: Take I-93 north, exit at Route 18, and turn left. The inn is on the left, several miles down the road. The inn is on Wells Road.

*

E: *The terrace in summer is so lovely for Sunday brunch or just cocktails. The inn dog is Deacon, a black Lab.*

Lovett's by Lafayette Brook
Franconia, New Hampshire
03580

Innkeepers: Mr. and Mrs. Charles J. Lovett, Jr.
Telephone: 603-823-7761
Rooms: 7 in main house; cottages and dorm.
Rates: $44 to $140, per person, double occupancy, MAP.
Facilities: Closed April to July, and after Columbus Day until after Christmas. Breakfast, dinner, bar. Swimming, game room. Tennis, golfing, riding, bicycling, fishing, and skiing nearby. American Express, MasterCard, and Visa accepted.

There are a lot of reasons for coming to the White Mountains and Franconia Notch, and one of the reasons is this inn. It was constructed circa 1784, even before a road was built through Franconia Notch. The inn is well into its second generation of 🖙 one-family ownership, and that says a lot.

Charlie Lovett runs a fine inn. As he says, they work hard at having the best table and the best cellar in the North Country. The menu changes daily. Every time I'm here I find they've come up with new temptations. They offer some old favorites like old-fashioned fresh vegetable soup and ratatouille, and some new ideas like 🖙 a cold black bean soup with rum. It's a wow! Roast loin of young pork with applesauce, and roast fresh turkey with wild rice and sausage dressing are two dinner entrees that taste just great. Fish, veal, and steak are offered, of course, but I think the roasts are so nice. The inn has its own ☞ herb garden. At last count there were thirty-seven different herbs at hand. No wonder the food is so good. Desserts, as you would expect, are heavenly.

There is a lovely terrace overlooking the mountains and the pool. Actually there are two pools. One is ☞ solar heated and the other fed from mountain springs. Oh, to be that hale and hearty for the latter.

Try to visit the New England Ski Museum, an excellent review of a sport that goes back 5,000 years. It is important to preserve these rare artifacts. It is right in the area.

How to get there: Take I-93 north, exit at Route 18 and turn left. The inn is on your right.

☙

E: *The bar, the bar! From the staircase in a Newport Mansion, the marble bar is the most inviting spot I've run into in a month of Sundays.*

> *I never thought of business when awakened at an inn*
> *by the three o'clock chime of a nearby church.*

Sugar Hill Inn
Franconia, New Hampshire
03580

Innkeepers: Jim and Barbara Quinn
Telephone: 603-823-5621
Rooms: 10, all with private baths; 6 cottages.
Rates: In summer, $37 to $40, per person, double occupancy, EPB. Rest of year, $55 to $75, per person, double occupancy, MAP.
Facilities: Open all year. Breakfast only meal in summer, breakfast and dinner in rest of year. Beer and wine license. No smoking in inn. Skiing, riding, fishing, canoeing, tennis, golfing, and hiking nearby. All major credit cards accepted.

The White Mountains are so beautiful and majestic, it is a joy to find the Sugar Hill Inn tucked into this loveliness. It is a charming inn. It was built in 1789 as a farmhouse by one of Sugar Hill's original settlers, and converted to an inn in 1929.

The inn has been carefully restored. The innkeepers have made the most of the beautiful old beams and floors and the handsome fireplaces. They have two comfortable living areas with cozy furniture, television, and lots of magazines. In one is an ☞ old pump organ that really works. In the dining room is a neat player piano with a lot of rolls. Really fun for a sing-along.

Guest accommodations in the inn and the country cottages

314

are lovely. Nice spreads, good mattresses, lovely antiques, and all super clean. The cottages are used from the middle of May through October.

Jim is the breakfast cook. He really does well. The blueberry pancakes I had were super. Be sure to try the fresh muffins. I had the ☛ applesauce and carrot muffins. Carolyn does the breakfast serving with help from their staff.

Dinner starters are shrimp and crab mousse, hot crab dip, and homemade soups. Try the delicious rolled stuffed chicken or lamb curry. Two fresh vegetables are served with dinner. Desserts are all made here. They are delicious.

The views of the mountain range from the porch are spectacular. The Appalachian Trail is nearby for invigorating hikes. Cannon Mountain is at hand for terrific downhill skiing, and cross-country skiing is everywhere. Other sports, such as horseback riding, fishing, canoeing, tennis, and golfing are only minutes away.

How to get there: Follow Route 18 through Franconia. Turn left on Route 117. The inn is one-half mile up the hill on the right.

❋

E: ☛ *Hot cider on the woodburning stove for skiers is so nice.*

Gunstock Inn
Gilford, New Hampshire
03246

Innkeeper: Tony Oliver
Telephone: 603-293-2021
Rooms: 23, plus 2 suites, all with private bath, air conditioning, television, radio, and telephone. Some rooms for the handicapped.
Rates: $45 to $110, double occupancy, EPB.
Facilities: Open all year. Full breakfast in season, and continental breakfast the rest of the year. Lunch in season, and dinner all year. Bar and lounge. Conference rooms, health spa, indoor pool. Downhill and cross-country skiing nearby. All major credit cards accepted.

Gunstock Inn is a different sort of inn. With a 🖜 seventy-five-foot indoor pool and a full spa, you'll love it. As a guest you will have 🖜 full privileges to use it all: whirlpool, sauna, steamrooms, and a fully equipped fitness room. For a modest charge you can have a massage or get a tan on one of the tanning beds. The inn offers package plans for a few days of this and the chef will give you a Naturally Fit menu. Nice? You bet it is. After eating my way through New England, this is just what I need.

The conference center is perfect for groups up to one hundred. Bring your family while you have meetings, for there is much for them to do. Fall is spectacular, but winter is king with breathtaking snowy views and cross-country and downhill skiing nearby.

All the rooms are different. Authentic antiques, hand-stenciled walls, rustic beams, and some have balconies. This inn really is a pleasant place to be.

After a day of skiing or exercising, you are sure to enjoy the living room. It has a beautiful view and tables for chess or checkers or perhaps a before-dinner cocktail.

Then on to the dining room. It is just lovely with a fireplace and views of the indoor pool and the out-of-doors. Lunch has good salads, clubs, and tea sandwiches. Dinner begins with appetizers like this: Seviche or creamed herring, and the beef teriyaki is a bit different. For entrees, scampi and linguine is a nice combination. Lord Britain's Chicken is lightly breaded breast of chicken, which is stuffed with asparagus and cheese, baked, and topped with sauce supreme. Desserts, well let's face it, we can't always be on a diet. They're good.

How to get there: The inn is located on Route 11 in Gilford.

✻

E: *Amazing inn, to have been built in the 1930s as a CCC and now turned into this fine place that has* ☞ *air conditioning, wake-up service, and all the conveniences in the rooms.*

Bernerhof Inn
Glen, New Hampshire
03838

Innkeeper: Bruce Gerrish; owners, Ted and Sharon Wroblewski
Telephone: 603-383-4414
Rooms: 10, 2 with private bath.
Rates: $25 to $30 per person, EPB.
Facilities: Closed mid-April to Memorial Day, and mid-November to
    mid-December. Lunch July through October, dinner, bar. Sauna.
    All major credit cards accepted.

The bar and lounge of the inn is fondly called the Zumstein
Room for Claire and Charlie Zumstein who once owned the inn
and introduced Swiss specialties here from their native land.
Almost thirty years later the restaurant still features some of
them. This is a lovely oak room, done in the style of a European
pub. It has its own menu.

Rooms are light and airy and individually decorated. There is
a sitting room with a television up here for your enjoyment. Or
perhaps you'd like to unwind with a visit to their ☞ Finnish
sauna.

The living room has a very unusual, tall, round coal stove
and a Steinway piano with a "Piano Corder" attached. It's an
ingenious tape-playing gadget that plays the Steinway.

318

☛ A Taste of the Mountains, a cooking school run by the innkeepers, is designed for lovers of fine food. If you want to know more, do call or write for a brochure.

Food here is something else, as you might expect from anyone who runs a cooking school. Shrimp Remoulade and Fettucine aux Herbs Provence are good, but the Delices de Gruyère—a smooth blend of Swiss cheeses, delicately breaded and sautéed and accompanied by a savory tomato blend—is superb. Swiss entrees include Emince de Veau au Vin Blanc, Weiner Schnitzel, and, of course, fondues. Veal Ragout is a stew made with braised veal, simmered slowly with vegetables and "old world" spices. ☛ Spaetzle is served with it. Noisettes of pork tenderloin are so tasty. The portions served are very generous.

You'll want to leave room for dessert, it's so good. Pot de Creme, Chocolate Fondue, or Profiteroles au Chocolat—tiny pastries filled with ice cream and topped with chocolate. ☛ The Soufflé Grand Marnier is outrageous. I could go on, but I'm getting hungry.

How to get there: From North Conway take Route 16 north. At Glen, turn left onto Route 302. The inn is on your right.

৵৵

E: *A free champagne breakfast in bed is yours on the third morning of your stay. It comes with eggs Benedict and fresh flowers. My, my.*

The John Hancock Inn
Hancock, New Hampshire
03449

Innkeepers: Glynn and Pat Wells
Telephone: 603-525-3318
Rooms: 10, all with private bath.
Rates: $55 to $65, double occupancy, EP.
Facilities: Closed one week in early spring, one week in late fall. Breakfast, lunch, dinner, Sunday brunch, lounge. Parking. Swimming, hiking, antiquing, summer theater, skiing, and tennis nearby. MasterCard and Visa accepted.

Operated as an inn since 1789, the John Hancock has been owned by Glynn and Pat since 1973. What a great job they do.

This is a nice old inn. Carefully preserved is ☞ The Mural Room, believed to date back to the early years of the inn. The Carriage Lounge is very unusual, with tables made from giant bellows from an old foundry in Nova Scotia. Seats are made from antique buggy seats. The name stems from the fact that John Hancock, the founding father, once owned most of the land that comprises the present town of Hancock. Set among twisting hills with a weathered clapboard facade, graceful white pillars, and a warm red door, the inn represents all that is good about old inns.

Warm welcomes, good food, sound drinks, and good beds, set in a quiet town that hasn't changed much in the last two centuries.

Sunday brunch is very popular with the townspeople as well as inn guests. They serve a variety of egg dishes, crepes, quiche, and French Toast à la Marie Antoinette (with pound cake).

Dinner is served by candlelight, and when winter storms howl through the hills the fireplace in the bar has a crackling fire to warm your heart and toes. Braided rugs cover part of the wide-board floors, and primitive paintings hang on the walls. There is a pastel of the inn, done in 1867, that the Wells were able to acquire.

Swim in summer in Norway Pond, within walking distance of the inn. Climb mountains, or just sit and listen to the church chimes during foliage time. Alpine and cross-country skiing are nearby in winter. Or browse in the antique shops on a cool spring morn.

How to get there: From Boston take Route 128, then Route 3 to 101 west. Hancock is located just off Route 202, 9 miles above Peterborough.

E: *The inn dog is a Lhasa named Nay-Daak Poo, which means "little innkeeper."*

> *We sat together around a single table and talked*
> *and heard each other in the quiet of the inn.*

Olive Metcalf

Colby Hill Inn
Henniker, New Hampshire
03242

Innkeepers: The Glover Family
Telephone: 603-428-3281
Rooms: 12, all with private bath.
Rates: $55, single; $85, double; EPB.
Facilities: Open all year. Dinner Tuesday through Sunday, bar. Television, swimming pool. Skiing, canoeing, fishing, ice skating, snowmobiling, and bicycling nearby. All major credit cards accepted.

This picturesque old house dates back to 1800. It leans and dips a bit here and there, but that only adds to the charm. The 🖝 wide floorboards are authentic. You cannot find boards like that nowadays. Don Glover, Jr., is chief innkeeper. He supervises the cooking and everything else that needs doing in a country inn. While researching this book I have found innkeepers up in trees, down in cellars, chopping wood, and even doing dishes. Don can be found at any one of these activities.

The food is all cooked to order, and it's as fresh as can be. The 🖝 vegetables come from their garden (and, as Don says, sometimes from a neighbor's). Chicken Colby Hill varies from day to day at the chef's whim. I've had reports back to me that all his whims are delicious. There is a nice selection of wines and spirits. The meal is topped off by homemade breads and desserts. They are famous for their cheesecake. I'm not surprised.

Henniker is a small New England college town. Indeed, New England College is here. There are many things to do in this area. Canoeing on the many lakes or rivers, white-water rafting in season, hiking or biking on the many trails or back roads, swimming in the inn's pool or in nearby lakes, fishing of all kinds (fly-fishing or ice-fishing), and, of course, there is ice skating, skiing, and snowmobiling. About ☞ forty-five miles of local trails are marked and maintained by Pole & Pedal. And back at the inn you can relax in the TV room, which is well stocked with games and puzzles. One is being worked on most of the time.

How to get there: Go up I-91 to Brattleboro. Take Route 9 east into Henniker.

∽

E: *The inn cat is Jelly Bean, and she has a few little beans around her.*

> With its swinging sign near
> the hills it stands,
> Vine-clad and filled with cheer.
> 'Tis a place to laze through
> fresh, golden days
> with sunlit peaks so near.
> So good-bye to cares,
> this spot is rare,
> and we thank kind fate
> for having brought us here.

The Meeting House
Henniker, New Hampshire
03242

Innkeepers: June and Bill Davis
Telephone: 603-428-3228
Rooms: 6, all with private bath.
Rates: $58 to $88, double occupancy, EPB.
Facilities: Open all year. Breakfast, lunch, dinner, Sunday brunch, bar, and lounge. Hot tub and sauna. White-water rafting, downhill skiing, antiquing, and theaters nearby. All major credit cards accepted.

You can sit in the bar and lounge area of this inn and watch the skiers coming down the hill. Now that's fun. This old barn that houses the restaurant and lounge is 200 years old.

Hanging on the walls are ☞ plastic bags in which students from New England College have collected shells, stones, sand, and volcano dust, and sent here for display. A nice thing to do. ☞ Little white Christmas lights are all over this area. They are so pretty and so unique. Only in a country inn.

When you want breakfast, it is ☞ delivered to your room in a basket, and what a surprise awaits you! (No, I'm not going to tell; you'll have to see for yourself.) There's a large lunch menu. I selected Meeting House Club Sandwich with a cup of soup. The club is a combination of lobster chunks, lettuce, bacon, and tomato with a delicate lemon mayonnaise served on special toast. And the soup was delicious. Brunch is another popular meal and ample.

And dinner.... Well, I had Bermuda Lobster. It was sautéed in butter, dark rum, and sherry peppers, and finished with heavy cream. Divine. The other seafood offerings also were ones you don't find very often, and the veal and chicken dishes looked great. Their salad dressings are super. I had an excellent hot bacon dressing. The fried cinnamon apples with ice cream, flavored with apple brandy, were the perfect ending to my dinner.

The rooms are filled with treasures from June's and Bill's former homes. I was delighted to find plenty of books and magazines and plump pillows for reading in bed, a favorite pastime of mine.

White-water activities are on the Contoocook River. Antique shops are nearby and two summer theaters are in neighboring towns. This really is a nice area.

How to get there: In Henniker take Route 114 South about 2 miles to Pat's Peak sign. Turn right onto Flanders Road. The inn is in about ½ mile on the right.

✳

E: *After a day of skiing, try the sauna and hot tub in the greenhouse. Sheer luxury!*

Stonebridge Inn
Hillsboro, New Hampshire
03244

Innkeepers: Nelson and Lynne Adame
Telephone: 603-464-3155
Rooms: 4, all with private bath.
Rates: $38, single; $45 to $50, double occupancy; continental breakfast
  included.
Facilities: Open all year. Closed Christmas Day. Sunday brunch, dinner,
  full license. Gift shop. Swimming and skiing nearby. MasterCard
  and Visa accepted.

Nelson and Lynne have owned the Stonebridge Inn for several years. They have a good bit of experience as innkeepers behind them, including the fact that Nelson's father was the innkeeper of the New London Inn in New London, New Hampshire for many years.

The inn was an old house that the Adames turned into a small inn. There are four rooms, two large and two small, all with private bath.

Downstairs there are three dining rooms. One is done in wrought iron and glass, unusual and very pretty. The main dining room is a 🖝 picture with ivory and chocolate napery dappled by flickering candlelight and enhanced by cut flowers. There are

326

a lot of windows in the inn, which are nice on a cloudy day and glorious on a sunny day.

Brunch at the Bridge is the name of the inn's Sunday brunch. It features eggs done many ways—eggs Benedict, Swiss eggs, and omelettes with a choice of fillings. It's nice to find chicken pot pie on a brunch menu. You'd prefer a hamburger or a salad? No problem.

The dinner menu lists an appetizer I really like—seafood stuffed in an artichoke. One of the entrees is veal prepared differently each day according to the season. You also can get a vegetarian entree. Their ☛ Stonebridge Inn Fried Chicken is superb. It is glazed with maple syrup. Now that's chicken with a New England difference! There is, of course, much more, and all of it delicious.

There is skiing nearby and summer swimming at Pierce Lake or Beard Brook. This is a very nice area of New Hampshire. Do try it.

How to get there: From western New England take I-91 north to Exit 3 and then follow Route 9 east for a bit better than 40 miles. You will find the inn on your left as you enter town. From the Boston area take Exit 5 off I-89 and follow Route 9 west for 17 miles to Hillsboro.

꙾

E: *There's a beautiful grandfather clock in the living room.*

The Manor
Holderness, New Hampshire
03245

Innkeepers: Jan and Pierre Havre
Telephone: 603-968-3348
Rooms: 24, all with private bath; 3 housekeeping cottages, 2 housekeeping apartments.
Rates: In season, $59 to $125; off season, $59 to $109; double occupancy, EPB. Cottages and apartments rented by week or month.
Facilities: Open all year. Lunch, dinner, Sunday brunch, bar, lounge. No pets. Swimming pool, tennis, boating, ice skating. Downhill and cross-country skiing nearby. All major credit cards accepted.

From the moment you drive up the long driveway to the inn you are enchanted with the surroundings. Then The Manor comes into view and your enchantment is complete, the inn is just so lovely. Built in 1903 by a wealthy Englishman, Isaac Van Horn, the house still has its original rich wood paneling, beautiful doors, some with mirrors, magnificently carved moldings, marble fireplaces, and old pedestal sinks. Thankfully, all details have remained unscarred over the years.

There are two handsome library-living rooms with fireplaces. The Tapestry Lounge is elegant. There also is a cocktail porch overlooking the lake, so nice on a moonlit night.

The dining rooms are lovely. Beautiful stemware, courteous staff, and good food. From where I had lunch I could look down on Squam Lake, made famous as the lake in ☞ "On Golden Pond." Oh my, I do like it here. I had the ☞ best grilled corned beef and Swiss cheese sandwich I ever had. The inn's tangy dressing and homemade pumpernickel bread made the sandwich memorable. Everything on the menu sounded so good, it was hard to choose. Dinner, I wouldn't know where to begin to describe it. The menu is extensive, so even the fussiest person would find it hard to complain. I hate to mention the desserts, they are sinfully good. I think I'll lose ten pounds and go back for a week.

The guest rooms are exceptional with handsome wall-coverings, and good beds and chairs. Some have ☞ lovely old pedestal sinks, and nine have fireplaces. The cottages are elegant.

There is everything to do here; swimming pool, tennis, shuffleboard, croquet, Ping-Pong, and much more. The Manor's own canoes, sailboat, and fishing dinghy are free for your use. There are thirteen acres for you to play in and 300 feet of sandy beach frontage for you to sunbathe on. If it rains, there are many games to play inside, Bogie the inn dog to visit with, or many places to just relax in at this beautiful mansion.

How to get there: Take Route 3 into Holderness. Cross the bridge, and on the right you will see the signs for The Manor.

❋

E: *The Lady of the Manor is a luxurious 28-foot pontoon craft, which is available for guided tours of "Golden Pond," parties, picnics, and transportation to* ☞ *Church Island for Sunday services in an outdoor setting. How I do like it here. Wow.*

The New England Inn
Intervale (North Conway),
New Hampshire
03860

Innkeeper: Kathy Rossi
Telephone: 603-356-5541
Rooms: 39, all with private bath; 10 suites with fireplace in village houses;
    4 one-room cottages with fireplace.
Rates: $43 to $69, double occupancy, MAP. EP is $15 less.
Facilities: Open all year. Breakfast, dinner. Entertainment on weekends
    and holidays. Conference room, three clay tennis courts, swimming
    and wading pools, skating rink, cross-country skiing and lighted
    trails for nighttime. American Express, MasterCard, and Visa ac-
    cepted.

    If you enjoy the charm of an authentic country inn where
cozy intimacy has been carefully preserved over the centuries by
conscientious innkeepers . . . if you relish the warm feeling of a
gracious country inn with a reputation for hospitality and friend-
liness . . . if you enjoy savoring hearty New England regional
foods, selected wines, and hearty drinks . . . if you like sports and
outdoor recreation . . . if you prefer just plain quiet and relaxation
. . . you'll love the village at The New England Inn.

It is said so well in their brochure, I just stole it.

When you arrive at the inn in any season, the sight is glorious, a white rambling country inn in the shadows of the White Mountains. The living rooms are gracious, with plenty of chairs and couches. Nice to curl up in with a good book, or, as I am prone to do, with needlework. The guest rooms are smashing, and all have recently been done over. After a full day they are a real pleasure to return to.

This is an all-American inn. The food and wine are as ☛ all-American as apple pie, and they have that, too. Try New England chicken and shrimp sauté, New England chicken pot pie, or Shaker cranberry pot roast. I've had the pot roast, and it's glorious. The wines, all-American, are served in crockery pitchers. A nice change from the ordinary.

They are involved with the ☛ Intervale Nordic Center. Between the inn and the Holiday Inn next door there are thirty-five kilometers of marked trails. Start off right by being outfitted in proper-fitting equipment, next take a lesson from a PSIA-certified instructor, and then go and enjoy cross-country skiing. The Intervale Tavern at the inn, with a blazing fireplace, serves skiers lunch and après-ski. A good hot chili is nice when you are cold.

Plan on a week at a time at this lovely inn. There is so much to do inside and out, and in any season.

How to get there: The inn is at the Gateway to the White Mountains, a Resort Loop, Route 16A, 3½ miles north of the village of North Conway.

∽

E: *Don't miss Gladys, who plays the piano in the lovely large lounge area.*

Christmas Farm Inn
Jackson, New Hampshire
03846

Innkeepers: Bill and Sydna Zeliff
Telephone: 603-383-4313
Rooms: 36, 14 in inn, 9 with private bath; 9 in 1771 saltbox, all with
private bath. Four suites in sugarhouse and barn. One log cabin,
and 7 cottages.
Rates: $42 to $68, per person, double occupancy, MAP. Special weekly
and package rates.
Facilities: Open all year. Breakfast, dinner, pub. Swimming pool, game
room, putting green, 80 kilometers of cross-country trails, golf, tennis, sauna, complimentary movies. Downhill skiing nearby. All major credit cards accepted.

Yes, Virginia, there is a Christmas Farm Inn, and they have
the Mistletoe Pub and the Sugar Plum Dining Room to prove it.
The food is fit for any Santa and his helpers, from the hearty, full
country breakfast, which includes ☛ homemade doughnuts,
muffins, and sticky buns, to gracious dinners that include three
entrees each evening, two homemade soups, a full salad bar,
homemade breads, and a complete dessert menu.

The food is excellent. The ☛ Medallions of Pork MacIntosh
is glorious, and it also has a hint of brandy. Veal and chicken are

so tender. Treats from the seas are real treats. The desserts do indeed make visions of sugarplums dance in your head, and all are made right here. How about apple pie, carrot cake, or the Christmas Farm special sundae? From here take a quick trip to the Mistletoe Pub for a nightcap.

Separate from the main building is the Christmas Farm function center. Perfect spot for not only medium to small business meetings, but also weddings, anniversaries, and the like. At one side of the room is a twelve-foot-wide fieldstone fireplace. There are also games of all sorts, a sauna, bar, and four nice suites.

Also separate are the three cottages, each with living room, fireplace, two bedrooms, and two baths. The rooms in the main building have Christmas names: Holly, Dasher, Prancer, Vixen, Donner, Cupid, Comet, and Blitzen.

Jackson is in the heart of the White Mountains, so bring your skis, or come in the summer for the annual Christmas-in-July Week. There's a magnificent gala Christmas party Wednesday night with an outside buffet and Christmas tree, as well as live entertainment, dancing, shuffleboard, and golf tournaments. Santa must live nearby, because he never fails to arrive in a most unusual manner. And when he comes, he's eagerly greeted by the inn dog, Daffodil.

How to get there: Go north on Route 16 from North Conway. A few miles after Route 302 branches off to your left you will see a covered bridge on your right. Take the bridge through the village and up the hill a quarter mile, and there is the inn.

*

E: Making 🐾 *memories is something Bill and Sydna and their staff know all about.*

Dana Place Inn
Jackson, New Hampshire
03846

Innkeepers: The Low family
Telephone: 603-383-6822
Rooms: 15, 8 with private bath.
Rates: $45 to $95, EPB; $90 to $140, MAP; double occupancy.
Facilities: Open all year. Breakfast, picnic lunch available, dinner, bar,
    lounge. Hot tub. Cross-country skiing, swimming pool, two all-
    weather tennis courts. Golf and downhill skiing nearby. All major
    credit cards accepted.

The inn is nestled at the foot of magnificent Mount Washington in a beautiful valley next to the Ellis River. The mountain
alone draws hikers and climbers and skiers who brave the big
spill to ski Tuckerman's Ravine each spring, and visitors who
journey to the top of the mountain via the Cog Railway or the
auto road. All of this plus this beautiful inn to stay in.

The inn was built in the mid-nineteenth century and surely
must have been a stagecoach stop. We know it was once a farmhouse, set in an apple orchard, and built by Antwin Dana. Set
your own pace along lawns, gardens, streams, meadows, and
woodland trails. Walk through the orchard, pass the swimming
pool, take the country road past the tennis courts along a mossy

tree-shaded path, through a clearing, and you'll be at a crystal-clear, rockbound pool in the Ellis River. Peace here is beyond description. If you want to go off for the day for other activities, you'll find golf, canoeing, kayaking, racquetball, family attractions like Storyland, outlet shopping in North Conway, as well as skiing.

The interior of the inn has been beautifully updated. The hot tub is in a room by itself and an indoor swimming pool is in its own room. It is a delightful addition to the inn. The dining rooms with pink napery and flowers are restful, and the food is good. ☛ Lobster bisque is a favorite of mine and very good here. I like unusual chicken and had their Rollintine of Chicken, rolled supremes of chicken with a cranberry walnut filling and a Riesling wine sauce. Desserts are wonderful. All baking is done right here. The breakfast menu is inventive. How about ☛ chocolate chip pancakes with Grade A maple syrup? Do come up and try this lovely inn.

How to get there: Take I-95 north to Portsmouth, then the Spaulding Turnpike to Route 16 north at Rochester. Follow Route 16 north past Jackson Village.

ɔℰ

E: *The hammock on the lawn overlooks the Ellis River. Lovely spot.*

The Inn at Thorn Hill
Jackson, New Hampshire
03846

Innkeepers: Bob and Pattie Guindon
Telephone: 603-383-4242
Rooms: 16, all with private bath, in 2 buildings; 3 cottage suites.
Rates: $60 to $68, per person, double occupancy, MAP.
Facilities: Open all year. Breakfast, dinner, bar. Swimming pool, cross-country skiing. Downhill skiing and golf club nearby. No small children. All major credit cards accepted.

Take a quiet country road, add a comfortable and friendly inn with a magnificent view of Mount Washington, blend in a gracious turn-of-the-century atmosphere, and enjoy at leisure. Their brochure says it so well. Mountains are everywhere you look from this inn. Relax on the porch in a ☞ New England rocking chair and enjoy the view. Even on a bad day it is spectacular. And the living room, with a generous fireplace, has a view that is unbelievable. There are movies and a VCR, games, puzzles, and a wonderful collection of bears. The pub called "The Snug" is cozy, with fireplace, four bar stools, and lots of cheer.

Elegant country dining by candlelight is what you get, and the food is grand. Crabmeat Ravioli or Chilled Shrimp with Snow Peas and Cantaloupe surely are different ways to begin your dinner. I find entrees such as Pasta Cepi enticing. It is linguine in fresh artichoke and basil butter, tossed with Saga cheese and julienned zucchini. ☞ Lobster pie in puff pastry is a nice lazy way to enjoy this fellow. Grilled quail is another imaginative dish. The desserts are wonderful.

Rooms here are large, decorated with lots of plants and good wallpapers. The beds are comfortable. The cottages are nice for those who want to be alone. One has a small screened porch.

They have a ☞ golf cart to shuttle guests back and forth to the nearby golf club. A shuttle bus for skiers is available, and cross-country skiing begins at the door. Tennis and riding are nearby. Just come and enjoy all of it with Albert, their golden retriever.

How to get there: Go north from Portsmouth, New Hampshire, on the Spaulding Turnpike (Route 16) all the way to Jackson, which is just above North Conway. At Jackson is a covered bridge on your right. Take the bridge, and just one block this side of the village center on the right is Thorn Hill Road, which you take up the hill. The inn is on your right.

❋

E: *A weekly ☞ clambake with all the fixings—lobsters, clams, chicken, corn on the cob, and cole slaw—is nice. Summertime only, you understand.*

> *"And now once more I shape my way*
> *Thro' rain or shine, thro' thick or thin,*
> *Secure to meet, at close of day*
> *With kind reception, at an inn."*
> —William Shenstone, 1714–1763
> (written at the Inn at Henley)

Olive Metcalf

Whitney's Village Inn
Jackson, New Hampshire
03846

Innkeepers: Terry and Judy Tannehill
Telephone: 603-383-6886 or 1-800-252-5622
Rooms: 36, 30 with private bath; 2 cottages with fireplace.
Rates: $49 to $69, per person, MAP. Packages available.
Facilities: Open all year. Breakfast, lunch in season or box lunch, dinner, bar, lounge. TV and VCR with movies. Skiing, ice skating, tobogganing, tennis, swimming, and summertime hayrides. American Express, MasterCard, and Visa accepted.

This is an authentic mountain hideaway nestled in among New Hampshire's White Mountains. It's pretty nice to be able to crawl out of bed, dress, have a sumptuous breakfast, and ☞ walk across to the lifts, trails, ski shop or ski school, all just a snowball's throw away. It is a real treat not to have to drive the car anywhere after you get here. Black Mountain, with its own snowmaking equipment, is right here. The lifts can handle about 3,000 skiers per hour, so there is hardly any waiting. There are many trails that serve the mountain, and all are kept in the best condition possible. A lighted skating rink is right beside the inn. Bring your own skates or borrow some here. The inn also has tobogganing and sleigh rides.

Summer fun is the inn's own swimming pond, which is in such a pretty setting on the lovely grounds. There are also all sorts of lawn games. Inside, there is a game room, well equipped with Ping-Pong, television, and all sorts of games. One of the parlors has puzzles in the making, nice comfortable furniture, a Steinway piano, and lovely old oriental carpets. There are Hunter Fans all over the inn. Then there is the Shovel Handle Lounge for après-ski fun and entertainment. Lunch in season is served out here.

Dining is superb in a casually elegant dining room. Mauve and tan are the napery colors. One of the soups is Yesterday's (Mom always said it was better the next day). Their Jackson-style Duckling is excellent, and how nice to find a delicious stew. ☛ Roast goose is also seldom seen on a menu. There is a lobster cookout by the brook once a week in the warm weather.

The guest rooms are carpeted and have comfortable beds. Some of the rooms have nice wingback chairs. Try it here. You will like it.

How to get there: Go north from Conway 22 miles on Route 16. Take a right on Route 16A through a covered bridge into Jackson Village. Take Route 16B to the top of the hill to the inn.

❧

E: ☛ *A really nice touch for families is a special children's table. Dinner at six o'clock is followed by a movie. Parents and children both can enjoy themselves. And remember, a family inn means children, not quiet solitude.*

olive Metcalf

The Wildcat Inn
Jackson, New Hampshire
03846

Innkeepers: Pam and Marty Sweeney
Telephone: 603-383-4245
Rooms: 16, 10 with private bath.
Rates: $28 to $32, per person, EPB.
Facilities: Closed weekdays in May. Lunch, dinner, bar. Music in lounge. Downhill and cross-country skiing, hiking, tennis, riding. All major credit cards accepted.

The brochure here at Wildcat says it so well, I'm just going to repeat it. Everything you need for a perfect vacation is within ☛ walking distance of the inn, so leave your car out back and save gas, money, and time. Begin in the Tavern Gardens, where you will be well fed and properly wined from breakfast through last call. Tennis, your choice of one hard and three clay courts. Golf at the beautiful Wentworth Hall course. Riding lessons, shows, and trail rides through mountain forests. There are package deals for all of the above. Fishing, hiking, or just meandering through town; good shopping is up here. And both downhill and cross-country skiing are nearby.

The tavern has two big fireplaces, nice couches, and on

weekends and holidays there is music. Accommodations are comfortable. All the rooms are different and each one has a view.

The Wildcat is a very popular dining spot. In fact, some years ago the big old front porch had to be converted into a dining room to make more dining space for all the people who wanted to eat here. The food here will titillate your taste buds. All meals are made to order and, as the chef says, patience is a virtue. Breakfasts are full, with all pastries baked right here. There are tavern specials at lunch. Lobster Benedict is different. I had it for lunch one day. Another day I tried one called Salmagundi; enough food for an army and delicious. Also, lovely lox on a bagel! Marvelous salads, six of them, all accompanied by homemade breads.

And at dinnertime good appetizers and soups. One entree is Baked Seafood Platter, which is different every day. Wildcat Chicken is chicken wrapped in puff pastry. Tempura is so good. A few of their desserts are Sour Cream Apple Pie, Rhubarb Pudding Cake, Frozen Raspberry Soufflé, so what are you waiting for?

How to get there: Take Route 16 north from North Conway. Take Route 16A to your right, through a covered bridge, and into Jackson. The inn is in the center of town.

❧

E: *There are a lot of inns in this area, but only this one serves lunch.*

. Olive Metcalf

The Monadnock Inn
Jaffrey Center, New Hampshire
03454

Innkeeper: Sally Roberts
Telephone: 603-532-7001
Rooms: 14, 7 with private bath.
Rates: $45 to $55, double occupancy, continental breakfast included.
Facilities: Open all year. Dining room closed on Sundays and Mondays
    for dinner in winter. Lunch Monday through Friday in summer and
    fall, dinner every day in summer and fall. Sunday brunch, bar.
    Cross-country skiing. MasterCard and Visa accepted.

From the minute you set foot on the wide front porch until
you sink into your comfortable four-poster at night you will be
happy at this lovely inn. There is so much to do. Have you ever
been to the Cathedral in the Pines? It's not far. Have you ever
wanted to get really involved in maple sugaring? This is the
place. It can be arranged with a snap of the fingers.

Sally does a terrific job as innkeeper. She likes to think The
Monadnock Inn is capable of taking you back in time. But it was
never this good.

The food is worth writing home about, and, as a matter of
fact, it's good enough to have been ☞ written up in *Gourmet*
magazine. Sunday brunch includes a nice twist: an ☞ omelette

bar, with choices of Swiss cheese, Havarti, cheddar, ham, mushroom, green onion, peppers, or prosciutto. What a super idea! Lunch is pleasant. I ran in from the rain one day and had their chili. It surely was good, but even better than that was a dessert special, a white chocolate mousse tart with strawberries. It was absolutely sinful! At dinner there are always specials, plus the menu. Braised Quail Duxelles, basted with grape preserves and served on a nest of rice, is one entree. Oysters Bartlett is fresh oysters simmered in a cream of spinach and tomatoes. Desserts, well, if what I had for lunch is an indication, order away.

In brisk winter weather there is always a roaring fire in one of the fireplaces and miles of cross-country trails for skiers. Or come in the fall for wonderful, glorious foliage. Autumn in New Hampshire should have a song all its own.

How to get there: The inn is located on Route 124, southeast of Keene, a scant 2 hours from Boston.

✳

E: ☞ *There aren't many places like this around. Cherish it.*

I was lost, I was tired, I was discouraged,
and then I found a friendly inn.

343

Beal House Inn
Littleton, New Hampshire
03561

Innkeepers: Doug and Brenda Clickenger
Telephone: 603-444-2661
Rooms: 14, 12 with private bath.
Rates: $35 to $75, double occupancy, EP.
Facilities: Open all year. Breakfast. Dinner for groups by arrangement
and on holidays. Antique shop. All major credit cards accepted.

The Beal House was built in 1833 as a farmhouse and barn.
Like most farms in New England, over the years the house and
barn became connected into one continuous building. Ultimately
it all became converted into an inn. The inn has an antique shop,
but is also an antique shop in itself, for all the furnishings are for
sale. You can ☞ sleep in a bed you may wind up buying. This is
a good way to go antiquing; try before you buy.

All the rooms are clean and neat. The front rooms have
☞ glorious four-poster beds. There also is an upstairs sitting
room, small but cozy.

Breakfast is bountiful. Doug is the chef, and his specialty is
popovers. Of course, he does all sorts of other good things. His
dining room has a fireplace, and is set with beautiful blue willow
plates. Off of this room is the porch, full of wicker furniture and

potted plants. Menus of all nearby restaurants are at hand for your perusal.

This is a lovely area to visit, not far from Franconia Notch and the Old Man of the Mountain. You also have Crawford Notch nearby. Do take a drive down the notch and look at the railroad they pinned to its west side. When you see it you cannot believe it.

The inn is in town so that you have the whole town of Littleton to walk about and see.

How to get there: From I-93 take Exit 42, turn right, and go one mile to the intersection of Route 18 and Route 302. This is Main Street and the inn is here.

∽

E: *The gazebo in the back yard is charming.*

The time between sunset and the completeness of night
should be spent around a well-laid board
with assurances of a warm bed to follow.

Edencroft Manor
Littleton, New Hampshire
03561

Innkeepers: Laurie and William Walsh, Jr., and Barry and Ellie Bliss
Telephone: 603-444-6776
Rooms: 6, 4 with private bath.
Rates: $35 to $60, double occupancy, EP.
Facilities: Closed two weeks in spring. Restaurant closed Sundays and
 Mondays in winter. Breakfast for house guests, dinner. Cross-
 country skiing, snowmobiling. American Express, MasterCard, and
 Visa accepted.

The grand old Victrola (and it works) sitting in the living
room took me back to my childhood with nice memories of wind-
ing ours up and listening to the records. The inn has a huge
collection of them. A large fireplace and plenty of books are also
in this room. All in all, very charming. For you garden buffs there
is a small solarium with plants and antiques just off this room.

The bedrooms have color names. The Brown Room has its
own fireplace. The Gold Room is yummy with two double beds at
angles to each other. Also, this is a bright, cheery room. In all the
rooms are ☛ homemade quilts. One is done with old neckties
and is just grand.

Sitting in the lounge-bar area you are overlooking both Cannon and Lafayette mountains. Beautiful in winter, and equally beautiful any other season with the hanging plants overhead.

Edencroft offers very enticing food. At dinner you'll find appetizers like mushrooms with crab and clams casino, followed by good soups. New England clam chowder is one. For entrees, wow—six beef choices and five of seafood. The salmon is prepared with a dill sauce. Shrimp creole has spicy Cajun vegetables. There are five veal selections. Veal Moutarde has a wine and cream sauce flavored with Dijon mustard. Very tasty. In addition to these are several listed as "something special." One that caught my eye was Chicken Citron—boneless breast of chicken with a lemon and wine sauce. Desserts are different each night and good. Cordials and special coffees are a glorious way to top off an evening.

How to get there: Take a left turn off of I-93 at Exit 43. The inn is one-tenth of a mile up Route 135 north.

✱

E: *Six appetizers, three soups, and a lovely dessert cart . . . too much.*

olive Metcalf

Lyme Inn
Lyme, New Hampshire
03768

Innkeepers: Fred and Judy Siemons
Telephone: 603-795-2222
Rooms: 15, 10 with private bath.
Rates: $60 to $75, double occupancy, with complimentary breakfast.
Facilities: Closed two weeks in late spring and the Sunday after Thanksgiving to Christmas. Dining room closed Tuesdays. Dinner, bar. Near Dartmouth College, golf course, canoeing, fishing, and skiing. No children under 8. All major credit cards accepted.

Lyme was the most productive sheepraising town in New England during the mid-1800s. Now it is mainly a quiet residential town, and close to Dartmouth College and Mary Hitchcock Regional Hospital in nearby Hanover. The inn dates back to 1809 and sits at the end of the common.

All of the inn's original rooms have been restored in keeping with the age of the building. The wide pine floorboards are handsome. The rooms are different in size and are full of antiques, quilts, four-poster beds, and hooked rugs.

The tavern—a really nice place to meet new friends—has a small fireplace. Great on a cold night. There are antique tavern tables in here.

Dining rooms wander about the inn. Good food is served in them. ☛ Deep-fried mushrooms or escargots are always a favorite. ☛ Fresh homemade soups are a plus, with a different one each day. The inn offers a light supper, which is nice when you are not very hungry. However, for the hungry, entrees like Alaskan King Crab Legs or Beer Batter Shrimp are good seafood choices. Hunter-style Veal is veal stuffed with Swiss cheese and ham, and served with a delicious herb sauce. Desserts, naturally, are good.

There is an extensive library for guests to enjoy. You are ☛ encouraged to take home a partially read book and return it when you are finished. This is nice.

There is much to do in the area. Great walking, great hiking, and wonderful skiing. But a few miles away is Dartmouth College with its Ivy League sports competition and fine cultural events. Locally you have a golf course, and there is canoeing on the Connecticut River. There are many secluded ponds for the fisherman to try his luck. And, of course, you have antique shops all about.

And do try a hot dog at the general store just on the other side of the common. Rare treat. So is Duffy, the real inn dog.

How to get there: Take Exit 14 from I-91. The inn is located east of the interstate on Route 10 right at the village common.

☙

E: *The wicker furniture on the huge screened porch is enchanting.*

You cannot hide a good country inn.

New London Inn
New London, New Hampshire
03257

Innkeepers: John and Maureen Follansbee
Telephone: 603-526-2791
Rooms: 30, all with private bath.
Rates: $40 to $45, single; $60 to $65, double; EP.
Facilities: Open all year. Breakfast, lunch, dinner, bar. Skiing, theater, golf, two public beaches, and water sports nearby. MasterCard and Visa accepted.

The owners of this college-town inn are restoring it back to the grandeur it had in 1792 when it began serving the traveler. What an undertaking, but they're doing it well, for what I've seen is very authentic.

As you enter the inn you immediately appreciate the long veranda. There's also another one upstairs with the rooms. Do come up and try the ☛ rockers. Rooms in the inn are large, airy, and comfortable. Each one is decorated differently from another.

☛ Cool cream and green are the colors of the dining room. It has large windows and the original fireplace is still working. For an almost 200-year-old fireplace, that's a lot of fires! The dining room's gracious ambience is well suited to the wonderful food.

The dinner menu features such enticing appetizers as Warm Asparagus Strudel with Light Wine and Herb Sauce, and Lemon Pepper Pasta with Fresh Vegetables and Italian Bacon. For soups they have ☛ Bisque of New England Spring Vegetables and Chilled Tomato Lime and Scallop Soup, among others. Oh, I love interesting soups. Entrees are innovative, like Grilled Marinated Monkfish served with Red and Yellow Pepper Coulis, Grilled Smoked Duck Breast served with Spicy White Beans and Corn Crepes, and Spiced Beef Medallions with Lime-Cilantro Butter and Avocado Sauce. Boy, it's hard to choose which one to eat! Desserts are very good and prepared daily. Breakfasts feature ☛ freshly squeezed orange or grapefruit juice.

The town of New London, home of Colby-Sawyer College, still has the feeling of a nineteenth-century village. From its wide main streets, fields, fences, and gracious houses to the beautiful mountains, it's just a lovely place to be. Its location in the Mount Sunapee lake region means there are three lakes close by that offer all the water sports. Golf is nice because there is no waiting, and there is good skiing.

This is a beautiful part of the world any time of the year, so come on up.

How to get there: Take Exit 8 at Ascutney, Vermont, from I-91. Follow signs to Claremont, New Hampshire. Take Route 11 east to Newport, Sunapee, Georges Mills, and New London. There is bus service via Vermont Transit from Boston, and from White River Junction, Vermont.

❧

E: *Living here are a Himalayan cat named Picasso and an American short-hair named Loco.*

When the stars are lost and rain seeps coldly upon the ground, how wonderful to find a lighted inn.

Pleasant Lake Inn
New London, New Hampshire
03257

Innkeepers: Grant and Margaret Rich
Telephone: 603-526-6271
Rooms: 13, 7 with private bath.
Rates: $40 to $50, double occupancy, EPB.
Facilities: Inn closed two weeks in April and two weeks in November. Dining room closed Tuesdays. Dinner, Sunday brunch, bar. Swimming, boating, fishing, and all winter sports. MasterCard and Visa accepted.

Pleasant Lake Inn is the oldest operating inn in this area. It began as a farm in 1790 and became an inn almost one hundred years ago.

Inn guests today are given privileges at the Slope and Shore Club on Pleasant Lake, just across the road, which offers tennis, boating, fishing, and swimming. There are iceboating and cross-country skiing here in the winter. The inn also has a nice pond for ice skating on the property and downhill skiing is close at hand. King Ridge is five minutes away. Mount Sunapee and Whaleback fifteen minutes away, Pat's Peak is twenty-five minutes away, and many more are within an hour's drive.

The view from the inn's front windows is magnificent, and

in the fall, it's 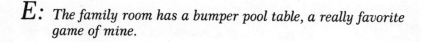 spectacular. The inn looks right out onto Pleasant Lake, and beautiful Mount Kearsarge is just on the other side of the lake.

There are antique furnishings, warming fireplaces, nice views, and very comfortable guest rooms throughout the inn. Two cockatiels are here. One is gray and one is white. They surely are pretty.

The food served in the pleasant dining rooms is good. Breakfast is hearty and includes a longtime favorite of mine, blueberry pancakes. Dinner appetizers include a beauty, escargots in mushroom caps with herbed garlic butter, baked in a pastry shell. All sauces and soups are prepared with fresh ingredients, no artificial agents, and sauces are thickened by natural reduction instead of with heavy starches. Entrees include steaks, chops, veal, chicken, and fish. They have nice liqueur parfaits for dessert and, as they say, if you have a favorite, they will try to make it.

How to get there: From I-89 take either New London exit. Halfway through New London, turn at the New London Trust Company. This is Pleasant Street. Go about 2 miles, and the inn is on your left.

🌸

E: *The family room has a bumper pool table, a really favorite game of mine.*

The Scottish Lion
North Conway, New Hampshire
03860

Innkeepers: David O'Connor; owners, Jack and Judy Hurley
Telephone: 603-356-6381
Rooms: 7, all with private bath.
Rates: $30 to $35, per person, EPB.
Facilities: Open all year. Closed Christmas Eve and Christmas Day.
    Lunch, dinner, bar. Parking. Import Shop, free catalogue available.
    All major credit cards accepted.

The rooms at The Scottish Lion are cozy. One has an eyelet-trimmed canopy bed, another a spool bed with a patchwork quilt. All are charming. The whole inn is full of fine ☛ Scottish paintings. Do not miss any of them.

Food, of course, features the best of Scottish touches. A hearty Scottish breakfast is served to house guests. Dinner is rated three stars in the Mobil Guide. Highland Game Pie, which is venison, beef, hare, and fowl simmered in wine and baked in puff pastry may sound strange, but a gentleman who had had it the night before reported to me, "Delicious." Hot Scottish oatcakes are served instead of bread or rolls. A marvelous dish named ☛ Rumbledethumps is one of the potato choices, what a taste. I must tell you one more: Forth Lobster Lady Tweedsmuir,

354

tender pieces of lobster in a delicate cream and Drambuie sauce, stuffed in the shell. You must try this dish.

For dessert, Scottish Trifle or Scots Crumpets with fresh fruit and honey are but a few. The inn also serves a very special coffee. The pub has a long list of tantalizing pleasures, such as Hoot Mon cocktail, St. Andrews Hole-in-One, or Loch Ness Monster.

The Import Shop features the finest of imports from Scotland, England, and Ireland. They have over ☞ 300 different tartan ties, plus wools, cashmeres, crystal, thistle pottery, and much more. Do go and enjoy.

How to get there: Take Route 16 to North Conway. The inn is one mile north from the center of town, on the left.

☙

E: *When you come down the road and see the magnificent flag streaming out in the wind you just can't go by. Stop for a drink, if you can't stay the night. You'll love it.*

olive Metcalf

The 1785 Inn
North Conway, New Hampshire
03860

Innkeepers: Charles and Rebecca Mallar
Telephone: 603-356-9025
Rooms: 13, 8 with private bath.
Rates: $55 to $80, double occupancy, EPB.
Facilities: Open all year. Dinner, bar, lounge. Golf, tennis, swimming pool, canoeing, fishing, and skiing nearby. American Express, MasterCard, and Visa accepted.

The 1785 Inn is one of the oldest houses in all of Mount Washington Valley. It was built in 1785 by Captain Elijah Dinsmore. Records indicate that Captain Dinsmore received a license to "keep a Publik House" in 1795. In addition to being a public house, the lovely old inn served as a stagecoach stop. The chimney and dining room fireplace with brick oven are original to the house. They form a beehive structure the size of an entire room in the center of the inn.

Guest accommodations are ample. The Mallars have just completely refurbished the inn. What a large undertaking! They have done such a fine job. There is a ☞ sink in all the rooms. I find this a very nice feature in rooms with shared baths.

There are two living areas; both have fireplaces, and one has a television set. They are furnished with attractive chairs and couches for your comfort. An old oak icebox is in here. It surely makes a beautiful piece of furniture. The tavern has a large bar, a woodburning stove, and good sitting areas. There is light classical music here at times.

The views from the porch-dining room are just lovely. The food is inventive and very good. I had a salad here once, crab and shrimp served on top of spinach and alfalfa sprouts, tomatoes, and herbed dill dressing. Wow, it was good. Another dinner dish is Raspberry Duck, duck roasted with a brandy-laced raspberry sauce and served on wild rice. There are several veal selections, and, of course, fish, chicken, and beef. The desserts are wild. Deep-fried ice cream. Honest, and it's great. So is the chocolate velvet.

How to get there: Take Route 16 north. The inn is on the left just before you come to Route 16A.

E: *A nice inn surrounded by many activities, good food—what more do you want.*

"Enough," he cried
and left with all speed
for the neighborhood inn.

olive Metcalf

Stonehurst Manor
North Conway, New Hampshire
03860

Innkeeper: Peter Rattay
Telephone: 603-356-3113
Rooms: 16 in the manor; 10 in the annex adjoining the manor; all but
    two with private bath, air conditioning, cable color TV, and radio.
Rates: $50 to $135, double occupancy, EP. MAP and package rates
    available in summer and fall.
Facilities: Open all year. Breakfast, dinner, bar. Meeting room for up to
    50 persons. Pool, tennis, shuffleboard, volleyball. All major credit
    cards accepted.

    This turn-of-the-century mansion is a fine country inn. Set
back from the highway among stately pine trees, it makes you
think you are going back in time, and in a way you are.
    The front door is huge. Once inside, you see beautiful oak
wood and wonderful wall-to-wall carpet. The room to the left is all
wicker and all comfort. Ahead of you is the warm living room,
with walls full of ☛ books, and a huge fireplace. The unusual
screen and andirons were made in England. To the right of the
fireplace is a twelve-foot, curved window seat of another era. The
lounge area has a two-seat bar, just the right size.
    Relax in a high-back wicker chair in one of the inn's four

dining rooms that have been awarded three stars in the Mobil Guide and also won the silver spoon award. Enjoy the fine gourmet dining with appetizers like Lobster Ravioli (I never had this one before; it's delicious) and wonderful soups. For entrees there are three veal dishes. The Veal Pêche won my vote: it's medallions of veal sautéed with peaches, cream, and cumin, and finished with peach brandy. Needless to say, there are many more, and all are divine.

The manor staircase is a beauty, and its large rooms are beautifully appointed. Fantastic wallpapers and beautiful carpets all add to this great inn. The third-floor rooms have windows at odd angles, dictated by the roof line of the house. Some rooms have porches, and one has a stained-glass door going out to its porch. There is a lot of lovely stained glass throughout the inn. On the second floor, in one of the hall bathrooms, is a wood-enclosed steel bathtub. Be sure to take a look at it. It is quite a sight.

Their pool, the largest in the Mount Washington area, is made of wood, the only wooden one I have ever seen. You swell it in the spring, just as you would a wooden boat. Cocktails are served around the pool in the summer. There are tennis courts, and shuffleboard and volleyball courts. Plenty of things will keep you busy, or, like me, you might want to just sit and relax.

How to get there: The inn is on Route 16 just a short distance north of North Conway.

❋

E: *The inn was the country estate of the Bigelow carpet family, so the inn cat's name is Mrs. Bigelow.*

Follansbee Inn
North Sutton, New Hampshire
03260

Innkeepers: Sandy and Dick Reilein
Telephone: 603-927-4221
Rooms: 23, 11 with private bath.
Rates: $55 to $65, double occupancy, EPB.
Facilities: Inn closed two weeks in April and two weeks in November. Restaurant closed Sundays and Mondays. Breakfast, dinner, lounge. Children over 8 are welcome. Cross-country skiing from the inn, swimming, boating. Downhill skiing and golfing nearby. MasterCard and Visa accepted.

This is a 🖝 nonsmoking inn. I commend the innkeepers for this.

The inn is an 1840 New England farmhouse located on Kezar Lake. It has its own pier and its own private beach. A windsurfer, paddleboat, rowboat, and canoe are provided for your pleasure. Or perhaps you'd like to take a 🖝 swim in this lovely lake? Maybe McCoy, the inn dog, will swim with you.

A woodburning stove makes the living room cozy and homey. The lounge has a small bar. Guests are encouraged to play the piano or guitar. The rooms are newly refurbished and are nice. The innkeepers have thoughtfully purchased very good mat-

360

tresses. The upstairs halls are wide enough to have space for some interesting furniture. There are plants all over the inn and lots of books.

The dining room has comfortable captain's chairs and touches of chintz and linen. These are very pleasant surroundings in which to relax and savor the food. ☛ The chef has been here for quite a while. This is always a good sign. Ask for your favorite dish and he will try to come up with it. The chalkboard menu changes daily. Roast pork, Chicken Parmesan, and baked stuffed shrimp are often available. Beef and veal are always on the menu. But you haven't had it all until you try the homemade desserts.

There is much to do in the area. You can go play a game of tennis or golf, take a hike or bicycle ride, or go picnicking. In winter alpine skiing is nearby, and cross-country skiing is from the door of the inn.

How to get there: Take I-91 north to Ascutney, Vermont. Follow Route 103 to Route 11 east, to Route 114. Proceed to North Sutton. The inn is behind the church.

❦

E: *North Sutton's old church is right next door. You might want to set your watch by its chiming clock.*

A night at an inn adds a tinge to the coming day that cannot be described, only be enjoyed.

Home Hill Inn
Plainfield, New Hampshire
03781

Innkeeper: Roger Nicolas
Telephone: 603-675-6165
Rooms: 6, 5 with private bath. Cottage with living room.
Rates: $60 single; $80 to $95, double occupancy; continental breakfast
 included. Cottage $95, per night; inquire about a weekly rental. Fall
 season and holidays slightly higher.
Facilities: Closed Sundays and Mondays, two weeks in March, and two
 weeks in November. Dinner, bar, lounge. Swimming pool, tennis
 court, cross-country skiing, fishing in Connecticut River.
 MasterCard and Visa accepted.

Roger's brochure said Home Hill Country Inn and French
Restaurant, and I could hardly wait to get there.

Roger was born in Brittany in northwest France, and he
speaks with a pleasant French accent. He has an ☞ authentic
French restaurant here. The food presentation is picture perfect
and the taste is elegant. No gravies, only sauces, and no flour,
cornstarch, or fillers are allowed. Roger believes in innovative
French cooking.

I started with a ☞ Fresh Fish Mousse with Lobster Sauce.
I have never had better. Next, cream of onion soup, then veal

slices, very thin and young with French mushrooms. You may have the salad before, with, or after dinner and the house dressing is gorgeous. Roger joined me at dinner and had duck prepared with white plums. I tasted it and it was very moist and delicious. Another dish served occasionally is veal stuffed with kiwi. Desserts, as would be expected, are superb. The wine list features both French and California wines.

In the kitchen is a lovely, long pine table where breakfast is served. What a homey spot at which to enjoy the continental breakfast of juice, croissants, butter, jams, and coffee.

The rooms are charming. The cottage is large enough for eight persons. There are French and American antiques, reproductions, and comfort. The lounge-library is lovely; in fact, you will find it hard to find any fault with this inn.

Roger's Great Dane is Big Mac. The inn is on twenty-five acres, only 500 yards from the Connecticut River. There are a swimming pool (a bar is out here), tennis courts, and cross-country skiing. Any season, any reason, head for Home Hill.

How to get there: Take I-89 to Exit 20. Follow Route 12A south to River Road and turn right. In 3½ miles you'll find the inn on the left.

✳

E: *Herman, the automatic tennis ball shooter, is a neat exercise encourager.*

Philbrook Farm Inn
Shelburne, New Hampshire
03581

Innkeepers: Connie Leger and Nancy Philbrook
Telephone: 603-466-3831
Rooms: 19, 8 with private bath; 5 cottages with housekeeping arrangements.
Rates: $33.50 to $42, per person, double occupancy, MAP. Cottages $250 weekly.
Facilities: Closed April and October 31 to December 26. Breakfast, lunch, dinner, BYOB lounge. Library, pool table, Ping-Pong, swimming pool, horseback riding, cross-country skiing, snowshoeing, hiking. Downhill skiing nearby. No credit cards accepted.

When you're traveling along Route 2, take a look across the fields and there you'll see this lovely inn that is listed on the National Register of Historic Places. And rightly so. In 1861 Philbrook Farm started as an inn. Today it is still an inn and still has ☞ Philbrooks living here, running it in fine New England tradition.

Everything you eat here is prepared from scratch in their kitchens. The baked goods are made daily. A huge garden provides good vegetables. One entree is served each night. Roasts of everything you can want—pork, beef, turkey—and on and on. The New England boiled dinner is also a favorite.

The downstairs playroom has Ping-Pong, a pool table, shuffleboard, puzzles, and fun. A lot of reading material can be found all over the inn. Fireplaces are also all over the inn. ☛ A player piano, an old pump organ, where else can you find such unique things except in an inn?

Rooms are furnished with a lot of old ☛ family treasures. There are some nice four-posters and a wonderful collection of ☛ old bowl and pitcher sets. All the cottages are different. They surely are nice if you want to linger here awhile. Some have dining rooms, some have fireplaces, and some have porches. If you are staying in a cottage you may bring along your pet.

With more than 1000 acres, the inn has plenty of room for you to roam any season of the year. Look across their fields to the Carter-Moriah and Presidential mountain ranges. Behind the inn rises the Mahoosuc Range. This is the Androscoggin Valley. Horseback riding lessons and trail riding are available at the Philbrook Farm stables. What a heavenly place for a horseback ride. I saw a foal about two weeks old when I was here. A real little beauty. The inn cats are Dustball and Fuzzy, and the inn dog, Leibschen, is a German shorthair pointer.

How to get there: The inn is 1½ miles off Route 2. Going west, look for a direction sign on your right, and turn right. Cross the railroad tracks and then a bridge. Turn right at the crossroads and go a half mile to the inn, which is on North Road.

☜☞

E: *The inn has a wonderful selection of Philbrook Farm puzzles made by ☛ Connie's grandfather. They have large, ¼-inch-thick pieces and are just beautiful.*

Snowvillage Inn
Snowville, New Hampshire
03849

Innkeepers: Frank, Peter, and Trudy Cutrone
Telephone: 603-447-2818
Rooms: 15, all with private bath.
Rates: $83 to $94, single; $69 to $76 per person, double occupancy;
   MAP. Special package rates available.
Facilities: Closed April and first two weeks of November. Breakfast,
   dinner, bar, lounge. Cross-country skiing, downhill ski rental and
   instructions, nature trails, tennis, hiking, canoeing, and fishing
   nearby. Children over 8 are welcome. All major credit cards ac-
   cepted.

The view from the inn is breathtaking. Mount Washington
and the whole Presidential Range, plus the rest of the White
Mountains, greet your eyes everywhere you look. In summer at
the top of Foss Mountain, right at the inn, you can eat your fill of
wild blueberries.

The guest rooms are comfortable and spacious, with 🖙 tons
of towels in luscious colors. Each room is named after a favorite
author of the innkeepers. The living room, with its huge fireplace
and nice couches all around, makes this an inn for rest and
relaxation. There are a service bar and a lounge, and plants are

everywhere. The game room has a television, and there is an extensive library. A huge porch surrounds the inn. I could sit here all day and enjoy the incredible view.

The cooking has an 🖝 Austrian flavor. One entree is served each evening. You may find pork tenderloin with sauerkraut, 🖝 curried chicken with peaches, beef tenderloin, chicken or veal piccata, and shrimp scampi, just to name a few. All breads and desserts are made here, and the soups also are homemade. This does make a difference.

Nice animals are here. The cats are Skunk, Harry, Virginia, and Shirlee, and dogs are to be added later.

How to get there: Out of Conway on Route 153, go 5 miles to Crystal Village. Turn left, go about 1½ miles, turn right at the inn's sign, and go up the hill ¾ mile to the inn.

🌻

E: *Peter, the son, makes the* 🖝 *best darn chili in the world. He sent some home with me and wow, it was good and hot. He also makes a mild-flavored one.*

Olive Metcalf

Dexters
Sunapee, New Hampshire
03782

Innkeepers: Frank and Shirley Simpson; Holly and Michael Durfor
Telephone: 603-763-5571
Rooms: 17, all with private bath.
Rates: $105 to $140, double occupancy, MAP. Package rates offered in off season.
Facilities: Closed mid-October to May 1. Breakfast, lunch in July and August, dinner, bar. Tennis, swimming pool, recreation barn. Fresh fruit and flowers in your room. MasterCard and Visa accepted.

The main house was built in 1801 by an artisan, Adam Reddington. He earned his living by carving from the huge knurls of the many fine maples on the grounds the bowls in which sailing ships carried their compasses. In 1948 the house became a small country inn.

Dexters is a nice family inn. The Simpsons, their daughter, Holly, and her husband, Michael, run the inn. They also have a new innkeeper, a very young one, Hartwell, who was born in July 1985. Never too soon to start learning.

Your day starts with ☞ juice and coffee served in your room at a time you set the night before. Or you can be really spoiled and have a New England breakfast tray in bed. These are rooms you'll want to linger in. They are a bit above average, with marvelous wallpapers and heavenly pillows made of 🖝 feathers. Most of the antique beds have come down through the Simpson family.

The living room library has over 500 books, magazines, and newspapers. It offers lots of comfort and charm along with a fireplace. There are two TV viewing rooms and a breezy screened porch.

Outdoor sports? You name it. Tennis is taken seriously here. Three all-weather 🖝 Plexicushion tennis courts with a pro and shop are provided for your enjoyment. Tournaments for seniors are just a few of the happenings going on up here. After a game there is a lovely outdoor swimming pool to cool off in. Croquet, a horseshoe pit, and shuffleboard are also available. In springtime the lake trout and salmon are close to the surface and hungry, so come all you fishermen. Spring is always late up here, so you have a longer season. For a good summer or fall activity there are some of the loveliest walking and hiking trails right on the inn's property.

There is a special recreation room in the barn for all ages, but it is keyed to those under seventeen who need a place of their own when the five o'clock cocktail hour begins.

How to get there: Take I-89 out of Concord and follow Exit 12 to Route 11, to 103B in Sunapee. Or take I-91 out of Springfield and follow Exit 8 to Claremont, New Hampshire, to Route 103. The turn to the inn is marked by a sign 200 yards south of the intersection of 103 and 11. The inn is about 1½ miles off Route 103.

∽

E: *Frank is a special innkeeper, right on top of everything. He has an outside terrace under the trees that is used for lunch. How nice!*

Olive Metcalf

Seven Hearths
Sunapee, New Hampshire
03782

Innkeepers: Marianne Morse Callahan and Miguel Ramirez
Telephone: 603-763-5657
Rooms: 10, all with private bath.
Rates: $73 to $138, per person, double occupancy, MAP in season. EP
    rates available for the rest of the year.
Facilities: Closed in April. Restaurant open Tuesday through Saturday.
    Breakfast, lunch July to October, dinner, Sunday brunch. Full li-
    cense. Swimming pool. MasterCard and Visa accepted.

    The inn was built in 1801 and remained in its original family
for almost one hundred years. It is nestled in a quiet and tranquil
part of the lovely area of Sunapee. The name Seven Hearths
came about from the fact that the inn has 🖙 seven working
fireplaces.

    Five of these fireplaces are in the rooms. Some rooms have
wide-board floors and exposed ceiling beams. Two rooms downstairs have an outdoor terrace overlooking the lake. 🖙 Fresh
flowers and bowls of fruit are set out to welcome you. There are
plants all over and lots of books to read.

    The living room has a massive fieldstone fireplace, a baby

grand piano just waiting to be played, and a library full of books and board games. ☞ Afternoon tea is served in here.

Breakfast and dinner are served in a lovely room that has another one of the seven fireplaces. This one has a beehive oven. A bay window overlooks the peaceful countryside. Hors d'oeuvres are served in the hearth room. The soups are divine. Creamy Scallop Bisque St. Jacques, or Spring Fiddlehead Cream Bisque are only two. They have more tasty offerings. Roast Duckling with Raspberry Glaze, or Seven Pepper Pork Tenderloin Medallions with Cumin and Serranos, followed by good salads and desserts. One I love is ☞ Chocolate Raspberry Torte. But I also love the Fresh Fruit Tart with Chantilly Cream. Oh, it's hard to choose between them.

The inn has a nice screened porch with rockers and a lovely swimming pool with a wooden deck all around it. The smell of the tall pines is heavenly. Care for croquet? It's here. Tennis anyone? It's to be built very soon.

How to get there: Take Exit 12 from I-89 and turn west on Route 11. In 4.2 miles, on the right, is a sign for the inn, which is in a few yards.

E: *In the living room is an album with menus going back to the 1930s. Thanksgiving dinner, five courses, $1.50. Wow.*

The Birchwood Inn
Temple, New Hampshire
03084

Innkeepers: Judy and Bill Wolfe
Telephone: 603-878-3285
Rooms: 8, 2 with private bath.
Rates: $40 to $50, single; $41 to $55, double; EPB.
Facilities: Closed three weeks in April. Dinner served Tuesday through Saturday. BYOB. Trout fishing, hiking, hunting, golf, summer theater, and lakes nearby. No pets. No credit cards honored, but personal checks accepted.

The inn is in the Mount Monadnock region of New Hampshire, so there is plenty to do and see here. From the top of the mountain you can see four states, a nice reward for you hikers. There are trout waiting for the fisherman, much game for the hunter, plus all those good things for the quieter type such as golf, summer theater, horseback riding, and walking.

Bill and Judy are the owner-chefs and are very good at what they do. I understand from my spies that their ☞ stuffed lobster is better than anywhere else. Chicken Piccata and Shrimp Parmesan served on green noodles are two more examples of their good food. They have She-crab Soup, which is hard to find north of South Carolina. It is excellent.

The inn has an 1878 square Steinway grand piano that is kept in perfect tune. The inn history stretches back some two centuries to circa 1775. During this time many people have come and gone, one notable personage being Henry David Thoreau. A room at the inn is named for him. Other rooms have rather different sort of names such as "The Bottle Shop" and "The School Room." The innkeepers will entertain you with the stories of how the rooms became so named.

How to get there: Take Route 3 out of Boston to Nashua, New Hampshire, Exit 7W. Follow Route 101 to Milford to Route 45 to Temple.

✺

E: *The dining room walls are covered with Rufus Porter murals. They are beautiful.*

The chill of a wood-stove-warmed bedroom evaporates in the crisp smell of bacon for breakfast.

The Chesterfield Inn
West Chesterfield, New Hampshire
03466

Innkeepers: Pamela Lendzion and Jeff Krock
Telephone: 603-256-3211
Rooms: 7, plus 2 suites, all with private bath, refrigerator, and telephone.
Rates: $85 to $135, double occupancy, EPB.
Facilities: Open all year. Full breakfast except on weekends when it's
continental. Dinner Wednesday through Sunday. Full license. Ice
skating. Fishing, boating, skiing, and swimming nearby. All major
credit cards accepted.

The original house was built in the 1780s. From 1798 to
1811 it was a tavern, and after that it was many things. Now it is
back to its original function of serving the public, but this time as
a lovely country inn.

Pamela has done a fabulous job of decorating the rooms. They
really are glorious. All are different, and all are color coordinated ☞ with thirsty towels. Two of the rooms have ☞ whirlpool
baths and four of them have fireplaces. Two of the rooms also
have balconies. One has stencils on the wall to match the bed-
spread and it is a beauty. Some of the rooms have walls paneled
with the wood that was in the old barn. There is a ☞ refrigerator
in all rooms with beer, wine, juice, and Perrier. This is an in-

374

credibly nice touch. The rooms have telephones, even 🖝 in the bathrooms. Cable TV is available.

Candlelight, crisp linen, and Waterford crystal make the dining rooms sparkle along with the food. Herring in a wine sauce, and assorted game pâtés of duck, rabbit, or venison, are just a sample of the appetizers. Boston Scrod Polignac is scrod baked with shrimp, garlic, tomato, and peppercorns. Boneless breast of duck is enhanced with an apricot stuffing and an apricot ginger sauce, making it so good and distinctive. Specials are always added to the menu.

The beautiful Connecticut River is a short walk from the inn, so bring along your canoe or fishing pole. Lake Spofford has boats for rent. Pisgah Park has hiking trails and two spring-fed ponds for swimming. In winter skiing is close at hand or go skating on the inn's lighted pond. Warm yourself with a hot toddy by the fire.

How to get there: Take Exit 3 off I-91. Take Route 9 west, going over the border from Vermont to New Hampshire. The inn is in two miles on your left.

∽

E: As soon as you see the entrance with a fireplace and comfortable couches and chairs, you have an idea what the rest of the inn is like.

Kimball Hill Inn
Whitefield, New Hampshire
03598

Innkeepers: Penny and Rick Preston
Telephone: 603-837-2284
Rooms: 8, 5 with private bath; 4 cottages.
Rates: $25 to $50, double occupancy, continental breakfast included.
Facilities: Closed in April. Restaurant closed to general public on Mondays and Tuesdays. Dinner, bar, lounge. Gift shop. Swimming, riding, golfing, and tennis nearby. American Express, MasterCard, and Visa accepted.

If you are looking for an inn that is comfortable, with good food and ☛ a fantastic view, look no further. I sat in the pub and had lunch looking out at the Presidential Range to the east and the Green Mountains to the west. Beautiful! The elevation of the inn is 1,390 feet.

Preston's Pub is finished inside with old barn wood. This is real barn-board, for they took down an old barn in Lancaster, New Hampshire, washed the wood, and refurbished the interior of the inn with it. The result is warm and cozy. If you look up you will see their ☛ standard gauge American Flyer train make a loop around the pub on almost one hundred feet of track. I love toy trains because I never grew up, and I am glad.

376

The dining room with its glorious views is pretty, serving good food. The pub also serves food. They have interesting Mountain Burgers, and a good chef's salad. The sweet and sour chicken is a different delight. There are also nice weekday specials in both the dining room and the pub.

For you inveterate shoppers they have a nice little gift shop right in the inn.

The rooms are comfortable, all different shapes and sizes, and all with spectacular views.

You will find many activities to entertain you a few miles down the road, or just sit in the pub and watch the world at peace.

How to get there: Take Route 116 east out of Littleton, New Hampshire, toward Whitefield. The inn is one mile south of town on Kimball Hill Road.

E: ☛ *The Mountain Rat is a special drink, and I mean special; orange, lemon, cranberry juice, light and dark rum, apricot brandy with 151-proof rum on top. It is served in a 22-ounce brandy snifter. Wow!*

> *"Drink wine, and live here blitheful while ye may;*
> *The morrow's life too late is, live to-day."*
> —Herrick

Spalding Inn Club
Whitefield, New Hampshire
03598

Innkeeper: Bill Ingram
Telephone: 603-837-2572
Rooms: 56, all with private bath and phone; 14 cottage suites.
Rates: Furnished upon request; MAP and AP.
Facilities: Closed mid-October to Memorial Day. Breakfast, lunch, dinner, bar, lounge. Swimming pool, four tennis courts, nine-hole par three golf course, eighteen-hole putting green, shuffleboard, lawn bowling. American Express, MasterCard, and Visa accepted.

I feel that everyone at some time should see how our parents and grandparents might have spent their summers years ago, and at the Spalding Inn Club you can have that experience.

The tables are set with ☛ fingerbowls, silver napkin rings, and white linen. The service is impeccable and the food is excellent. The choices are myriad, reminding me of a cruise ship where you have unlimited food. Breakfast alone is outstanding. Hot from the bakery come popovers, doughnuts, and Danish pastries. Dinners are baked stuffed lobsters, beef, veal . . . you name it, and it's here.

The rooms and cottages are tastefully appointed, with fresh flowers, direct dial telephone, and turn-down service at night.

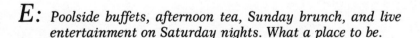 Extra pillows and blankets are so nice. All rooms have private baths with tub and shower, and very special soaps. The cottages have living rooms, bedrooms, and baths. All have their own fireplace, and some have their own porch.

The newly decorated living room has an abundance of books and magazines, baskets of apples, jars of candy, and a 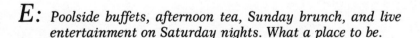 barometer for tomorrow's weather. In the card room are lots of puzzles. One puzzle or another is always ready for you to add a piece or two. Downstairs is a lounge with a huge television screen.

Golf anyone? The inn's own eighteen-hole putting green and nine-hole par three course are here, and you never have to worry about starting times. Lawn bowling is a unique sport found here at the inn. There is a 120-square-foot bowling green where championship games are often played. Swimming, tennis, fishing in miles of trout streams, and hunting in the fall are at hand. There is so much to do, one need never leave the inn's 500 acres.

To the south lies the Franconia range with its famous Old Man of the Mountains. To the west is the Dalton Ridge, gateway to the Connecticut Valley. On the far horizon are the Green Mountains of Vermont, and to the north the Kilkenny ranges with over sixty peaks known as "the Yankee Alps."

How to get there: Take I-93 north to Exit 41. Follow Route 116 through the village of Whitefield. Continue 1½ miles north of town, turn right onto Mountain View Road.

∽❧∾

E: *Poolside buffets, afternoon tea, Sunday brunch, and live entertainment on Saturday nights. What a place to be.*

The Ram in the Thicket
Wilton, New Hampshire
03086

Innkeepers: Andrew and Priscilla Tempelman
Telephone: 603-654-6440
Rooms: 9, 3 with private bath.
Rates: $45 to $55, double occupancy, continental breakfast included.
Facilities: Open all year. Dinner, bar. Indoor swimming pool, hot tub,
    horseback riding, hiking. Summer theater nearby. MasterCard and
    Visa accepted.

The unusual name of the inn is taken from the old Bible
story of Abraham and Isaac. As a substitute for his son Isaac's
death, Abraham finds "a ram caught in the thicket" sent by the
Lord. Andrew and Priscilla founded the inn as a substitute for a
life in the Midwest from which they wanted a change.

Luckily for all inn lovers the Tempelmans' move has results
in another better-than-nice inn. This old Victorian mansion has
been carefully restored and now has lovely dining rooms with
crystal chandeliers, ☞ a hand-carved fireplace, and many other
Victorian touches. One dining room has lovely blue delft tiles.
The innkeepers are Dutch. The New Hampshire lounge has
plants hanging from the ceilings.

Some of the dinner dish names are great. They taste good,

380

too. How about China Garden Chicken, stir-fried chicken with fruit, or Lamb Rawalpindi, lamb in a sweet curry sauce, or Hampton Beach, seafood newburg in puff pastry. These are just an example of what you can expect. In the summer, all this good food can be savored on the screened porch.

This good inn is set in eight acres of wonderful country for roaming. Horses and sheep are in the lower pasture and you also have Jaws II, the cat, and her friends. Summer theater is close by. If you love to walk, there are many trails right at hand.

How to get there: Take Route 3 and just about at Nashua take Exit 7 west on 101A to 101 about 15 miles to Wilton. Watch for the inn's signs.

❀

E: ☞ *An enclosed swimming pool is my idea of heaven.*

When life dwindles thin and you wonder
if the sun will rise on another day,
seek perhaps an unfamiliar but rejuvenating bed
in a nearby country inn.

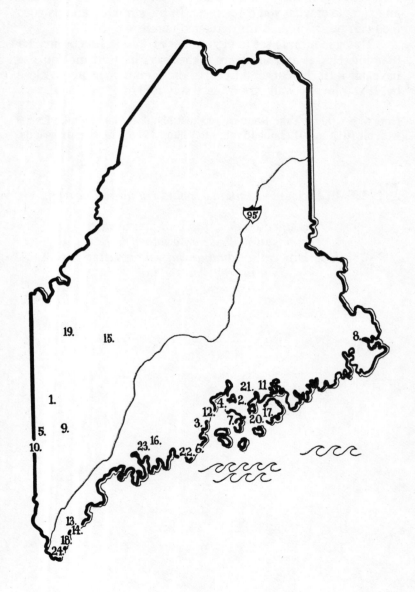

19. 15.

8.

21. 11.
4. 2.
12.
3. 7. 20. 17.
5. 9.
10.
23. 16.
22. 6.

13.
14.
18.
24.

Maine

Numbers on map refer to towns numbered below.

The Bethel Inn
Bethel, Maine
04217

Innkeepers: Dick Rasor; manager, Ray Moran
Telephone: 207-824-2175
Rooms: 70, all with private bath, telephone; 16 with fireplace.
Rates: $48 to $95, per person, double occupancy, MAP. Package rates
   available.
Facilities: Open all year. Breakfast, lunch, dinner, bar, lounge. Golf,
   tennis, swimming pool, lake house with sailfish and canoes, cross-
   country skiing, sauna, indoor games, supervised activities for children. Own walking tour guide. Downhill skiing nearby. All major
   credit cards accepted.

   The Bethel Inn faces the village common of Bethel, Maine,
which is a National Historic District complete with beautifully
restored churches, public buildings, and private homes. The rear
of the inn overlooks its own eighty-five acres, which include a
nine-hole par thirty-six golf course.
   Guest rooms have private baths and direct dial telephones.
They are well done and very comfortable. A number of rooms
have been recently redecorated with country print wallpaper,
thick carpeting, and fresh paint.
   The huge living room, music room, and library are beauti-

fully furnished for the utter comfort of the guests. The piano, by the way, is a Steinway.

Dining is a pleasure, either in the charming main dining room or on the fully screened porch overlooking the golf course. You'll find such entrees as prime ribs, roast duck, and lobster and crabmeat casserole on their extensive menu. Just before sunset, look out over the golf course. You'll see literally hundreds of swallows diving into the chimney of the utility building next to the course.

Downstairs is the Mill Brook Tavern. Jim Stoner, a blind jazz pianist, plays the piano here, June through October. Mill Brook cuts through the golf course and was the site of Twitchell's mill erected in the early 1700s in Sudbury, Canada, which is now Bethel, Maine.

Down here in the bar and lounge there is a light supper menu, which is nice for the late hiker or skier. In the winter you can have hot cider, hot buttered rum, and glögg. Lunch is nice in the new screened-in terrace lounge, but the drinks are even better. They're called the Kool Krazy Bouncy and Hot drinks. I managed to taste three of them. Oh boy.

The lake house, three miles away on Lake Songo, features clambakes and barbecues. The downstairs patio on summer weekends also has a bar.

Skiing is super up here with Sunday River (I love that name) and Mount Abram right at hand. The inn has special ski packages. Do check them. And as a special special, they have over twenty kilometers of groomed cross-country trails for your pleasure.

How to get there: Bethel is located at the intersection of U.S. Route 2 and Maine Routes 5 and 26. From the south take Exit 11 off the Maine Turnpike at Gray and follow Route 26 to Bethel. The inn is on the green.

❀

E: *Afternoon teas, punch parties, and lobster bakes are nice to find in an inn.*

The Sudbury Inn
Bethel, Maine
04217

Innkeepers: Cheri and David (Fuzzy) Thurston
Telephone: 207-824-2174
Rooms: 11, all with private bath; 2 suites.
Rates: $47 to $90, double occupancy, EPB.
Facilities: Open all year. Dinner, bar, lounge. Skiing, ice skating, ca-
   noeing, tennis, golfing, and hiking nearby. All major credit cards
   accepted.

This inn is located in the very pretty village of Bethel in the
mountains of western Maine. The town is home to Gould Academy, one of Maine's foremost prep schools, which was founded
in 1836. Near the inn are miles of maintained cross-country ski
trails, downhill skiing, ice skating, canoeing (flat and white-
water), tennis, golfing, and hiking the Appalachian Trail. The
inn provides easy access to the White Mountain National Forest.
The fall foliage around this area is breathtakingly beautiful.

The whole inn has been refurbished and renovated, quite a
task. The bar is made of ☞ bird's-eye maple and is a one-of-a-
kind beauty. A fireplace is in here, and on cold nights this is the
place to be.

Rae is the chef, and the food she serves is good and plentiful

386

Yankee cooking. Everything from soups and breads to desserts is homemade. Rae is famous for her ☛ chowder. I like inventive cooking and Sole Roujolet (sole wrapped around scallop and shrimp mousse in phyllo dough and topped with a white wine sauce) is a good invention. So is her Chicken Chardonnay— boneless chicken breast in a chardonnay sauce topped with julienne carrots, small braised onions, and mushrooms. Fuzzy's favorite is ☛ barbecue country-cut spareribs, and I love them, too.

The guest rooms are clean, neat, and comfortable. There is a gallery off the lobby where local craftspeople display their work for sale. This is a very nice touch.

How to get there: Take Exit 11 off the Maine Turnpike and follow Route 26 to Bethel. The inn is on lower Main Street.

∽

E: *Rockers on the front porch. You can sit and watch the world go by.*

A day by the fire, a hot ale in hand,
and the idiot cares of the world are as nothing.

olive Metcalf

Blue Hill Inn
Blue Hill, Maine
04614

Innkeepers: Rita and Ted Boytos
Telephone: 207-374-2844
Rooms: 10, all with private bath.
Rates: $53 to $58, double occupancy, EP.
Facilities: Open all year. Full breakfast and dinner. Restaurant closed
  Mondays. BYOB. Cross-country skiing, swimming, boating, golf,
  tennis, and concerts nearby. All major credit cards accepted.

It is always nice to have an inn back in the book. Rita and
Ted, the new innkeepers, are doing a great job. I like happy
innkeepers, and Rita and Ted are a happy pair. They make you
feel right at home.

An inn since 1840, this is a lovely old place, made nicer by
the innkeepers who think of everything to keep their guests comfortable. They thoughtfully provided setups for their BYOB
guests. They have stocked their TV room with lots of games and
puzzles, and encourage guests to play the piano here. Or you can
feel free to curl up in one of the comfy chairs or couch in the
living room in front of the nice fireplace, and read one of their
ample supply of books. It is a relaxed inn, and ☞ children are
welcome.

388

The rooms are cozy, well furnished, and all have private baths.

Their lovely dining room features things like cream of cucumber soup, spinach or tossed green salad, broiled scallops, baked halibut, and beef tenderloin. Beef goulash was something I had not had in many a country mile, so I was glad to find it here. And now for the best—Rita has quite a following for her pies. Lemon Meringue is only one of them and it's spectacular.

This is a lovely section of Maine. Any time of the year there is something to do. For music lovers there is the Kneisel School of Music, offering concerts several times a year. The famous potters, Rowantrees and Radcliff, are nearby. Golf and tennis, also swimming and boating, are close at hand. Winter brings good cross-country skiing in nearby Acadia National Park.

How to get there: From Belfast, follow Route 3 through Searsport to Bucksport. Bear right after crossing the Bucksport Bridge. After a few miles turn right onto Route 15 to Blue Hill. Turn right on Main Street, then bear right again onto Route 177. The inn is the first building on your left at the top of the hill.

*

E: *Maine is so beautiful and Blue Hill is a gem.*

Olive Metcalf

Camden Harbour Inn
Camden, Maine
04843

Innkeepers: Sal Vella and Patti Babij
Telephone: 207-236-4200
Rooms: 22, 16 with private bath.
Rates: $45 to $145, double occupancy, EPB.
Facilities: Open all year. Full breakfast, dinner, Sunday brunch, bar. Television in lounge. Entertainment. Golfing, skiing, and sailing nearby. MasterCard and Visa accepted.

Camden Harbour is one of the best known ports in Maine, and one of the prettiest, too. In the late nineteenth century when Camden was bustling with cargo and fishing schooners, the inn was built to accommodate passengers who traveled from Boston to Bangor by steamship. Today, boats of yesteryear, both sail and power, as well as beautiful yachts of today, moor here by the rolling mountains that come right down to the rocky shores. The inn sits up high above all this and provides a ☞ panoramic view all around.

The original guest rooms are small and clean and neat as a pin. In 1984 ☞ four larger guest rooms were added. Two overlook the harbor and bay and have outside decks. Another is a suite with a foyer, wet bar, sitting room adjacent to a large deck, and a comfortably furnished bedroom with a working fireplace. The fourth room has a large sitting area and a brick patio that overlooks the outer harbor.

The Thirsty Whale Tavern serves simple suppers. The menu is posted on the chalkboard each evening. The new dining room, which has beautiful views, has its own menu. The appetizers are interesting. Shrimp Tsukeyaki, skewered shrimp marinated in a Japanese sauce and grilled, is outstanding. Oysters and mussels are prepared in some very different ways. Some entrees are Crab Dijon; three deliciously different lobster dishes, including Lobster Grapefruit Salad; and Duck with Raspberry Cassis, a new way with duck. Shrimp Fettucine alla Romano is great; add mushrooms and prosciutto and it's a plus. There are good beef and veal selections on the menu.

There are walking tours, bicycle trips, and nature walks in and around Camden. ☞ There is hardly a spot in this whole lovely Maine town that is not worth a visit. In July the Penobscot Folk Festival draws crowds to the Rockport Opera House.

This is a wonderful town to muddle about in for days.

How to get there: From Route 1, which runs through the center of town, turn up Bay View Street to number 83.

✺

E: *Sunday brunch has lobster stew on the menu. Those who know me know I'm a real lobster person. Champagne is nice with it.*

Come back in one hundred years and stay at my inn.

Olive Metcalf

The Manor
Castine, Maine
04421

Innkeepers: Paul and Sara Brouillard
Telephone: 207-326-4861
Rooms: 12, 10 with private bath.
Rates: $55 to $95, double occupancy, EPB.
Facilities: Open all year. Breakfast buffet, dinner by reservation only,
  bar, lounge. Children and pets welcome. Harbor tours. MasterCard
  and Visa accepted.

There is a lot of history in Castine. Champlain was here in
1604, and Castine is on a map he drew in 1612. The Manor, a
major architectural landmark, was built at the turn of the century by Commodore Fuller of the New York Yacht Club as a
summer cottage. It is listed in the ☛ National Register of Historic Places.

Sara was raised here, and after The Manor was sold to Paul,
they fell in love and were married. Now Sara and Paul are raising
their children in this lovely place.

All of the rooms are large and airy, with views of the islands
in the bay. One huge room has a king-sized bed and a grand
window to see the lovely views. Another room has its own porch.

Paul invites guests into his lovely retreat, the Hunting and

Billiard rooms. There is a very 🖘 fancy billiard table, and on a wall in the adjoining room are a lion's head, stuffed owls, and more. The Manor also has a large living room with a fireplace and tons of books.

On the front porch is a nice green marble and mahogany oyster bar, serving a variety of hors d'oeuvres, wines, and cocktails. There is also a porch for summer sipping, while you look out at Oakum Bay.

The food is glorious. 🖘 Portuguese Tomato Shrimp Soup is a house special, and it is special. The menu has some other unusual offerings. Duck Breast Armagnac, Salmon Fillet with French Sorrel, and Acadian Lobster Pie, which is lobster meat, butter, sherry, and Gruyère baked under a golden crumb crust. These are followed by very nice desserts.

🖘 Children and pets are welcome. This is a nice change. They, of course, have an inn cat, Mickey, who loves cars. I found him sleeping in mine.

How to get there: Take I-95 from Portland to the "Coastal Region—Brunswick, Bath, Route 1" Exit. Follow Route 1 to Bucksport. In 2 miles, turn right onto Route 175. Take Route 175 to Route 166, which takes you into Castine.

❋

E: *The innkeepers also own Dennets wharf, a lobster pound and Maine's longest oyster bar. It is right on the harbor.*

The Pentagöet Inn
Castine, Maine
04421

Innkeepers: Virginia and Lindsey Miller
Telephone: 207-326-8616
Rooms: 18, 12 with private bath; 1 suite.
Rates: $55 to $85 per person, double occupancy, MAP.
Facilities: Closed January through March. Breakfast, dinner, bar. Extensive wine list. Seven queen-sized beds. Fishing, sailing, and golfing nearby. American Express, MasterCard, and Visa accepted.

The Pentagöet is a lovely inn located on the unspoiled coast of beautiful Penobscot Bay. Built in 1894, this Victorian inn offers the traveler warmth and a very friendly atmosphere.

Part of the inn is Ten Perkins Street, the building next door, which is more than 200 years old. The suite is here. I stayed in it and it's a gem. All the rest of the rooms in both buildings are lovely, too. Some have little alcoves with views of the town and harbor. Some are small and have odd shapes, but this goes well with a country inn. There are ☞ working fireplaces in most of the rooms at Ten Perkins Street, and wood is supplied so you can light yourself a fire some cold evening.

There is a library to the right as you come in the door of the main inn. Lots of books, a piano, nice and soft stereo music and very restful couches give this room the perfect relaxed atmosphere. The sitting room is to the left with a woodburning stove and a beautiful picture window.

The wraparound porch is a delight. Good food is served in the new dining room. Breakfast when I was here included ☛ Maine strawberries, which arrived early in the morning, freshly picked at a local farm. Homemade granola, sourdough blueberry pancakes, and homemade jellies add up to a good breakfast. All baking is done right here. Good dinner appetizers include Shrimp Piccata—prepared with little Maine shrimp—lobster crepes, and Maine crabmeat crepes. Pork tenderloin, peppered ribeye steak, and lobster thermador are some of the entrees. I had ☛ lobster pie, a lazy and delicious way to have lobster.

The Maine Maritime Academy is located here and its training ship, the State of Maine, is docked at the town wharf. The local professional theater group, ☛ Cold Comfort Productions, performs four nights a week. The Downeast Chamber Music School also summers in Castine. Sometimes on a Sunday afternoon you will find them performing on the inn's porch.

How to get there: Take I-95 from Portland to the "Coastal Region—Brunswick, Bath, Route 1" Exit. Follow Route 1 to Bucksport and 2 miles beyond turn right onto Route 175. Take Route 175 to Route 166, which takes you into Castine.

౿

E: *The innkeepers and Bilbo Baggins, the inn cat, will really make your stay a pleasant one.*

Trifles make an inn, but an inn is no trifle.

Westways Country Inn
Center Lovell, Maine
04016

Innkeeper: Nancy Tripp
Telephone: 207-928-2663
Rooms: 7, 3 with private bath; 5 cottages.
Rates: $114 to $145, double occupancy. MAP. Package plans available.
Facilities: Closed April and November. Breakfast, dinner, full license.
Swimming, boating, sailing, tennis, handball, recreation building
with bowling, Ping-Pong, pool, and card room. Two marinas on
Lake Kezar. All major credit cards accepted.

Westways was built in the 1920s as the executive retreat of
the Diamond Match Company. It is a look into the past that is a
pure delight.

The living room overlooking Kezar Lake is large, with a huge
stone fireplace and comfortable couches and chairs. On cool
nights in winter your ☛ five-course dinner is served in here on
glorious ☛ Spode china. The appetizers might be quiche or
stuffed mushrooms. The soup may be stracciatella. Your salad is
served with homemade dressings, and the entrees consist of two
nightly choices. One day I was there one of the choices was
lobster. But your choice may be Veal Cordon Bleu, or fresh red

snapper, prime ribs, or steak. Great, creative desserts and coffees come next. This is indeed the way to live.

All of the rooms are gracious, most overlook the lake, and all have libraries. The president of Diamond Match was quite a reader, and his collection is here for you to enjoy. By the way, all of the rooms are different, some have wicker headboards and some have four-poster beds. All are comfortable.

The boathouse overlooks the lake and is comfortable for reading or just idle meditation. ☞ The view of the White Mountains from here is fantastic. There are over one hundred acres in all that go with the inn, plus a sandy beach, and a picnic area where a seaplane once was kept.

How to get there: Coming either way on Route 302 turn north at Fryeburg, Maine, onto Route 5. Fourteen miles north the lake will appear on your left, and the inn's entrance (marked with a sign) is on your left about 6 miles up the lake.

❧

E: *There is a body shower in the bath on the first floor that is unbelievable. It is certainly one of a kind.*

The Craignair Inn
Clark Island, Maine
04859

Innkeepers: Norman and Terry Smith
Telephone: 207-594-7644
Rooms: 17, all share baths.
Rates: $40 to $43, per person, double occupancy, MAP.
Facilities: Open all year. Breakfast, dinner for six or more in winter.
Special diets furnished upon reasonable notice. BYOB. Swimming, skiing, tennis, riding, and golf nearby. MasterCard and Visa accepted.

This isn't a fancy inn, but it is comfortable. It was built about fifty years ago as a boarding house for quarry workers. It hangs on the edge of the water, with rocks, tidal flats, an ocean inlet, and loads of peace and quiet. The quarry has long since been worked out, but you can swim there in the salt water that rises and falls with the tide. If you worry about old wooden buildings, sleep relaxed here.

There is always something to do at Craignair. If the fog rolls in, cozy up to the fire in the sitting room. When it snows, the Camden Snow Bowl Ski Area is a short drive away. Nearby towns and villages offer diversified activity stops, including antique shops, art galleries, museums, and specialty shops. Or you could attend a concert, play golf or tennis, ride horseback, bicycle, sail, or catch one of the numerous festivals paying homage to seafood, blueberries, chicken, sailboats, and history.

If tidal pools, clam flats, islands, meadows, and spruce forests invite you, come to Craignair in any season.

No excuse now, if you are a weight watcher, or on a salt-free diet, Terry will stick to your diet if you let her know a day or two ahead of time. There's one entree only each evening, but what variety. And on Saturday, enjoy that traditional Maine dinner, fresh lobster with steamers. The dining room is cozy, done in blue and white with lots of windows looking to the sea.

How to get there: Go to Thomaston on Route 1, then take Route 131 south for about 6 miles, and turn left on Route 73 for about a mile to Clark Island Road. Take a right, and the inn is at the end of the road.

❁

E: *The living room–library is very comfortable. This is a real Maine Coast inn with its own Maine Coast dog, a black Lab named Delia.*

Having had an excellent meal and a lovely evening,
I tucked myself in bed knowing I had sinned
but it did not seem to matter.

The Pilgrim's Inn
Deer Isle, Maine
04627

Innkeepers: Jean and Dud Hendrick
Telephone: 207-348-6615
Rooms: 13, 8 with private bath; 1 cottage.
Rates: $62.50 to $72.50, per person, double occupancy, MAP. Cottage
  $125, EP; $175, MAP.
Facilities: Closed end of October to mid-May. Full breakfast, dinner,
  bar, lounge. Bicycles, sailboats for charter, swimming nearby. Golf
  or tennis at the island country club as their guest. No credit cards
  honored, but personal checks accepted.

In 1793 Ignatius Haskell built this lovely house, following the specifications of his wife who ☛ demanded the luxuries of city living on their country estate. He had his own sawmill nearby and built the house out of northern pine. Today you are welcomed to this rambling inn by the glowing hearths of its many fireplaces.

The inn is heated by wood stoves and each room has one. The beds are very comfortable. All of the rooms are different and have a view of the pond or Northwest Harbor. The third floor has marvelous views and a great room. Actually, there are five rooms on the third floor, but one is huge.

400

Deer Isle, Maine

The inn has all the right touches, such as tons of 🖝 books, a huge fireplace, and soft well-worn wood floors and walls in the common rooms and taproom. There is a small service bar and the 🖝 honor system is in effect. If it's before the six o'clock cocktail hour you know to leave your tab on the bar.

Crisp linens and flowers are on the tables of the candlelit dining room, which once was a barn. It just glows. Dinner may be poached salmon or tenderloin of beef, done many ways. One night is lobster night. Soups are interesting. Billi-bi, cream of celery, and more, accompanied by a different bread each night. All the baking is done right here. A full breakfast is served. It is a 🖝 sumptuous buffet, with baskets of muffins, homemade granola, meats and cheeses, melons, and fruit. You are also offered eggs. You may never want to leave.

How to get there: From Route 1 turn right after Bucksport onto Route 15, which goes directly to Deer Isle. In the village turn right on Main Street. The inn is on your left.

∾

E: The inn dog is Mr. Beaudandy, and he sure is a dandy.

A well-run inn and a man on a diet
go together about as well as
an arsonist and a bale of hay.

olive Metcalf

Lincoln House Country Inn
Dennysville, Maine
04628

Innkeepers: Mary Carol and Gerald Haggerty
Telephone: 207-726-3953
Rooms: 6, all share 4 semiprivate baths; 2 with wood stove; 2 with
   fireplace.
Rates: $55 to $65, per person, double occupancy, MAP.
Facilities: Open all year. Breakfast for house guests, dinner daily by
   reservation. Full bar, wine list. MasterCard and Visa accepted.

When you walk in the side door of the inn you are in what
once was the summer kitchen and now is a library full of books
with a huge fireplace hung with old cooking equipment and one
Japanese wok! On through Mary Carol's kitchen you find two
delightful dining rooms. Beyond is a large living room with a
baby grand piano. This is an inn where you can feel totally at
home.

Mary Carol's kitchen really turns out exceptional food, including the best ☞ lamb I have ever had. It was prepared quite
differently and only Mary Carol can tell you how. Her breakfast
muffins almost outdo her lamb.

The inn is a handsome, yellow, foursquare Georgian Colonial perched above the Denny River, one of the few rivers where

402

you can find the Atlantic salmon. John Audubon once stayed here and was so impressed he named the "Lincoln Sparrow" for his hosts. The inn was built by an ancestor of President Lincoln in 1787.

Jerry is a master restorer and perfectionist. It shows all over the inn. The woodshed, a village pub, has a bar that Jerry carved from a 4,000-pound elm trunk with a bear's head carved at one end. The woodshed has fun on Thursday nights in the winter. It is "open mike" time and local amateurs come and do their thing. On Sundays it is international dart shoots with neighboring Canada. The U.S. seems to always win and whether this is their ability or Jerry's liberal beers we do not know.

You will love this inn, but it is a long way off, so do make reservations ahead.

How to get there: Route 1 goes right by Dennysville. Driving up take the second sign into Dennysville, just after you have crossed the Denny River. Turn left and you will find the inn almost immediately on your right.

✳

E: ☛ *Bald eagles and osprey are seen here, and families of seals swim in the river. It is a long way up here but worth every mile.*

The Waterford Inne
East Waterford, Maine
04233

Innkeepers: Barbara and Rosalie Vanderzanden
Telephone: 207-583-4037
Rooms: 9, 6 with private bath.
Rates: $45 to $70, double occupancy, EP.
Facilities: Closed March 1 to May 1. Breakfast, dinner. Hiking, hunting, fishing, swimming, bird watching, and skiing nearby. No credit cards accepted.

This is a beautiful part of the world. It is secluded, quiet, and restful. The inn offers a fireplace in the parlor and a library full of books and good music for your relaxation. And when the weather is warm, you can while away your days in the rockers on the porch.

But if you're looking for activity, The Waterford Inne can offer that, too. The area provides hiking, hunting, fishing in the summer and winter, downhill and cross-country skiing, swimming, and bird watching.

This is a first for me, a mother and daughter who are the innkeepers. They bought the inn in 1978 and have done a masterful job of restoring and renovating it. There are antiques in all the rooms, nice wallpapers, and some stenciling. For your com-

404

fort there are electric blankets in the winter, and for your visual pleasure ☞ there are fresh flowers in the summer.

Rosalie, the mother, does the cooking. The dinner is a fixed price with one entree served each evening. She is a very good and creative chef. All baking is done right here and all the vegetables are grown in the inn's garden. Barbara does the serving, and you may be seated at a table for four in the ☞ attractive dining room with a fireplace, or in a secluded corner just for two.

How to get there: From Norway, Maine, take Route 118 west for 8 miles to Route 37. Turn left and go one-half mile to Springer's General Store. Take an immediate right up the hill. The inn is about one-half mile.

❧

E: *Tansey and Teasel are the two inn cats lucky enough to live in this beautiful part of the world.*

The crackle of an inn's hearth
can melt the chilliest of minds and bodies.

olive Metcalf

The Oxford House Inn
Fryeburg, Maine
04037

Innkeepers: John and Phyllis Morris
Telephone: 207-935-3442
Rooms: 5, 3 with private bath.
Rates: $50 to $65, double occupancy, EPB.
Facilities: Open all year. Full breakfast, dinner, Sunday brunch in winter only, lounge with a full license. Canoeing, swimming, fishing, and antiquing nearby. All major credit cards accepted.

John and Phyllis have a lot of innkeeping experience, having managed a nearby inn for several years. They know just how to make an inn inviting and comfortable. There's one thing for sure: They have put together a ☛ marvelous brochure. It says, this is the way The Oxford House might have appeared back in 1923, looking through the windows of a spanking new Jordan motor car.

The rooms are charming and very comfortable. All of them are named after the names of rooms on the original blueprints. Perhaps you'll sleep in the Sewing Room. The tub in one shared bathroom is the largest I've ever seen. Care for a swim?

At dinnertime you'll delight as I did in the outstanding and creative dishes offered on the menu. For example, Turkey Waldorf is an entree you'll not find many places. It is medallions of turkey breast sautéed with apples and walnuts, then splashed with applejack and cream. Pork, Pears, and Port is another entree done in a rich port and ginger sauce. How about ☛ Canadian Steak Pie? This is an individual pie made of pieces of choice sirloin and mushrooms in a rich wine sauce. Very nice indeed. Three innovative steaks are also offered. House Pâté of the Day might be how you'd like to begin your meal. I think it's nice to find variations in pâtés. Or maybe ☛ Maine Crab Chowder will catch your eye. It's good and different. Needless to say, the desserts are all homemade.

In warm weather the screened porch is used for dining. I really like porches, and this one is a beauty. You can sit here and look out at the beautiful surrounding mountains or the lovely gardens. Peace and quiet are at hand.

How to get there: The inn is on Route 302 in Fryeburg, 8 miles east of North Conway.

❀

E: *The inventive menu is really a joy.*

> *To eat merely to live*
> *is a crime against man*
> *for which the gibbet is*
> *inadequate punishment.*

Olive Metcalf

The Domaine
Hancock, Maine
04640

Innkeeper: Nicole L. Purslow.
Telephone: 207-422-3395
Rooms: 7, all with private bath.
Rates: $140, double occupancy, MAP.
Facilities: Open May to October. Full breakfast, dinner, bar, lounge.
   Fifty-five acres to roam in. Boating, swimming, and fishing nearby.
   All major credit cards accepted.

How nice to find a provençale auberge this far up in Maine. On the first floor are the bar and lounge, and a grouping of wicker furniture is around the wood stove. Nicole has one of the wine coolers and servers that are so handy, and someday I'm going to have a small one like it for my home. The French provincial dining room has crisp linens, gleaming copper, and fresh flowers.

Now for the best part, and that is the food. Nicole, a graduate of the Cordon Bleu school of cooking in Paris, runs one of the finest French restaurants in the East. It was started in 1946 by her mother, who died in 1976. Over the years, the inn has received accolades from many publications. The most important accolade of all comes from the many returning guests.

Nicole's ☞ exquisite entrees and appetizers change with the

seasons. Pâté de Foie Maison or Saumon Fumé d'Ecosse are just two of the appetizers. Move on to Coquilles St. Jacques Provençale, Veal à la Crème, or Steak Bordelaise. There is no way I can say enough about her food. It is divine. Breakfast can be had in the dining room, your 🖝 own table in your room, or on the decks overlooking the pines and gardens. The inn's honey from its own hives or homemade jams go on croissants, muffins, or scones. They come with 🖝 French café au lait or pots of tea, making you feel you are in a true European auberge.

Each room has its own character. They are named for herbs. They all have a library and several have private porches.

There are many things to do in this area and Nicole will be glad to help you plan your day.

How to get there: The inn is about 9 miles above Ellsworth on Route 1.

∽

E: *In the huge fireplace in the dining room are a* 🖝 *rotisserie and a grill Nicole had made in France. On cool evenings she cooks here. Very nice touch!*

Olive Metcalf

Isleboro Inn
Dark Harbor, Isleboro, Maine
04848

Innkeeper: Kathleen Waterman
Telephone: 207-734-2222
Rooms: 14, 11 with private bath; 1 suite.
Rates: $105 to $195, double occupancy, MAP.
Facilities: Closed end of October to Memorial Day. Full breakfast, din-
    ner, afternoon tea, bar. Tennis court, croquet, shuffleboard, bicycles
    and small boats available at no cost, larger boats by charter. Guest
    moorings. Swimming and golf nearby. No credit cards honored.

Isleboro is a secluded thirteen-mile-long island in Penobscot
Bay. It has wonderful pine forests and magnificent turn-of-the-
century summer "cottages." The inn was originally such a "cottage," built by a Philadelphia millionaire.

There are ☞ twelve fireplaces in the inn. What a homey
feeling they give. Seven of them are upstairs and no two mantels
are alike. The Gold Room is lovely. Of course it has a fireplace,
plus chairs and tables for games. Very cozy. The lounge and bar
area overlook the water. I had breakfast on the terrace and the
view from here looking west to the Camden Hills is awesome. I
was also treated to an ☞ unbelievable sunset the night before.

Most of the guest rooms have this same view. Most also have

410

a working fireplace. This is a real treat on a cool Maine evening.

During the day living is very informal, but at dinnertime gentlemen wear jackets and ladies wear dresses. There is a less formal area to eat, but I like dressing for dinner, and especially for wonderful food like this. Chicken Monticello—chunks of chicken breast sautéed with mushrooms, blended with sherry and cream, and finished with Swiss cheese under the broiler—yum yum. Good rack of lamb. Baked haddock or lobster, and the ☞ lobster bisque is divine. So is the ☞ blueberry vinaigrette for your salad. Strawberries were in season when I was here, and I had shortcake that was out of this world. Sometimes they serve Chocolate Pot de Crème, a real favorite of mine. I'll have to come back for it. Breakfast is not just ho-hum. Belgian waffles with maple syrup caught my eye, and they were superb. All the baking is done here. The staff is very nice. This is a no-tipping inn.

How to get there: The ferry terminal is about 4 miles north of Camden. The ferry takes 25 minutes and runs every hour until 5:00 P.M. After you leave the ferry, take the first three *paved* right turns to get to the inn.

✳

E: The peace and quiet and views from here are unsurpassed.

The Kennebunk Inn
Kennebunk, Maine
04043

Innkeepers: Arthur and Angela LeBlanc
Telephone: 207-985-3351
Rooms: 31, plus 3 suites, 27 with private bath, all with air conditioning.
Rates: Off season, $30 to $70; in season, $35 to $80; double occupancy, EP.
Facilities: Closed Christmas Day. Full breakfast June to October; continental breakfast off season. Lunch and dinner every day except Sunday. Sunday brunch October through June, and Sunday dinner in off season. Bar, lounge. Fishing and swimming nearby. All major credit cards accepted.

The inn is located right smack on Route 1 in the heart of town, convenient to everything. Even the beaches are very close at hand.

Built in 1799, the inn was in total disrepair when the LeBlancs bought it. With a tremendous amount of work and attention to detail, they have restored the inn to its current state of being a proper in-town country inn.

All of the beds have ☞ new mattresses and all bedrooms are air conditioned. A modern touch like air conditioning in an old inn is great. There are some brass headboards, and if I know

Angela, there will be more. Now Angela has put ☞ hair dryers in all the bathrooms. Throughout the inn the wallpapers are ☞ French imports, and they are beautiful.

The upstairs foyer is a nice spot to gather. There are couches and chairs, television, puzzles, games, and books. Family photographs hang on the walls here, and it is quite a family. When you are at the inn, do read the back of the menu. It tells you all about the family.

The dining room has colorful tablecloths, and the food served here is impeccable. For breakfast, among many dishes, is Omar Pacha, baked eggs on sautéed onions and topped with cheese. Another dish is King Neptune's Delight, two fresh eggs enthroned on crab meat on English muffins and crowned with hollandaise sauce. There are also ☞ croissants and scones baked daily. Luncheon is equally interesting, with burgers, soups, salads, and some hot specials. For dinner, do try an appetizer named ☞ Pheasant Terrine with Lingonberry Sauce, or Smoked Trout with Tangy Horseradish Sauce. Follow it with Angela's Fillet of Veal Béarnaise or Amira's Duckling with Liqueur Sauce, flamed at tableside, of course. Perhaps you'd like King Arthur's Boneless Breast of Chicken? There are more selections from the sea, beef, and a vegetarian garden medley. You will love whatever you order.

How to get there: Take Exit 3 from I-95 (the Maine Turnpike) to Kennebunk. The inn is at 45 Main Street.

E: *Lunch is served in July and August in the courtyard. Cocktails too. There are Perrier umbrellas to ward off the sun.*

The Captain Jefferds Inn
Kennebunkport, Maine
04046

Innkeeper: Warren Fitzsimmons
Telephone: 207-967-2311
Rooms: 12, 8 with private bath; carriage house with 3 apartments.
Rates: $65 to $90, double occupancy, EPB. Long-term rental fee for apartments.
Facilities: Open most of the year. Closed in November. Full breakfast only meal served. BYOB. No children under 12. No credit cards honored, but personal checks accepted.

The inn was built in 1804. Its style is Federal, complete with a magnificent Federal fence. It is absolutely fabulous throughout. To go along with all of this are 🖝 three inn dogs whose names absolutely convulse me. Jenny Millstone, Maggie Street, and Isabelle Necessary were strays; I have never seen anything funnier than the three of them. There is also a long-haired Maine coon called Tessie.

Warren was in the antique business before he became innkeeper and he furnished the inn from his stock, except for mattresses and box springs. There's a spectacular 🖝 majolica collection of more than 1,000 pieces. Cupboards overflow with antique china and pottery. The mirror in the dining room is most unusual; a landscape scene with overhanging trees is painted right on it. An unusual étagère that is made of shells and holds boxes made of shells is a work of art. There is a captain's bridge stairwell, reminiscent of a sea captain's lookout post. It is all just beautiful.

The guest rooms are color coordinated. Laura Ashley wallpapers, the finest sheets that can be obtained, extra pillows, magnificent antique bedspreads, and the furniture is as you would expect, beautiful. White wicker on the porch, a Steinway grand piano in the living room, six fireplaces, a lovely sun porch, and a brick terrace all add to the exceptional ambience of the inn. The plants remind me of home; they are trees.

Breakfast is good and it is fun. It is served at a huge mahogany table. Warren cooks. If you stayed a week your breakfast would be different every day. Blueberry crepes, French toast with Grand Marnier, New England flannel (corned beef hash with dropped eggs), Italian eggs, and it goes on and on.

The inn provides setups for your drinks. There are plenty of restaurants nearby for lunch and dinner.

How to get there: Take Exit 3 from the Maine Turnpike. Turn left on Route 35 south to Kennebunkport. At the traffic light, turn left. Go over the drawbridge. Look for the sign for Ocean Drive. Take it one-third mile to Arundel Wharf. The next left is Pearl Street, where the inn is located.

❋

E: *I think you can tell I sure do like it here.*

Captain Lord Mansion
Kennebunkport, Maine
04046

Innkeepers: Beverly Davis and Rick Lichfield
Telephone: 207-967-3141
Rooms: 16, all with private bath, 11 with working fireplace.
Rates: $89 to $149, double occupancy, continental breakfast included.
Facilities: Open all year. Breakfast only meal served. BYOB. Gift shop.
Perkins Cove and Rachel Carson Wildlife Refuge nearby. No children under 12. All major credit cards accepted.

This is a truly grand inn. The mansion was built in 1812, and has had such good care that the front bedroom still has the wallpaper that dates from that year. Another room has its wallpaper that dates back to 1880. Some of the original Lord furniture is in the house. For example, the ☛ handsome dining room table with carved feet and chairs belonged to Nathaniel Lord's grandson, Charles Clark, and is dated 1880. Throughout the inn are portraits of past owners in the Lord family.

A three-story suspended elliptical staircase, a ☛ hand-pulled fireplace that works, a gold vault, and double Indian shutters are but a few of the wonderful things to be found in the inn. There are fireplaces, oriental rugs, old pine wide-board floors, and claw-footed tables. It's almost a comfortable museum. The

416

innkeepers give 🖝 conducted tours a couple of times a week. Rick knows the history of the house and loves to tell it.

Eleven of the guest rooms have working fireplaces. There are fourteen throughout the inn. Most of the rooms have padded, deep window seats, a great place to relax and daydream. One of the beds is a four-poster twelve feet high. Rugs and wallpaper, thanks to Beverly's eye for decoration, are well coordinated, 🖝 thirsty towels are abundant, and extra blankets and pillows help make your stay better than pleasant.

Breakfast is the only meal served in the inn, but what a meal! It is family style. Two long tables in the kitchen are set with Wedgwood blue. There are two stoves in here side by side, a new one and an old coal one about a hundred years old. You'll start your day with good baked food like Rhubarb Nut Bread, French Breakfast Puffs, Pineapple Nut Upside-Down Muffins, Oat and Jam Muffins, or Strawberry Bread. The recipes are available in the lovely gift shop, so now I can bake some of these yummies at home. All this, plus an exquisite mansion, good staff, and great innkeepers, makes this an inn you shouldn't miss.

How to get there: From I-95 take Exit 3 to Kennebunk. Turn left on Route 35 and drive through Kennebunk to Kennebunkport. Turn left at the traffic light at the Sunoco station. Go over drawbridge and take first right onto Ocean Avenue. Go ³⁄₁₀ mile and turn left at the Mansion. Park behind the building and take the brick walkway to guest entrance.

〜

E: *This is a bring-your-own-bottle inn, and from the* 🖝 *scenic cupola on its top to the parlors on the first floor, you will find many great places to enjoy a drink.*

Old Fort Inn
Kennebunkport, Maine
04046

Innkeepers: David and Sheila Aldrich
Telephone: 207-967-5353
Rooms: 14, all with private bath, kitchen, and television; 1 suite.
Rates: $75 to $125, double occupancy, continental breakfast buffet included.
Facilities: Closed mid-December to mid-April. Suite available all year. Continental breakfast only meal served. BYOB. Swimming pool, tennis, antique shop. Bikes for rent, ocean nearby. All major credit cards accepted.

When you enter the Old Fort Inn you are in an excellent antique shop. Next you are in a huge living room that overlooks the swimming pool. The pool has ☛ a solar cover that enables the inn to stretch its swimming season a bit. I know it works because I have one on my pool. This is a lovely, comfortable living room with a fireplace, a super spot to curl up and read a book.

The rooms are charming, and all are fully equipped with a kitchen. This is so nice when you plan a longer stay than overnight. The beds have antique headboards of brass or wood along with good, comfortable mattresses. The towels are ☛ color coordinated, which I always love. There is a nice library in the foyer.

The inn provides a laundry. Until you have been on the road a week or so, you do not know how convenient such a facility is. The inn also provides a place to shower and change if you are checking out and still want to swim in the pool or the ocean that is only one block away.

There is a television in each room, and the suite has color cable. To go with these modern touches is the inn cat, Bogart. And to go with the cat is the great inn child, Shana. She is some innkeeper. You will love her.

Although you may want to prepare your own food in your fully equipped kitchen, the inn does provide you with the menus of all the area restaurants.

How to get there: Take Exit 3 from the Maine Turnpike (it is marked Kennebunk), turn left on Route 35 to Kennebunkport, and follow the signs to the inn. It is on Old Fort Avenue.

✳

E: *The breakfast buffet is super. You can pick and choose from all types of teas and juices, fresh fruit, baked breads, crois-sants, and* *sticky buns, which are fantastic.*

One Stanley Avenue
Kingfield, Maine
04947

Innkeepers: Dan and Sue Davis
Telephone: 207-265-5541
Rooms: 6, 3 with private bath.
Rates: $45 to $50, double occupancy, EPB.
Facilities: Inn open all year. Restaurant closed April 1 to July 4 and third
    week of October to Christmas. Breakfast, dinner, bar. Skiing, ice
    skating, golfing, mountain climbing, and white-water rafting nearby.
    MasterCard and Visa accepted, but personal checks preferred.

     The house at Three Stanley Avenue is a lovely Queen Anne
Victorian house, built in circa 1899. It is one of the three Stanley
homes in Kingfield. Here are the guest rooms for the inn, neat,
clean, and comfortable.

     One Stanley Avenue, right next door, is the restaurant for
the inn. This house is in the National Register of Historic Places.
In the front hall is a ☛ beautiful old oak reach-in refrigerator
that holds the inn's wine collection at perfect temperatures.
There's a real beauty of a piano, a Chickering square piano, refurbished and ready to play. The small bar is also here.

     The restaurant rates three stars in the Mobil Travel Guide.

420

Dan is a rather inventive chef. ☛ Roast Duck with Rhubarb Glaze. I never would have thought of this combination in a hundred years, but it is excellent. Pork with Port Wine and Juniper Berry Sauce. Another entree is Atlantic Salmon with Dan's own sauce McIntire, named after his maternal heritage. Blackberry chicken sounds divine. I do love to cook with fruits.

The desserts are also magnificent. Rhubarb Strudel, Crème Celeste, Indian Pudding à la mode, and many more. Come on up here and enjoy Dan's fine cooking.

Sugarloaf Mountain is close by, providing superb downhill and cross-country skiing. An eighteen-hole golf course is on the Sugarloaf property. White-water rafting is an exciting spring and summer sport, and many lakes surrounding the area provide other water sports. No matter what season you come, you'll always find an abundance of things to do.

How to get there: Take the Maine Turnpike to the Belgrade Lakes Exit in Augusta. Follow Route 27 through Farmington to Kingfield. In town, turn right on Route 16. Cross a bridge, and turn right to stay on Route 16. Stanley Avenue is the first street on the left.

❧

E: *There are three charming dining rooms in which to enjoy Dan's food.*

Winter's Inn
Kingfield, Maine
04947

Innkeeper: Michael Thom
Telephone: 207-265-5421
Rooms: 12, 9 with private bath.
Rates: $50 to $75, per person, MAP. Twenty-one-day cancellation notice. EP rates and white-water rafting packages available.
Facilities: Closed after Easter to mid-June and end of foliage to before
Thanksgiving. Breakfast, dinner, Sunday brunch in summer, bar,
lounge. Swimming pool, tennis, cross-country skiing. Downhill skiing, hunting, fishing, hiking, golfing, white-water rafting, canoeing, and Stanley Steamer Museum nearby. All major credit cards
accepted.

Located in the heart of the western Maine mountains
Bigelow, Sugarloaf, and Saddleback sits Winter's Inn on top of a
ten-acre hill on the edge of town. A Neo-Georgian manor house
built at the turn of the century for Amos Greene Winter, it had
fallen into sad disrepair when it was rescued in 1972 by Michael
Thom, a young architect. Michael has restored the house beautifully, yet every time I come up here I find something he's
improved. ☞ Much to his pride, the building has now been listed
in the National Register of Historic Places.

Elegant without being stiff or pretentious, the inn has been decorated with ☞ handsome wallpapers. The walls are hung with a fine collection of oil paintings and gold-framed mirrors. The view from the dining room windows of the western mountains is breathtaking. The view is the same from the swimming pool.

☞ Food served in Le Papillon is delightful, a continuing surprise in this faraway inn at the back of beyond. Guests can spend their days climbing mountains, come home to the inn for a swim and a drink, then dress for dinner and dine elegantly, savoring the best of both worlds.

Balthazar's Pub is an elegant place to have a drink, play backgammon, chat, and enjoy. There is a unique corner fireplace in here.

Hunting, fishing, hiking along the Appalachian Trail, and canoeing welcome outdoors people. Downhill skiers are especially happy here, but so is the lady guest ensconced by the pool with her needlepoint or book.

Each year, as the inn reopens in June, Michael gives a Great Gatsby Party. This is such a fun party, I'd like to attend every year. Everyone dresses in Great Gatsby-period attire for a formal garden party around the pool. The food is divine—one year poached Norwegian salmon was served—and a band plays the greatest dance music. One year the party raised funds for the Hartford, Connecticut, Ballet. The ballet troupe performs in the area for several weeks in the summer.

How to get there: Kingfield is halfway between Boston and Quebec City, and the Great Lakes area and the Maritimes. Take the Maine Turnpike to the Belgrade Lakes Exit in Augusta. Follow Highway 27 through Farmington to Kingfield. The inn is on a small hill near the center of town.

❀

E: *Balthazar died, and Michael has a new buff-colored kitten. I helped Michael pick him out. He will be Balthazar II.*

The Newcastle Inn
Newcastle, Maine
04553

Innkeepers: Frank and Sylvia Kelley
Telephone: 207-563-5685
Rooms: 20, 9 with private bath.
Rates: $45 to $65, double occupancy, EP.
Facilities: Closed in January and on weekdays in February. Full breakfast, dinner June through September and weekends the rest of the year by reservation. Swimming and cross-country skiing nearby. MasterCard and Visa accepted.

The inn is in the lovely Boothbay region, only fourteen miles from Boothbay harbor and sixteen miles to Pemaquid with its famous lighthouse, fort, and sandy beach. This is a very interesting and distinctive part of Maine.

The lovely porch, full of white wicker furniture, has a view of the ☞ Damariscotta River. This is a nice place to while away the time talking to other guests and making friends. The Stenciled Room has some beauties on the floor. There is a TV in here and while I was visiting a lively bridge game was going on. The living room with a fireplace has a very comfortable couch and some very attractive chairs. The dining room is at the end of this room.

Breakfast is a joy. French toast has an orange flavor. Scrambled eggs are done with cheese and broccoli. ☛ Dutch pancakes come with a blueberry sauce. Baked eggs are prepared with ham and Swiss cheese. Blueberry muffins. Wow. One good entree is offered at dinner. Desserts, well, if you're lucky Sylvia will have made a Key lime pie. Stupendous.

The rooms are clean and comfortable. White curtains, white spreads, extra pillows, and an electric fan if needed. Well-behaved children are welcome at the inn.

How to get there: When going north on Route 1, take the Newcastle exit to the right. Stay to your left; the inn is about 4 blocks down the road on River Road.

∽

E: *Casey Jones and Dekin are cousins. Both are miniature schnauzers.*

The glowing carriage lamp beside the door
of a country inn when viewed through a cold rain
erases the rigors of the day
and promises a fine, fine evening.

Asticou Inn
Northeast Harbor, Maine
04662

Innkeeper: Dan Kimball
Telephone: 207-276-3344 or 276-3702
Rooms: 50, 48 with private bath. Suites available.
Rates: $130 to $135, double occupancy, MAP.
Facilities: Open June 21 to September 14. Cottages and topsiders open May 2 to November 2. Breakfast, lunch, dinner, Sunday brunch, bar, lounge. Trail lunches available. Boating, swimming, tennis, and golf nearby. No credit cards honored, but personal checks accepted.

For over one hundred years, the inn has been situated at the head of Northeast Harbor. I do believe I could sit forever on the deck that overlooks the harbor, without ever getting tired of the view.

There are many sitting areas in the inn. All of them are very comfortable. The cocktail lounge has the same ☞ beautiful view that the deck has. It certainly is a nice place to gather and have some cheer. Another cozy area has a television and tables for backgammon or cards and other games.

Dinner is served in a lovely dining room with floral murals, crisp linens, and fresh flowers. The dinner menu changes every

426

day. I love bacon-wrapped scallops and they were here. Chicken in a lemon cream sauce with mushrooms was different and good. Roast prime ribs of beef are always nice to find on a menu. Believe me, there is something for everyone on this menu. Chocolate Decadent Cake was scrumptious. And in the morning when you're ready for breakfast, you'll find anything you could possibly want available. There's nothing ho-hum about breakfast here.

Accommodations are varied. Some are large, and some are small, and all are comfortable and clean. The cottages are nice and private.

During the day you can take a cruise from the town dock. A real beauty is the *Black Jack,* a friendship sloop. From Bar Harbor there are nature cruises, a cruise to Baker Island, and dinner and clambake cruises. These are a lot of fun.

How to get there: From Augusta follow Route 3 east through Ellsworth to the Trenton Bridge and Mount Desert Island. Continue on Route 3, and just before you get to Northeast Harbor turn left and the inn will be on your right.

E: *A sumptuous roast beef and seafood buffet is offered on Thursday nights, followed by dancing. That's for me!*

olive Metcalf

The Old Village Inn
Ogunquit, Maine
03907

Innkeepers: Benjamin J. Lawlor and Catherine L. Nadeau
Telephone: 207-646-7088
Rooms: 9, plus 6 suites, all with private bath, television, and air conditioning, in 2 buildings.
Rates: $50 to $60; suites $55 to $80; double occupancy, continental breakfast included.
Facilities: Closed in January and two weeks in February. Dining room closed Mondays in winter. Full breakfast available. Dinner, bar, lounge. Fishing, swimming, boating, and summer theater nearby. MasterCard and Visa accepted.

Ben Lawlor and Cathy Nadeau have a good in-town inn that dates back to 1833. Recently they have added a ☞ guesthouse to provide more rooms for sleeping. They are doubles and have television and air conditioning. In the main inn six very nice suites are available. One of the beds has a headboard made from four ladder-back chairs. Several have views of the Ogunquit River and ocean.

The Ogonquit Room is a perfect spot for a private party for up to twenty persons. It has nice views. The Greenhouse is one of the dining rooms, and, of course, you eat here surrounded by lovely greenery. It has a great ocean view. The Bird & Bottle is another one of the dining rooms. The full breakfast that you can order includes many of the usual things, plus some extras like the inn's Egg Frittata or a fluffy parmesan, crab, or zucchini quiche served with home fries. Texas French Toast is served with cream cheese and fruit and topped with brown sugar. Yum.

One dinner appetizer I love is Fresh Main Crab au Gratin. Add the special salad—Caesar, which I adore—and entrees like Shrimp and Scallop Kebab or Baked Haddock with Thyme Walnut Butter, or fresh Maine lobster. The chef's special of the evening always gets rave reviews.

Hard on the rock-bound coast of Maine, this inn has interests for all. The famous Ogunquit Playhouse is here, as is the newer off-Broadway repertory theater. There is plenty of fishing and swimming, and two unusual walking trails.

The Marginal Way winds you along the spectacular bay and sea, and the Trolley Trail follows an abandoned line through the woods. I have never gone by, or even near, Ogunquit without a stop at this good inn.

How to get there: The inn is at 30 Main Street in the middle of Ogunquit. Main Street is Route 1.

✳

E: *A picture of the inn, done by John Falter, was on the cover of the August 2, 1942* Saturday Evening Post.

olive Metcalf

The Rangeley Inn
Rangeley, Maine
04970

Innkeepers: Ed and Fay Carpenter
Telephone: 207-864-3341
Rooms: 36, all with private bath.
Rates: $42 to $70, single; $49 to $80, double occupancy; EP. MAP
available.
Facilities: Inn open all year. Dining room closed Easter to Memorial Day
and Thanksgiving to Christmas. Breakfast, dinner, bar, lounge,
banquet facilities. Fishing, boating, swimming, hiking, tennis,
golfing, hunting, skiing, and snowmobiling nearby. American Express, MasterCard, and Visa accepted.

As their brochure says, "From out of the past. Try our old-
fashioned comfort and hospitality." The Carpenters really mean
it. The Rangeley Inn is in a lovely part of the world, 1600 feet
above the ocean. Two daughters help run the inn; Susan is the
chef and Janet tends the front desk and is headwaitress. Ed and
Fay are everywhere.

The bar and lounge area is quite large. Here, Ed and I enjoyed a ☛ few games of pool. A nice woodburning stove takes
the chill off the air and the bar stools are really comfortable.

There also is a nice television room, furnished with couches and lounge chairs and decorated with plants that add a lot of charm.

Almost all the rooms are carpeted and all are ☛ very clean. The baths have wonderful claw-footed tubs; some rooms have showers. A bath in an old bathtub is heavenly. You can be up to your neck in water; you can't do this in a modern tub.

Susan is a fine chef. She prepared a chicken dish when I was here that was delicious. I topped it off with a favorite dessert, ☛ strawberries dipped in chocolate, served with whipped cream flavored with Kahlua.

Spring brings superb fishing for brook trout and landlocked salmon. Some brooks are open only to fly-fishing. Wildflowers and migrating birds are plentiful, so bring a camera. Summer is boating, swimming, and hiking, or tennis and golf. Fall is spectacular fall foliage and hunting. Winter, of course, brings snow activities. Saddleback is nearby for downhill skiing, and cross-country skiing and snowmobiling are everywhere.

In any season of the year, Angel Falls, twenty miles away, is impressive and worth a visit. It is a fifty-to-sixty foot fall. Beautiful!

How to get there: From the Maine Turnpike, take Exit 12 at Auburn. Pick up Route 4 and follow it to Rangeley.

∾

E: *There is organ music Memorial Day to Thanksgiving, and a dance band in ski season.*

431

The Claremont
Southwest Harbor, Maine
04679

Innkeeper: John W. Madeira, Jr.
Telephone: 207-244-5036
Rooms: 30, 3 suites, 9 cottages, all with private bath.
Rates: In season, $100 to $135, double occupancy, MAP. Off season, $40 to $55, double occupancy, EP.
Facilities: Open mid-June to end of September. Off-season is May 15 to mid-June and after Labor Day to October 15. Breakfast, lunch July 15 through Labor Day, and dinner. Service bar, full license. Tennis court, dock and moorings, croquet courts, badminton, bicycles, row-boats, library. Three golf courses, sailing, freshwater swimming, summer theater, and Acadia National Park nearby. No credit cards honored, but personal checks accepted.

The Claremont has been a landmark on the shores of Somes Sound, the famous fjord of beautiful Mount Desert Island, for more than a century. It was entered in the National Register of Historic Places in 1978.

There is so much to do and see up here. Every year there is a ☞ croquet tournament. The Claremont Croquet Classic has gained wide recognition as the home of nine-wicket croquet, one of America's few truly amateur sports. You can sit in a cozy chair at the bay window in one of the upstairs suites, and watch this event in sheer comfort.

The library and game room has a nice fireplace. There are a lot of places here to sit down and just relax. Most activities center around the waterfront, where a dock, float, and deep-water moorings are available for guests. The boathouse is nice for lunch and pre-dinner cocktails.

The dining room, done in pink and white napery, offers marvelous views of the mountains of Acadia and Somes Sound. The joy you'll get from the views will be well matched by your pleasure in the excellent food. Iced Maine Crabmeat Cocktail caught my eye, and so did the Seafood Crepes—lobster, scallops, crabmeat, and white fish in an herbed crepe. Baked Chicken Champagne was another winner. Of course, the king of them all, boiled Maine lobster, is served here.

How to get there: Take the Maine Turnpike to Augusta, Exit 15, at Route 3. Follow Route 3 east through Ellsworth to the Trenton Bridge and Mount Desert Island. Once over the bridge, take Route 102 to Southwest Harbor and follow signs to the Claremont.

✳

E: *The inn has known only three owners in its lifetime. The current owner is Mrs. Allen McCue.*

olive Metcalf

Surry Inn
Surry, Maine
04684

Innkeeper: Peter Krinsky
Telephone: 207-667-5091
Rooms: 13, 11 with private bath.
Rates: $48 to $58, double occupancy, EPB.
Facilities: Closed four days at Christmas. Box lunch available, dinner,
    bar. No pets. Swimming, canoeing, rowboats, horseshoes, croquet.
    Cross-country skiing and Acadia National Park nearby. MasterCard
    and Visa accepted.

Peter has done wonders with this handsome and sprawling
inn that dates back to 1834. Its lawns sweep right down to the
inn's private beach in Contention Cove. The driveway, called
☞ Stagecoach Lane, dates back to the time when the stage met
the Boston steamboat at the landing here at the inn.

There is a sixty-foot porch overlooking the cove. I could sit
here night after night to watch the beautiful sunsets. On special
occasions a chamber concert is out here.

The inn is full of good books, warming fireplaces, and restful
chairs and couches. There are three fireplaces in the living rooms.

A multi-windowed room is the dining room. Here is a fireplace and a view. ☞ *Gourmet* and *Bon Appetit* magazines have

both requested recipes from the inn. Obviously this is good food! Onion soup, lentil vegetable soup, or gazpacho are but three of the soups you may find on the menu. Veal Tarragon or Normande—these are good ways to prepare veal. Chicken Paprika, which is seldom seen on a menu, is good here. Shrimp Sambucca is so different. The shrimp are laced in a tomato and Sambucca sauce. Viennese Chicken is sautéed in lemon butter. In the morning the breakfasts are as popular as the dinners.

The rooms are lovely with a lot of charm. The whole inn has that. There is much to do in the area, but I think to just relax here would be equally pleasant.

How to get there: Follow Route 1 north to Bucksport, Maine. Seven miles north of Bucksport, turn right onto Route 176 (Surry Road), and follow it to its end. Turn left onto Route 172 and the inn is in 2½ miles.

E: *Maine autumns are spectacular, and they are especially so here.*

Hark, which are common noises
and which are the ghosts of long contented guests.

Olive Metcalf

The East Wind Inn
Tenants Harbor, Maine
04860

Innkeepers: Tim Watts and Ginny Wheeler
Telephone: 207-372-8800
Rooms: 26, 12 with private bath; 3 suites and 1 apartment; in 2 build-
ings. All have telephones.
Rates: $46 to $134, double occupancy, EP.
Facilities: Open all year. Breakfast, lunch, dinner, lounge with full li-
quor license. Deep-water anchorage for boats. MasterCard and Visa
accepted.

The inn was built in 1890 and stood vacant for twenty years.
Tim, a native of the town, watched the old house deteriorate and
dreamed of restoring it so others could share the charm of "the
country of the pointed firs." He's been able to do just that.

Today you can sit on the ☞ wraparound porch of the inn
and enjoy the view. Tenants Harbor should be on a ☞ postcard,
it's so beautiful. The inn is within walking distance of the village,
where you will find a library, shops, post office, and churches.

The Meeting House is so nice for a relaxed conference or
seminar. The guest rooms are very clean. Some have oak bureaus
and Victorian side chairs, while others have brass beds. Almost
all the rooms have good views of the harbor.

The lunch I had here was memorable because the view and the food were so terrific. My lobster salad plate was loaded with this king of fish. The chef's salad is also very good served with ☛ raspberry vinaigrette dressing. Dinner has marvelous offerings from the sea. One I really liked was New England Crab and Shrimp Casserole—native shrimp and crabmeat baked in a mild white sauce and lightly breaded. Desserts—of course they are excellent.

The inn is open all year, so winter sports enthusiasts can just step outside to go cross-country skiing or snowshoeing. The Camden Snow Bowl is only a short drive away. ☛ The ketch *Izzy* sails twice a day from the pier at the East Wind. These are three-hour cruises on a thirty-three-foot ketch with comfortable accommodations for up to six persons. The captain really knows these waters and can tell you all you want to know. Go and enjoy.

How to get there: From Route 1, just east of Thomaston, take Route 131 south for 9.5 miles to Tenants Harbor. Turn left at the post office and continue straight to the inn.

☙

E: Watching the working fishing boats is a nice pastime.

olive Metcalf

The Ledges Inn
Wiscasset, Maine
04578

Innkeeper: Laurie Stewart
Telephone: 207-882-6832
Rooms: 3, all with private bath.
Rates: $60, double occupancy, EPB.
Facilities: Closed two weeks in February. Breakfast, lunch, dinner, bar, lounge. Boating and swimming nearby. All major credit cards accepted.

Every time I used to drive up Route 1 to Wiscasset I would check for a new look at The Ledges. I finally found it in time for this edition. Laurie has taken over this old inn and gotten rid of the ugly neon signs that once defaced it. It is now just as lovely as I had thought it could be.

The porch is a joy, and is furnished with ☞ rockers. Sit here and rock awhile, enjoy a good book, or do some needlework, while the rest of the world rolls by on Route 1.

Inside, the pub is very nice, and its beamed ceilings and stenciled curtains add to its friendly ambience. The dining rooms have their own distinctive look. The Bay Room with its lovely bay window is done in soft rose and the Mirror Room features a floor-to-ceiling mirror. Whatever room you eat in, the food served

438

here is good. At lunch try ☛ Chicken à la King served in a popover. I think it's a great idea. Fried Maine shrimp roll is another lunchtime dish. There are specials like these each day of the week. At dinner, besides all the starters, are Veal Parmesan served with pasta, or (if you're good and hungry) two jumbo shrimp, baked and stuffed or fried, and a ten-ounce sirloin steak. The possibilities are many. Popovers are also special here.

The three guest rooms have pine wide-board floors, braided rugs, old-fashioned print wallpapers, and nice sunny windows. They are homey and very pleasant.

You'll find much to see in the area. Historic houses, antiques, and two old four-masted schooners whose watery grave is in Wiscasset. The *Luther Little* is the one closest to shore. It is 204 feet long, and *Hesper* is six feet longer. They were the last two four-masted schooners built in New England. Sailors believe that a ship can be jinxed, and both of these qualify.

How to get there: The inn is on Route 1 in Wiscasset.

❋

E: *I hope Laurie's daughter will grow up to be a good inn-keeper, too.*

York Harbor Inn
York Harbor, Maine
03911

Innkeepers: Joe, Jean, and Garry Dominguez
Telephone: 207-363-5119
Rooms: 20, 8 with private bath.
Rates: $45 to $120, double occupancy, continental breakfast included.
Facilities: Open all year. Dining room open daily in summer and fall; after November 1, dining room open Thursday through Sunday. Lunch, dinner, Sunday brunch year round. Bar, cocktail lounge. Entertainment on weekends. Gift shop. Public beach, fishing, boating, golfing, tennis. All major credit cards accepted.

Wow! Three dining rooms with a ☞ view of the Atlantic. This is a cozy and comfortable inn with good food and good grog. Sitting there looking over the Atlantic should be enough, but when you add the excellent food it is ☞ heaven. Everything is made to order and baked right here. The appetizers are glorious. Tortelleni, an Italian classic, is oh, so good, and there are several more. By his own words, Chef Gerry Bonsey creates incomparable homemade soups. You can imagine what the rest is like. I wish I had more space to tell you more. Do go, I know you will enjoy.

The cellar, which once was a livery stable, is the lounge. A friendly bartender is at the beauty of a bar, made of solid unstained cherry wood joined with holly and ebony woods. The carpenter even put an inlaid tulip in a corner—out of tulip wood, of course. Happy hour is fun. The local people come in and I really enjoyed talking with them. The fireplace corner is so nice and cozy with the furniture clustered around the fireplace. There is listening-type music down here.

The inn is old; 1637 is the date for the room into which you first come. Originally a fisherman's house, it has sturdy beams in the ceiling, not for holding up the roof, but instead to hold up wet sails to dry before the large fireplace.

The rooms are comfortable and from some you can see the sea. On a quiet night you can hear the sea breaking on the generous beach below the inn. The annex next door has been beautifully remodeled. What a monumental job. All the rooms over here have a private bath. There are two working fireplaces and one room has its own patio.

When you arrive at the inn you are given a ☛ book, with information about the inn and area and a few poems, all lovingly put together. This is a really nice touch. Another one is the ☛ decanter of sherry in the hall for a thirsty guest.

How to get there: From I-95 take the Yorks Berwicks Exit. Turn right at the blinking light, left at the first traffic light (Route 1A), and go through the village about 3 miles. The inn is on the left.

E:· *York Harbor and all the areas around are beautiful. Be sure to bring your camera so you can remember it all at home.*

Indexes

Alphabetical Index to Inns

Romantic Inns

Inns Serving Lunch

Inns Serving Sunday Brunch

Inns Serving Afternoon Tea

Riverside Inns (* Denotes on the River)

Lakeside Inns (* Denotes on Lake)

Inns on or near Salt Water (* Denotes on Beach)

Inns Owning Boats for Guests' Use

Inns with Swimming Pools

Inns with Golf Course or Tennis Court

Inns with Cross-Country Skiing on Property

Inns with Health Clubs or Exercise Rooms
(* Denotes Health Club)

Inns with Meeting Rooms or Conference Facilities

Inns with Separate Cottages

About the Author

The "inn creeper" is the nickname Elizabeth Squier has earned in her almost fourteen years of researching this guide to the inns of New England. And a deserved name it is, for she tours well over 200 inns every year from top to bottom, inside and out, before recommending the best ones to you.

A recognized author on fine food and lodging, Elizabeth is a gourmet cook and has written travel and food columns for many periodicals. Like you, she recognizes readily the special ingredients that make a good inn exceptional.

Guests—

Ye are welcome here,
 be at your ease
Go to bed when you're ready
 get up when you please.
Happy to share with you
 such as we've got
The leak in the roof
 the soup in the pot.
Ye don't have to thank us,
 or laugh at our jokes
Sit deep and come often
 you're one of the folks.

found in an inn, Brookline Mass